# Innovative Business School Teaching

Dr. Elaine Doyle lectures primarily in the area of taxation in the Kemmy Business School, University of Limerick in Ireland. After completing a Masters in Accounting at the Smurfit Business School in UCD, training as a chartered accountant and completing her professional taxation qualification, she spent six years working as a tax accountant before joining the UL faculty in 2002. She has completed a PhD in moral reasoning in a tax context through the University of Sheffield in the UK. She designed and is the course director for the Master of Taxation program and was awarded the University of Limerick's Teaching Excellence award in 2010. She is the current Chair of the Kemmy Business School Research Ethics Committee. In 2012 she spent 3 months as an International Research Scholar with the Open University Business School in Milton Keynes, UK. Her research interests include inter alia, professional ethics and risk management in tax practice, the tax aggression of tax practitioners, research ethics, procedural justice, ethical reasoning and ethics education. She has published nationally and internationally in these areas in journals such as '*Journal of Business Ethics*' and '*Innovations in Education and Teaching International*' and has secured national and international funding to support her research activities.

Dr. Patrick Buckley lectures in the area of information management in the department of Management and Marketing in the Kemmy Business School, University of Limerick, Ireland. He was awarded the Dave McKevitt Scholarship to pursue his doctoral studies on the organizational deployment of prediction markets, which he completed in 2011. Patrick's research interests include the use of technology to address the challenges of large group teaching. He has received national research funding to pursue this interest. His work in this area has been published in books such as '*Technologies for Enhancing Pedagogy, Engagement and Empowerment in Education: Creating Learning-Friendly Environments*' and peer-reviewed journals such as '*Journal of Teaching in International Business*' and '*Computers and Education*'.

Dr. Conor Carroll lectures in the area of marketing at the Kemmy Business School, University of Limerick in Ireland. He is the winner the 2010 National Award for Excellence in Teaching (*The prestigious NAIRTL Award*), and twice winner of the University's Teaching Excellence award. He is a prolific case study writer, having written over 75 published marketing case studies, many of which are used extensively in leading European and International Universities such as Notre Dame, University of Hong Kong & National University of Singapore. He has won numerous accolades for his case study writing, winning awards at both national and international case study competitions. These competitions included McGraw-Hill, Ernst & Young, Newstalk, Enterprise Ireland and The Case Association case writing awards. Furthermore, Conor has presented case study writing seminars at Harvard Business School. His research interests include crisis communications, strategic sales management, digital marketing, and marketing case studies.

# Routledge Advances in Management and Business Studies

*For a full list of titles in this series, please visit www.routledge.com*

25 **Managing Technological Development**
Hakan Hakansson and Alexandra Waluszewski

26 **Human Resource Management and Occupational Health and Safety**
Carol Boyd

27 **Business, Government and Sustainable Development**
Gerard Keijzers

28 **Strategic Management and Online Selling**
Creating competitive advantage with intangible Web goods
Susanne Royer

29 **Female Entrepreneurship**
Implications for education, training and policy
Edited by Nancy M. Carter, Colette Henry, Barra Ó. Cinnéide and Kate Johnston

30 **Managerial Competence within the Hospitality and Tourism Service Industries**
Global cultural contextual analysis
John Saee

31 **Innovation Diffusion in the New Economy**
The tacit component
Barbara Jones and Bob Miller

32 **Technological Communities and Networks**
International, national and regional perspectives
Dimitris G. Assimakopoulos

33 **Narrating *the* Management Guru**
In search of Tom Peters
David Collins

34 **Development on the Ground**
Clusters, networks and regions in emerging economies
Edited by Allen J. Scott and Gioacchino Garofoli

35 **Reconfiguring Public Relations**
Ecology, equity, and enterprise
David McKie and Debashish Munshi

36 **The Pricing and Revenue Management of Services**
A strategic approach
Irene C. L. Ng

37 **Critical Representations of Work and Organization in Popular Culture**
Carl Rhodes and Robert Westwood

38 **Intellectual Capital and Knowledge Management**
Strategic management of knowledge resources
Federica Ricceri

39 **Flagship Marketing**
Concepts and places
*Edited by Tony Kent and
Reva Brown*

40 **Managing Project Ending**
*Virpi Havila and Asta Salmi*

41 **AIDS and Business**
*Saskia Faulk and Jean-Claude
Usunier*

42 **The Evaluation of Transportation Investment Projects**
*Joseph Berechman*

43 **Urban Regeneration Management**
International perspectives
*Edited by John Diamond, Joyce
Liddle, Alan Southern and Philip Osei*

44 **Global Advertising, Attitudes, and Audiences**
*Tony Wilson*

45 **Challenges and Controversies in Management Research**
*Edited by Catherine Cassell and Bill Lee*

46 **Economy, Work, and Education**
Critical connections
*Catherine Casey*

47 **Regulatory Governance and Risk Management**
Occupational health and safety in the coal mining industry
*Binglin Yang*

48 **Risk Management and Corporate Governance**
*Edited by Abolhassan Jalilvand
and A.G. Malliaris*

49 **Careers in Creative Industries**
*Chris Mathieu*

50 **Marketing without Advertising**
Brand preference and consumer choice in Cuba
*Joseph Scarpaci and Emilio
Morales*

51 **Pioneers in Marketing**
A collection of biographical essays
*D. G. Brian Jones*

52 **Mergers and Acquisitions**
The critical role of stakeholders
*Edited by Helén Anderson, Virpi
Havila and Fredrik Nilsson*

53 **Management in Africa**
Macro and micro perspectives
*Edited by Terri R. Lituchy, Betty
Jane Punnett and Bill Buenar
Puplampu*

54 **Organizations and Working Time Standards**
A comparison of negotiations in Europe
*Jens Thoemmes*

55 **Recession at Work**
HRM in the Irish crisis
*William K. Roche, Paul Teague,
Anne Coughlan, and Majella
Fahy*

56 **Innovative Business School Teaching**
Engaging the millennial generation
*Edited by Elaine Doyle, Patrick
Buckley and Conor Carroll*

# Innovative Business School Teaching

Engaging the Millennial Generation

Edited by
Elaine Doyle, Patrick Buckley
and Conor Carroll

NEW YORK AND LONDON

First published 2013
by Routledge
711 Third Avenue, New York, NY 10017

Simultaneously published in the UK
by Routledge
2 Park Square, Milton Park, Abingdon, Oxon OX14 4RN

First issued in paperback 2018

*Routledge is an imprint of the Taylor & Francis Group,
an informa business*

© 2013 Taylor & Francis

The right of the editors to be identified as the author of the editorial material, and of the authors for their individual chapters, has been asserted in accordance with sections 77 and 78 of the Copyright, Designs and Patents Act 1988.

All rights reserved. No part of this book may be reprinted or reproduced or utilized in any form or by any electronic, mechanical, or other means, now known or hereafter invented, including photocopying and recording, or in any information storage or retrieval system, without permission in writing from the publishers.

**Trademark Notice:** Product or corporate names may be trademarks or registered trademarks, and are used only for identification and explanation without intent to infringe.

*Library of Congress Cataloging-in-Publication Data*
Innovative business school teaching: engaging the millennial generation / edited by Elaine Doyle, Patrick Buckley and Conor Carroll. — First Edition.
    pages cm. — (Routledge advances in management and business studies; 56)
Includes bibliographical references and index.
ISBN 978-0-415-53399-7 (hbk.) — ISBN 978-0-203-11368-4 (ebk.)
1. Business education. 2. Business schools. I. Doyle, Elaine.
HF1106.I584 2013
650.071'1—dc23

ISBN 13: 978-1-138-61723-0 (pbk)
ISBN 13: 978-0-415-53399-7 (hbk)

Typeset in Sabon
by Apex CoVantage, LLC

**Dedicated to our families**

# Contents

*List of Tables*   xiii
*List of Figures*   xv

1   Introduction   1
ELAINE DOYLE, PATRICK BUCKLEY AND CONOR CARROLL

## PART I
## Large Group Teaching

2   Introduction to Large Group Teaching   13
PATRICK BUCKLEY

3   Keeping Everyone Engaged: The Challenges and Opportunities of Large Group Teaching   18
HELENA LENIHAN AND SARAH MOORE

4   Engaging Large Groups of Individual Learners Through an Online Environment: An Emerging i-Learner Generation?   30
FRAN MYERS, MIKE PHILLIPS, PAUL RABY AND CAREY STEPHENS

5   Prediction Markets in Management Courses: Opportunities and Challenges   41
DORIT GEIFMAN AND DAPHNE R. RABAN

## PART II
## Dynamic Learning Environments

6   Introduction to Dynamic Learning Environments   55
CONOR CARROLL

7 Encouraging Enquiry-Based Learning: A Ten-Sentence Case That Expands Itself 59
KRISTINA MAIKSTENIENE

8 The Live Case Study Approach in Business Education 70
PETER DALY

9 Authentic Assessment—Key to Learning 81
GRACE MCCARTHY

10 The Worst Day of My Life: The Future Leaders' Experience 93
JON TECKMAN

# PART III
# Critical Thinking

11 Introduction to Critical Thinking 105
PATRICK BUCKLEY

12 'The Game Is Afoot!'—Playing the Sleuth in Creative Problem-Solving Performances by Business Economics Students 109
DANIEL BLACKSHIELDS AND MARIAN MCCARTHY

13 Action-Based Learning for Millennials: Using Design Thinking to Improve Entrepreneurship Education 128
BLAŽ ZUPAN, ANJA SVETINA NABERGOJ, ROK STRITAR AND MATEJA DRNOVŠEK

14 Enquiry-Based Feedback 139
ANDY ADCROFT

# PART IV
# Ethical Citizenship

15 Introduction to Ethical Citizenship 153
ELAINE DOYLE

| | | |
|---|---|---|
| 16 | Actively Engaging Learners in Exploring Business Ethics<br>MICHAEL K. MCCUDDY | 158 |
| 17 | Articulating Competence–Insight in Business Education Through Social Entrepreneurship<br>THERESE MOYLAN | 168 |
| 18 | Live Projects—Bringing Learning to Life for Contemporary Marketing Students<br>DEIRDRE O'LOUGHLIN | 178 |
| 19 | Making Play Work: Classroom Use of a Board Game to Teach Corporate Social Responsibility<br>SHEILA KILLIAN AND JOHN LANNON | 189 |
| 20 | Conclusion<br>PATRICK BUCKLEY, ELAINE DOYLE AND CONOR CARROLL | 200 |
|  | *Appendix* | 207 |
|  | *Contributors* | 211 |
|  | *Index* | 219 |

# Tables

| | | |
|---|---|---|
| 5.1 | Results of Postactivity Questionnaire | 49 |
| 7.1 | Student Evaluation of the Ten-Sentence Case Process and Learning Outcomes | 67 |
| 9.1 | Responses to Questions Relating to Assessment | 88 |
| 13.1 | Key Findings of the 2012 Postgraduate Survey | 131 |
| 14.1 | Percentage of Students Doing Better and Worse in the Exam Compared to the Assignment | 147 |

# Figures

| | | |
|---|---|---|
| 1.1 | Macro Trends in Higher Education Leading to Pedagogical Challenges | 8 |
| 5.1 | Hidden Profile Task Trading Patterns | 44 |
| 5.2 | The Knapsack Problem Screens | 45 |
| 12.1 | A Diagrammatic Representation of the Sherlock Holmes Investigative Model in a Problem-Solving Performance | 111 |
| 12.2 | The Teaching for Understanding Framework | 114 |
| 12.3 | A Teaching for Understanding Graphic Organizer for the Economist as Detective | 116 |
| 13.1 | The Design Thinking Process | 130 |
| 14.1 | The Three-Step Process of Enquiry-Based Feedback | 141 |
| 14.2 | An Example of the Detailed Marking Scheme | 142 |
| 14.3 | An Example of Generic Feedback | 144 |
| 14.4 | Diagrammatic Conceptualization of a Body of Literature | 146 |
| 14.5 | Distribution of Action Planners' and Non–Action Planners' Change in Performance Between the Assignment and Exam Across Nine Bands | 148 |
| 18.1 | Alcohol and Identity Poster (Responsible Drinking Campaign) | 182 |
| 18.2 | Connectedness to the Community Poster (Student Volunteering Campaign) | 184 |

# 1 Introduction

*Elaine Doyle, Patrick Buckley and Conor Carroll*

## BACKGROUND TO THIS EDITED COLLECTION

This edited collection was conceived from our passion for teaching and learning. We believe that some of the critical problems facing higher education in contemporary times require innovative techniques and novel pedagogical approaches. Each academic year seems to add new burdens to faculty already struggling to juggle quality teaching, impactful research and burgeoning service roles in an era of shrinking resources (both financial and human). Nonetheless, a cursory observation of some of the teaching and learning activities taking place within our institution alone gives plenty of cause for optimism. Faculty members with a passion for teaching and learning are doing amazing things to encourage student learning and engagement. This is happening despite the fact that high-quality teaching is often unrewarded in the context of an academic career, while the pressure to publish in high-quality journals intensifies annually. Like so many academics, we strive every year to find innovative and effective ways to engage our students, encourage them to be critical thinkers, acquire mastery of their subject discipline, equip them with the knowledge and skills they need to develop successful careers in business, and ensure they have the opportunity to develop as well-rounded individuals. This book is our attempt to draw together in one place some of the techniques being used in contemporary business school teaching. It provides a resource that we can all use when seeking to develop or reinvigorate our teaching. We hope you find it as stimulating to read as we found it to edit.

## BROAD CONTEXT

Some of the challenges in business education are timeless. Synthesizing the latest disciplinary thinking into a coherent whole, providing effective learning environments and offering encouragement, motivation and feedback to students are perennial challenges. Business school graduates need to not only be technically excellent but also have the ability and confidence to question the status quo, critically evaluate alternatives, be beyond question ethically, work effectively as part of a team and be open enough to respond to and embrace change. Contemporary business school teaching must therefore create a classroom environment that generates enquiry by constantly challenging and stimulating students. Educators must strive toward generating deep, active and reflective learning experiences that engage this new generation, developing learning platforms that encourage interaction and blend with students' new learning styles. In essence, business educators need to arouse their students' intellectual curiosity and imagination as they embark on a learning odyssey at university level.

However, a number of trends are dramatically affecting the pedagogical environment of the 21st-century business school. These trends include the new generation Y or millennial generation of students currently sitting in our classrooms, the changing financial models funding universities, and the massification and globalization of education. These trends are fundamentally changing the content of courses and the delivery mechanisms being deployed within the university sector. Educators need to be acutely cognizant of these developments and to adapt to these changing dynamics. The purpose of this book is to enumerate these trends, identify their impacts on teaching and present pedagogical innovations that allow higher education teachers and educational institutions to meet these challenges in an effective and rigorous manner under a number of distinct headings.

## THE MILLENNIAL GENERATION

Influenced in their formative years by events, people and places that have developed an enduring cultural and social resonance, members of a generation are seen as sharing values and behaviors (Lancaster & Stillman, 2002). There is academic consensus that a new generational group has developed (Elam, Stratton, & Gibson, 2007; Howe & Strauss, 2000). It is commonly referred to as the millennial generation but can also be termed 'generation Y', the 'Net generation', the 'Dot-coms', the 'Echo-boomers', the 'me generation', 'digital natives', 'generation-D' (for digital) and the 'Nexters' (see, for example, Shaw & Fairhurst, 2008). While there are variations in the literature as to how the millennial generation is described and the start and end birth dates that are used to identify it, consistent with Shih and Allen (2007) and others, we categorize them as having birth dates between 1982 and 2003. This demographic is seen as having a number of distinctive characteristics.

Socialized by their parents and peers to expect success, members of the millennial generation are seen as being generally hard-working. Goal oriented, they expect highly structured processes for evaluating their educational achievement and receiving feedback (Coomes & DeBard, 2004; Howe & Strauss, 2000). In general, they have received enormous support from their parents (Elam, et al., 2007; Howe & Strauss, 2000). This support has allowed them to engage in a wide variety of social and extracurricular activities, which has aided the development of excellent social and interpersonal skills. They are widely viewed as being team oriented and socially networked (Howe & Strauss, 2000, 2003; Shih & Allen, 2007). The variety of activities in which they engage has developed their multitasking skills, and this generation is seen as being adept at rapidly shifting between tasks and challenges. This is the first generation that has been exposed to the accoutrements of information technology, such as computers and cell phones, from birth. 'It is more than technically literate; it is constantly wired, plugged in, and connected to digitally streaming information, entertainment and contacts' (Eisner, 2005, p. 6). It is widely accepted that members of the millennial generation are the first 'digital natives' of a world increasingly mediated by the tools of information technology. This digital literacy has altered their relationship with content, in that they perceive they can access knowledge instantaneously and free from restriction. However, the deluge of information at their disposal makes it hard for this generation to navigate, critically evaluate, and correctly synthesize the material.

Researchers have also identified negative traits that are shared by members of the millennial generation. Accustomed to rapidly switching between different activities, their hectic lifestyle has led to multitasking behavior, which has shortened their attention span (Elam et al., 2007). Their symbiotic relationship with information technology is seen as having contributed to this. Typically able to acquire factual information at a moment's notice, the millennial generation lacks the time or/and the skill to engage in the concentration and reflection required for the acquisition of in-depth knowledge. Their goal-driven nature has led to a lack of appreciation of the importance of critical reflection and self-analysis in the learning process. Learning is seen as a means to an end rather than a journey of exploration. This weakness has been exacerbated by standardized assessment mechanisms that focus on rote learning at the expense of critical analysis and reflection, particularly in the primary and secondary education sectors. These factors result in individuals who don't develop the introspective and analytical skills associated with being critical thinkers (Elam et al., 2007).

## CHANGING FINANCING MODELS

Universities are facing ever-increasing financial demands (Altback, Reisberg, & Rumbley, 2009). In particular, the European model of state-funded universities is coming under mounting pressure (Cornuel, 2007). Demographic changes mean that government revenue is falling, with consequent pressure on all state-funded activities. Government tax revenues are simply not keeping pace with the increased cost of providing students with a quality academic education (Altback et al., 2009). This has a number of effects. Faced with declining income from traditional sources, universities inevitably seek cost savings. Recruitment restrictions mean increased teaching loads for lecturers (Altback et al., 2009). These increased loads come in two forms: more classes to teach and larger class sizes. This occurs in an environment that is becoming increasingly dominated by the 'publish or perish' model, which stresses research outputs in the form of journal articles and successful research funding applications as the primary metric of academic success for lecturers.

Universities also seek to address the changing financial environment by developing new revenue streams (Altback et al., 2009). In a pedagogical context, this has two primary effects. First, universities in general, and business schools in particular, are encouraged to run postgraduate programs and executive education courses that are not state funded and are thus seen as being a source of additional revenue. Second, many universities seek to attract foreign students from outside their home country, as these students may not qualify for free or subsidized education and may therefore be seen as being more financially attractive than indigenous students. This has led to educators grappling with greater levels of diversity within the classroom.

Many jurisdictions have seen a shift from a state funding model to student funding of higher education through the introduction of course fees (Altback et al., 2009). One of the consequent effects of this is that students become consumers of education rather than participants in education, thereby changing the nature of their expectations in terms of the level of service expected from faculty and staff. The increased financial burden on students may also mean that they need to undertake part-time work, reducing the time available for study.

## THE MASSIFICATION OF EDUCATION

The concept of mass higher education is traditionally seen as describing the enrollment of students beyond the levels required to repopulate academia and certain other high-status professions (Cornuel, 2007). Until relatively recently, only a very small minority of the population studied at higher education institutions. In recent decades, this has changed in the developed world, where attaining a higher-level education qualification is increasingly seen as a prerequisite for most careers. The proportion of adults with higher-level education qualifications in the OECD countries almost doubled from 22% to 41% between 1975 and 2000, while globally, the percentage of the relevant age cohort enrolled in tertiary education has risen from 19% in 2000 to 26% in 2007, with some 150.6 million tertiary students globally, roughly a 53% increase over 2000 (Altback et al., 2009, p. vi).

The massification of education at the level of the traditional school leaver means that the selection criteria used at enrollment are becoming less stringent. Assisting these students to develop their potential and providing them with the support they need in the face of static or diminished resources poses grave challenges to teachers who have traditionally seen their role as educating 'the best and the brightest'. In addition to continued increases in the proportion of school leavers participating in higher education, two other major demographic groups seeking to attain higher-level qualifications can be identified. First, school leavers in increasingly affluent countries such as China and India are seeking university degrees. Second, in OECD countries, the rise of the knowledge economy means that lifelong learning is becoming more important. Many people outside the traditional school leaver demographic are seeking higher-level qualifications to improve their career prospects. Increasingly, mature students and nontraditional learners are becoming part of campus life (Altback et al., 2009). Many of these students may not have experienced formal education for a long period of time. This may require the provision of specialized supports to help them reacclimatize to the educational process. Students may be balancing career and family commitments with the pursuit of educational achievements. It is increasingly common for individuals to undertake a university program while also working in full-time jobs. Enabling these students to succeed may require the provision of nontraditional learning environments. E-learning and other technologies may be required to support these learners. Novel teaching structures such as block release, distance learning or evening and weekend classes may be required to facilitate access to academic staff. Again, providing these supports must be balanced against the resource constraints that most modern universities are facing.

## THE GLOBALIZATION OF EDUCATION

The ever-increasing interconnectedness and interdependence of modern countries, economies and societies is most commonly referred to as globalization. As with virtually every other sector of society, globalization is having a major impact upon higher education institutions (Altback et al., 2009). Globalization offers the possibility of attracting students and faculty from around the world and sending our students and academic faculty to study and teach abroad, significantly broadening the learning experience. In 2005 the number of students from OECD countries studying abroad reached 1.9 million. Altback et al. (2009) report that 2.5 million students are studying outside their home countries, with this figure estimated to rise to 7 million international students by 2020. However, the increased mobility of students also means that universities are forced to engage in competition for students, particularly foreign students, who may be financially lucrative for the institutions involved (Adnett, 2010). In the context of globalization, it is increasingly important that curricula become more international in nature, which leads to the need for teaching faculty to be more international (Cornuel, 2007).

Beyond the education context, globalization has made the world a very small place. Decisions made by individuals, organizations and countries may frequently have a global impact. Some issues, such as climate change, are global in nature and require action at a global level; however, local interests often override the common good. Scientific advances such as cloning and genetic engineering raise many important ethical questions. Taking a consequentialist position, this new environment presents a number of profound ethical challenges. The interconnectedness across nations and cultures implied by a global world introduces a new sense of urgency and extends the notion of a duty of care toward other peoples beyond national borders. Meeting the challenges posed by these issues requires moral and ethically sensitive individuals who think and act in a responsible manner. Since business schools are the primary source of the business leaders of the future, equipping students to meet these challenges is a paramount concern of all business schools.

The globalization of education means that international students are now also an increasing proportion of the student body (Healey, 2008). Such students may need to adjust to the cultural norms of their host country. There are often significant language barriers in these situations. Again, universities and individual teachers need to be cognizant of the diverse needs of these students. In many cases, the increasing diversity of student cohorts represents an exciting opportunity for higher-level teachers. With careful utilization of peer learning, students' different backgrounds and skills can be leveraged to provide the whole student body with novel perspectives that would be otherwise unobtainable. Mature students with professional experience can offer insights into the business world to younger students. Students from different countries can explore together the challenges and opportunities of intercultural exchanges. However, these benefits can only be attained by nuanced and targeted teaching practices that recognize and embrace the increased diversity of student bodies.

To summarize, the challenges facing contemporary business education mean that business lecturers must find ways to teach both large and small groups of diverse learners effectively so that they become ethical citizens who can think critically. This provides the rationale for the breakdown of the key sections of this book.

## RATIONALE FOR CHAPTER BREAKDOWN

Against the background of the macro trends in higher education outlined above, teachers must continue to make the content of courses and modules stimulating and interesting while maintaining academic rigor. The role of the teacher has evolved into a facilitator helping to guide students through subject material, encouraging the development of knowledge through self-directed learning rather than simply passively receiving information and subsequently dumping it into assessment instruments. These objectives can be fulfilled through a combination of lectures, practice through tutorial exercises, case studies, presentations and projects, feedback to students through assessment mechanisms, peer reflective learning environments, real business case discussions, simulations and students' own reflections on their learning experience. Learning is a cumulative experience, necessitating multiple delivery formats and assessment instruments. Modern pedagogy has evolved into something that enriches the learning experience for students, equipping them with critical thinking and analytical skills while being simultaneously richly engaging. Bennis and O'Toole (2005) argue that we need to develop students' conditioned reflexes to the business contexts they face.

The macro trends explored above that are driving the evolution of business schools have created new pedagogical challenges. These challenges are global in nature and reflect underlying demographic and social changes that are evident in virtually all higher education environments. Against the backdrop of the macro trends in education outlined above, this book synthesizes the emerging issues in contemporary business teaching into four pedagogical challenges that will serve to categorize the sections within the book. Each pedagogical challenge represents a distinct theme. These themes are: Large Group Teaching, Dynamic Learning Environments, Critical Thinking, and Ethical Citizenship.

While each of the macro trends in education impact on multiple pedagogical challenges and themes, some of the more obvious relationships are illustrated in Figure 1.1. Driven by trends such as the massification of education and globalization, educators are increasingly finding themselves responsible for teaching larger and larger classes. At the undergraduate level, such classes are often measured in hundreds of students. Dealing with classes of this scale requires educators to reevaluate how they engage with their students and manage the educational process. This is the concern of our first section.

To engage with the millennial generation, educators must move from the traditional model of education, which was predicated on the notion that the teacher's role was to provide facts and information to students. With rote learning rendered a relic of a bygone age by the pervasiveness of information technology, the role of an educator has evolved. Teachers must now create dynamic, realistic and emotionally engaging learning environments. Techniques and methodologies for creating such environments are presented in the second section of this book.

New technological developments have led to an abundance of information at students' fingertips with rapid access to data available. Teaching students to process this data into knowledge is an important challenge. There has been a substantial shift from generating information to being able to differentiate the varying quality of information and analyzing it (see, for example, Johnston & Webber, 2003). In other words, the skill that students need to acquire today is that of critical thinking. How we can help students

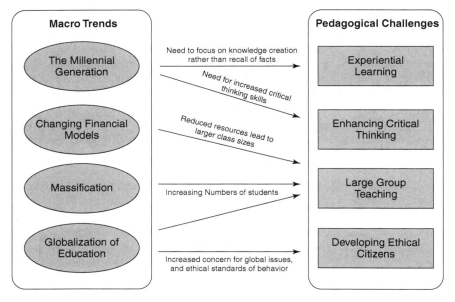

*Figure 1.1* Macro Trends in Higher Education Leading to Pedagogical Challenges

to develop their critical faculties and think at a meta-cognitive level is the focus of the third section of this book.

Finally, the advent of globalization and the creation of a tightly connected, networked world mean that business schools must accept the burden of developing in their graduates the ethical and moral sensitivities required of productive and constructive members of modern society. Business schools have a public responsibility to ensure that their graduates are not just technically skilled but are also aware of and take responsibility for the social implications of their actions. Approaches and techniques for inculcating these traits is the subject of the fourth and final section of our book.

## CONCLUSION

This edited book showcases the latest pedagogic innovations that actively engage the millennial generation in learning within the business domain. In the context of the contemporary macro issues facing higher education, it presents some of the latest teaching practices and tools used in higher education business teaching, clearly illustrating the practical ways in which business teachers can confront current pedagogic challenges. All of the contributors to this collection have outstanding track records in teaching. Many have won national and international awards for teaching excellence, as well as published widely on pedagogy. Best practice teaching from multiple jurisdictions across a broad spectrum of business schools is represented. Each contributor shares his or her innovative teaching tools and techniques in a manner that emphasizes how these tools can be adapted to other contexts, thus presenting readers with a valuable teaching resource. Enjoy reading these chapters and using them within your own discipline to engage your students.

## REFERENCES

Adnett, N. (2010). The Growth of International Students and Economic Development: Friends or Foes? *Journal of Education Policy, 25*, 625–637.
Altback, P. G., Reisberg, L., & Rumbley, L. E. (2009). *Trends in Global Higher Education: Tracking an Academic Revolution*. Paris: UNESCO.
Bennis, W., & O'Toole, J. (2005). How Business Schools Lost Their Way. *Harvard Business Review, 83*(5), 96–104.
Coomes, M. D., & DeBard, R. (Eds.). (2004). *Serving the Millennial Generation: New Directions to Student Services*. San Francisco: Jossey Bass.
Cornuel, E. (2007). Challenges Facing Business Schools in the Future. *Journal of Management Development, 26*, 87–92.
Eisner, S. P. (2005). Managing Generation Y. *SAM Advanced Management Journal, 70*, 4–15.
Elam, C., Stratton, T., & Gibson, D. D. (2007). Welcoming a New Generation to College: The Millennial Students. *Journal of College Admission, 195*, 20–25.
Healey, N. (2008). Is Higher Education in Really 'Internationalising'? *Higher Education, 55*, 333–355. DOI:10.1007/s10734-007-9058-4.
Howe, N., & Strauss, W. (2000). *Millennials Rising: The Next Generation*. New York: Vintage.
Howe, N., & Strauss, W. (2003). *When Millennials Go to College: Strategies for a New Generation on Campus*. Washington, DC: American Association of Collegiate Registrars.
Johnston, B., & Webber, S. (2003). Information Literacy in Higher Education: A Review and Case Study. *Studies in Higher Education, 28*, 335–352.
Lancaster, L. C., & Stillman, D. (2002). *When Generations Collide: Who They Are. Why They Clash. How to Solve the Generational Puzzle at Work*. New York: Harper Business.
Shaw, S., & Fairhurst, D. (2008). Engaging a New Generation of Graduates. *Education and Training, 50*, 366–378.
Shih, W., & Allen, M. (2007). Working with Generation-D: Adopting and Adapting to Cultural Learning and Change. *Library Management, 28*, 89–100.

# Part I
# Large Group Teaching

# 2 Introduction to Large Group Teaching

*Patrick Buckley*

Large group teaching is a growing phenomenon in higher education, and, whatever our view of it, it is here to stay. In the introduction, we identified two key trends that are causing class sizes to swell. The first is the massification of higher education (Cornuel, 2007). The proportion of students undertaking higher-level education increased by an average of nearly 25 percentage points in OECD countries between 1995 and 2010 (OECD, 2012). In the developed world, the attainment of at least an undergraduate degree is increasingly becoming the norm. An average of 62% of young adults in OECD countries will enter higher-level programs (OECD, 2012). Globally, the percentage of the relevant age cohort enrolled in tertiary education grew from 19% to 26% between 2000 and 2007 (Altbach, Reisberg, & Rumbley, 2009). Most developing countries are on a similar trajectory. In China, tertiary enrollments by school leavers are expected to rise from 24% to 38% between 2007 and 2020, while corresponding enrolments in India are expected to rise from 16% to 23%. It is expected that the five largest tertiary education systems in 2020 will be China (*37 million students*); India (*28 million students*); United States (*20 million students*); Brazil (*9 million students*); and Indonesia (*7.8 million students*) (The British Council, 2012).

At the same time, third-level institutions face changing funding models. There has been a philosophical shift from viewing tertiary institutions as public goods, which provide utility to society as a whole, to that of private goods, where the primary benefit is received by an individual—the graduate (Altbach, 2009). This philosophical shift, allied to the increased financial pressures brought about by long-term trends such as demographic shifts and medium-term effects such as the global financial crisis, has led to a diminution of state support and an increasing emphasis on universities as economically independent, self-financing entities. For example, tuition fees have been introduced in countries where higher education was formerly free or heavily subsidized (*China in 1997, United Kingdom in 1998, Austria in 2001*).

The expansion in student numbers and the shift in funding models have presented a major challenge for systems traditionally providing access to free or highly subsidized tertiary education (Altbach et al., 2009). In the face of these challenges, many institutions have adapted the obvious strategy: increasing the size of classes without allocating increased teaching resources (McAvinia & Oliver, 2002; Yanamandran & Noble, 2006). As such, it is quite common for undergraduate courses in popular subjects such as business and arts to measure in hundreds of students (Hogan & Kwiatkowski, 1998). Increasing austerity in universities and other postsecondary institutions leads to other negative side effects such as overcrowded lecture halls, outdated library holdings, less support for faculty research, the deterioration of buildings, the loss of secure faculty positions, and a faculty brain drain as the most talented move abroad (Altbach, 2009). Educators across a broad range of higher-level institutions and spanning all disciplines are increasingly facing the challenge of dealing with large classes while armed with pedagogical strategies designed for smaller groups (Phillips, 2005).

Increasing student–staff ratios present numerous challenges (Gibbs, 1992). First, students can lack clarity of purpose. In small classes, in addition to formal communication structures such as course outlines, students and lecturers can build informal relationships based on face-to-face contact. In larger classes, these informal communication channels can break down. As a result, students may lack clarity as to the module's purpose and the associated learning objectives of a module.

Students may find it more difficult to gauge their personal progress through a large group module. In small classes, students can rely on feedback from the lecturer and their peers to give them an indication of how they are progressing. The more tenuous student–teacher relationship associated with large groups can damage this process. This is particularly the case where the class is sufficiently large that the traditional feedback mechanisms such as midterm assessments, projects, and pop quizzes become difficult or impossible to conduct due to logistical constraints. Reduced communication between students and teaching staff may also lead to a dearth of advice on strategies for improvement. A critical part of learning any skill is the ability to interact with a domain expert who can demonstrate how to perform a particular task. Students in a large group context who are struggling with material may find it difficult to obtain the appropriate level of assistance. In large groups, students may feel intimidated and may be unwilling to approach the lecturer or tutors with problems. In turn, lecturers and tutors may lack the time to help students to resolve issues they encounter, or they may not even realize that there is a problem in the first place.

Larger class sizes lead to increased diversity within the class. There may be huge differences in the underlying educational or professional qualifications, academic and practical abilities, and cultural backgrounds of students. Students have different needs based on cultural and linguistic needs as well as ability. In large groups, it can often be difficult for teaching staff to identify an individual's needs, much less address them. Individual learners may find the pacing of content delivery too fast or too slow, leading to distraction on the part of the learner and a diminished learning experience

(Hadley, 2002). However, it is important to note that the diversity inherent in large groups can be extremely positive. Students learn from their peers in a diverse group. The size of the group, however, remains an issue.

Large groups often lead to an inability to support independent study optimally. There are a wide variety of tried and tested pedagogical tools that prompt and support independent learning, such as projects, critical essays, and problem-based learning. However, such activities require at least some one-on-one guidance from teaching staff, which becomes progressively more difficult to offer as class sizes grow larger and larger. Discussion also suffers in large groups. Students may be intimidated by the presence of large numbers of their peers and may be unwilling to engage in or contribute to a discussion. Lecturers may fear that discussions will quickly spin out of control. Finally, and perhaps most perniciously, motivation suffers in large groups. Deprived of a rich communicative relationship with teaching staff and their peers, learning can become a solitary experience. Students can feel isolated or *part of a crowd*, and these negative emotions inevitably damage the learning experience.

The traditional model of university education is predicated on small classes, or at least the opportunity for large classes to be broken into smaller groups via tutorials and seminars, facilitating the development of a strong working relationship between the student and the teacher that allows for the exchange of detailed and complex conceptual knowledge. Higher education teachers must increasingly come to terms with teaching large groups with limited resources and begin to evolve pedagogical strategies to deal with this new reality.

In this section, we examine novel methods for addressing the challenges associated with large group teaching. In their chapter 'Keeping Everyone Engaged: The Challenges and Opportunities of Large Group Teaching', Lenihan and Moore accept that large groups are here to stay. They are particularly cognizant of the importance of maintaining motivation and engagement in large groups and the academic necessity of encouraging active learning. They discuss a range of methods for bolstering the student–teacher relationship. They provide a host of techniques that can be applied to improve interaction in the classroom and, in their own words, overcome 'the passive learning experience that students often associate with instruction in large classes.'

Lenihan and Moore also note the potential of e-learning systems and other technology-enabled approaches for dealing with the challenges of large group teaching. In this context, the contribution by Myers et al., 'Engaging Large Groups of Individual Learners through an Online Environment: An Emerging i-Learner Generation?' is particularly appropriate. Technology has often been suggested as being an avenue worth exploring to address the challenges posed by large group teaching (Rouet & Puustinen, 2009; Tsai, 2008; Wang, 2009). Others have been more skeptical (Lemak, Reed, Montgomery, & Shin, 2005). The Open University is a globally recognized leader in distance education. Myers et al. draw on this institutional knowledge to describe, compare, and contrast the range of tools used at the Open University to enable online learning in very large classes. Of particular note is their use of a large data set to explore in detail some of the assumptions underlying online learning and the millennial generation. Such insights are valuable to all practitioners who seek to use e-learning tools to deal with the challenges of large group teaching.

An innovative e-learning tool is described by Geifman and Raban in their chapter 'Prediction Markets in Management Courses: Opportunities and Challenges'. Multiple-choice questions have a long history of being used in large group teaching contexts. Of particular note is their scalability. Once designed, a multiple-choice quiz can be distributed to a thousand students as efficiently as ten. Prediction markets in a pedagogical environment share this scalability but have a number of additional advantages. They can be used to ask students to calculate values rather than simply select from a set menu of choices. They operate in real time and allow students to reconsider their answers. Most importantly in terms of encouraging motivation, engagement with a prediction market is a group activity. Geifman and Raban describe a number of ways in which prediction markets can be integrated into existing course structures to improve the learning experience while ensuring that students remain focused on learning objectives.

The chapters in this section provide in-depth commentary from experienced teachers dealing with the challenges of large group teaching. More positively, however, the considered judgment of these authors is that large group teaching is a challenge that can be addressed. A variety of techniques and tools generally applicable across disciplines and class sizes are presented and provide academics and educational practitioners with a range of tools that can be adapted to meet the challenge of large group teaching in their own context.

## REFERENCES

Altbach P. G. (2009). The giants awake: The present and future of higher education systems in China and India. In Organisation for Economic Co-operation and Development, *Higher education to 2030: Vol. 2. Globalization* (pp. 179–203). Paris: OECD, Centre for Educational Research and Innovation.

Altbach, P. G., Reisberg, L., & Rumbley, L. E. (2009). *Trends in global higher education: Tracking an academic revolution.* Paris: UNESCO.

The British Council. (2012). The shape of things to come: Higher education global trends and emerging opportunities to 2020.

Cornuel, E. (2007). Challenges facing business schools in the future. *Journal of Management Development*, 26(1), 87–92.

Gibbs, G. (1992). *Teaching large classes in higher education: How to maintain quality with reduced resources.* London: Kogan Page.

Hadley, N. (2002). An empowering pedagogy sequence for teaching technology. *Journal of Computing in Teacher Education*, 19(1), 18–22.

Hogan, D., & Kwiatkowski, R. (1998). Emotional aspects of large group teaching. *Human Relations*, 51(11), 1403–1417.

Lemak, D. J., Reed, R., Montgomery, J. C., & Shin, S. J. (2005). Technology, transactional distance, and instructor effectiveness: An empirical investigation. *Academy of Management Learning & Education*, 4(2), 150–159.

McAvinia, C., & Oliver, M. (2002). 'But my subject's different': A web-based approach to supporting disciplinary lifelong learning skills. *Computers & Education*, 38(1–3), 209–220.

Organisation for Economic Co-operation and Development. (2012). *Education at a glance 2012: Highlights*. Paris: OECD Publishing.

Phillips, R. A. (2005). Challenging the primacy of lectures: The dissonance between theory and practice in university teaching. *Journal of University Teaching and Learning Practice*, 2(1), 1–12.

Rouet, J., & Puustinen, M. (2009). Introduction to 'Learning with ICT: New perspectives on help seeking and information searching.' *Computers & Education*, 53(4), 1011–1013.

Tsai, C. (2008). The preferences toward constructivist Internet-based learning environments among university students in Taiwan. *Computers in Human Behavior*, 24(1), 16–31.

Wang, Q. (2009). Design and evaluation of a collaborative learning environment. *Computers & Education*, 53(4), 1138–1146.

Yanamandran, V., & Noble, G. (2006). Student experiences and perceptions of team-teaching in a large undergraduate class. *Journal of University Teaching and Learning Practice*, 3(1), 49–66.

# 3 Keeping Everyone Engaged
## The Challenges and Opportunities of Large Group Teaching

*Helena Lenihan and Sarah Moore*

### INTRODUCTION

Despite the emergence of many new teaching and learning modes and tools, large group lectures remain a central and pervasive part of students' formal learning experiences in higher education. In particular, first-year classes tend in most universities to be very large. Despite smaller group interactions in tutorial and other settings, often these large arenas are where learners are exposed to the core curriculum. Many critics have called for an end to large classes of this nature, saying that they are outdated, 19th-century forums for learning and that they are inappropriately applied in current settings, where information can be accessed through a much wider and arguably much more engaging range of media. In the words of Cooper and Robinson (2000, p. 7), who have been among the many critics of the large lecture experience: "It is a sad commentary on our universities that the least engaging class sizes and the least involving pedagogy are foisted upon the students at the most pivotal time of their undergraduate careers: when they are beginning college."

In a higher education context that should enable students to develop modes of thinking that they would not otherwise acquire, is this the best way to develop students' learning in any discipline or subject? A university education should encourage students to engage in critical analysis, problem solving, exploration and effective dialogue. Education should instill intellectual skills in a setting where effective communication and creative engagement are valued. All of these dynamics can be difficult enough to achieve in small class settings, where the instructor has more scope for interacting with all students, but achieving these outcomes in large class settings can be very challenging indeed. Foreman (2003) summarizes such challenges, saying that large group lectures provide an environment that is in direct conflict with ideal learning environments that are characterized by one-to-one attention, immediate feedback, and individually customized pace and modes of learning. So why, then, do large group lecture formats persist? Commentary suggests a number of reasons, some of which are economic, others of which are social and/or organizational. Large classes may not provide the most pedagogically effective environment, but they remain the most cost-efficient way of interacting with students on key aspects of their learning and their curriculum (Moore, Walsh & Risquez, 2007). In addition, despite emerging tools and technologies, the social importance of a synchronous gathering of students, all attending in the same social space at the same time, may have been underestimated. The difficulties of ensuring that a cohort of students gain access and pay attention to the same material may be greater than even our information-rich age can tackle, and the problems of gaining student attention outside as well as inside the classroom has been well documented (e.g., Fransson 1977; Moore, Armstrong & Pearson, 2008; Urdan & Schoenfelder, 2006). We argue that (1) large group teaching as a forum for student learning is likely to persist, and (2) there are achievable ways to ensure that large group teaching is effective and impactful, leading to positive learning and teaching outcomes.

This chapter presents strategies for dealing with large groups and describes innovative methods for overcoming the challenges associated with the large group environment. We argue that, while good learning may well be influenced by class size, what underlies this influence are the dynamics of motivation and engagement and that if these are tackled in large group settings, then it is also possible to minimize the negative impact of large class size. We show how it is possible to make a large group environment interactive, engaging and active. Our own experience shows us how interactive environments encourage students to question, think critically and act creatively.

Before we outline our thoughts on the large group teaching environment, we begin by sharing some core aspects of our teaching philosophy (developed over a combined teaching experience of almost 50 years). We share these insights for two reasons: First, it shows what we try to achieve in our classes, and, second, it highlights our overriding belief that our teaching philosophy prevails and is relevant in all the teaching contexts in which we operate, regardless of class size. Delivering on our philosophy is undoubtedly more challenging in large group settings, which is why we will subsequently explore some of the techniques and approaches that we have used to address those challenges.

Good teaching is immensely rewarding, both intellectually and emotionally; being an effective teacher is critical to our role as academics. Our teaching has many aims. We need to work to enable students to achieve the learning outcomes that have been declared in the curriculum. We need to ensure that the pace and momentum of the subject is manageable. We need to direct students to material, ideas, research and data that help them to develop a command over the subjects that we teach. But, possibly most importantly, we need to provide an environment that stimulates student motivation, that encourages effort and that provides pathways for independent learning. Both theory and practice show us that this is rendered more achievable when students engage actively with their teaching and learning experiences through interaction and participation (e.g., Barrett & Moore, 2010).

Critical thinking is an active approach to learning and a skill that we commit to developing among our students. We know that critical thinking is much more likely to be fostered when we engage in interactions with people whose views and perspectives we do not always share (Bean, 2011) and that, almost by definition, it is more likely to be a competence that is developed in interactive environments. So for us, the challenge of large group teaching lies largely in fostering functional interaction among students in such settings.

## THE LARGE CLASS ENVIRONMENT

There is no agreed-upon numerical definition of what constitutes a large class. For some teachers, any number that exceeds that associated with the 'ideal group' (over 8 members) is considered larger than is pedagogically desirable, especially when goals relate to developing positive, meaningful teaching relationships, sustaining intensive interaction and giving detailed customized feedback to each student. For others, a group is still considered small when it contains up to 50 students, notwithstanding the need for students to break into subgroups for the kinds of small group activities that promote optimal engagement. However, for most higher education teachers, the large class experience is characterized by classes of typically a hundred or more students all learning in the same space, led by a single teacher. The relatively arbitrary definition of 100 or more students seems to have persisted in the literature for many decades (see, e.g., Carbone & Greenberg, 1998; Edmonson & Mulder, 1924).

Because budgets for higher education are being cut in most countries and because fiscal austerity in all education sectors is now broadly the norm, and despite existing and developing technologies, it seems that educators will be charged with teaching more hours and to larger groups of students. As outlined by authors such as Murdoch and Guy (2002) and Borden and Burton (1999), large classes are frequently viewed as a cost-efficient way of teaching large numbers of students, particularly in first year. All the evidence points to large classes becoming ever more prevalent in the future.

## ACTIVE/INTERACTIVE LEARNING

While a plethora of definitions of active learning abound, we largely agree with Harris (2010), who defines it as 'anything taught within the classroom other than an instructor's lectures to passive students' (p. 13). Much research in cognitive psychology (e.g., McGlynn, 2005) has demonstrated that active engagement promotes deeper levels of processing and learning, creating stronger cognitive connections than those that occur when learners are simply exposed to information without interaction. Although research on the effect of large classes on student performance is inconclusive, much of the evidence recognizes large classes as a deterrent to both student engagement

(Cooper & Robinson, 2000) and students' sense of belonging and motivation (Moore & Kuol, 2005). There is also overwhelming agreement that the key to effective instruction and student learning, regardless of class size, is engaging students in active learning (De Caprariis, Barman & Magee, 2001; Stanley & Porter, 2002). The importance of engagement, critical thinking and interaction with students and of stimulating active rather than passive learning are more important than ever. And despite the challenge of the large group context, it is still possible to create active learning environments in these settings.

In the forthcoming sections, we share some of the techniques that we have used in large classes to unlock more energy from students, help them feel a sense of belonging, enhance the teacher–class relationship and ensure that students have more opportunities to experience the lecture as a formal learning session that adds real value.

## INCREASING CONNECTION BETWEEN TEACHER AND STUDENTS, ENHANCING A SENSE OF BELONGING

A major challenge in large group teaching is balancing instructor-centered teaching with student-centered learning. Only when we get such a relationship right can we begin to interact with our students.

### Explain the Rationale of Classroom Activities and Teaching Approaches

If students are to be asked to interact in large group settings, such interactions must be not only carefully designed but carefully explained. Many students are still not accustomed to being asked to interact in a large group, a context in which they have learned to expect a rather passive experience, and they may not be prepared for the rigors that interactive activity brings. Thus, not only do interactive experiences need to be carefully designed, planned and paced in situations where large numbers of learners are involved, but students need to understand why an instructor is asking them to engage interactively. Experience has taught us that embarking on a series of interactive exercises must be accompanied by negotiation and explanation. It seems to be consistently important to share with students the rationale for whatever teaching approach is being adopted.

### Be Available Before and After Class

To improve the teacher–class relationship, we have found that being available to answer student questions for 10 minutes before and after class can be very useful. Other helpful techniques include walking around the teaching space during class and greeting students outside of class.

### Walk Around During Class

Walking around the lecture theater (which generally requires a clip-on microphone) has improved our communication and relationship with students, perhaps because it reduces the feeling of 'them' versus 'us', which is frequently mentioned by students when discussing their experiences of large classes. We become more of a 'guide in the aisle' than the traditional 'sage on the stage'.

### Greet Students Outside of Class

To mitigate the impersonal nature of large classes, we make a big effort to greet our students outside of class. In our large first-year microeconomics class, for example, it is compulsory for students to purchase the textbook so that they have access to a unique identifier online learning code, which they need for completing online assessments throughout the semester. Because the textbook is only used by first-year students studying this particular module, students carrying or using the book (e.g., in the library or computer labs or more informally in the student cafés throughout the campus) are readily identified by the lecturer as being part of that particular large class. Sometimes the lecturer merely greets these students; at other times she uses it as an opportunity to derive some informal feedback about the module delivery or accompanying tutorials to the module.

While it may be difficult to see how small actions like this relate to the quality of the student experience, our evidence shows that these are the kinds of interventions that can make all the difference, particularly at the early stages of students' time at university. Students respond to these early moments of contact, and the increased levels of rapport set the scene for more engaged, more positive and more connected learning experiences (Moore et al., 2007).

## TECHNIQUES FOR ENCOURAGING INTERACTION

This section provides details regarding some of the interactive techniques we use in our large classes in economics and organization behavior. These are the teaching strategies for which we have received very positive feedback from generations of students and which have had a demonstrated impact on their perceptions of our disciplines and their learning experiences. The main aim here continues to be examining ways of overcoming the passive learning experience that students often associate with instruction in large classes.

We believe that if hard-nosed economists in business schools can try out some of these methods and techniques, then anyone can! Indeed, as outlined by Watts and Becker (2008, p. 285), 'relative to other instructors, economists rely more on lecture'. Other published surveys of economists, such as those by Stead (2005) and Benzing and Christ (1997), have supported this view. In a similar vein, Salemi (2009) argues that 'one of the most important challenges facing college instructors of Economics is helping students engage' (p. 385).

All of the interactive techniques outlined below have been used by us in classes of 500 students or more. In our large economics modules, one of our key objectives from the outset is to introduce students (primarily through interactive exercises and techniques as outlined below) to the 'economic way of thinking'. The overriding aim of the economic way of thinking is that it helps students to think in terms of alternatives (or, more precisely, alternatives foregone, in the lingo of economists—'opportunity cost'). This is an extremely valuable way of thinking, because the logic can be applied to various types of decisions by employing different economic frameworks, concepts and tools. The economic way of thinking provides a very logical approach to making decisions and putting a value on the best alternative foregone. This way of thinking becomes much clearer to students if they engage with it in an interactive group learning environment. The economic way of thinking rarely comes alive for students if they are merely passive learners (as part of a gannet culture of 'feed me more and more information'), suffering 'death by bullet point' as they gaze at one PowerPoint slide after another.

## Warm Calling

To encourage interaction, we engage in 'warm calling' of students. On our way into the lecture room, we ask a couple of students to interact with us during the session. We boost their confidence by explaining possible responses to our questions. Students essentially become our 'partners in crime' by interacting with us during the lecture; once interaction begins, other students join in. By week three of the semester, such initial warm calling is no longer necessary because interaction becomes standard practice in class.

As a general rule, when interaction does occur, we are very open and encouraging. We thank the student for his or her contribution and proceed to repeat verbatim the question asked (or comment made). This is imperative in a large class, because not everyone hears the original question or comment. We always get as close as possible to the person who asked the question. Once students realize that we are open to interaction, much enlightening discussion follows.

## Buzz-Group Exercises

We provide student-specific tasks to work on during the class. From our experience of buzz-group exercises, our advice is to go for easy targets at the beginning of the semester and then for more difficult exercises as the semester progresses once students' confidence has improved and an appropriate interactive teaching/learning environment has been created. For example, when introducing an economics concept such as elasticity for the first time, there is no point in asking students to give the formula for the price elasticity of demand. A better starting point would be to ask what key factors determine whether you will purchase a product such as an iPad. Using questions with no correct or incorrect answers can help students to engage more deeply with material.

During buzz-group discussions, we wander among the students, listening and clarifying the tasks where necessary. We also encourage students to ask questions about points that were not clear to them earlier in the lecture. Whenever appropriate, we try to incorporate students' comments and contributions into our wrap-up. In our opinion, students need to know that the lecturer is interested in their analysis and that their insightful contributions do matter. From our experience to date, active listening and flexibility in discussion leadership are key elements of this.

To ensure that those at the front of a class do not dominate, we invite students from different parts of the lecture room to answer different questions. We have found that as the semester progresses, calling on students to participate becomes less of an issue as they will voluntarily contribute once an interactive teaching/learning environment has been created and they feel safe and no longer intimidated. We find this to be true even in very large classes. When requesting students to answer questions, whether as part of a buzz group or on an individual basis, we find that it is best to allow them to prepare questions and answers before going public. An inverted pyramid approach works particularly well in this regard: students work on their own initially, then in pairs, then in fours and finally as a whole class. By building up to open discussion in this way, students develop their ideas and, as their confidence grows, are more likely to contribute productively. If students find this threatening, we emphasize that it is our competence as teachers and not their competence as learners that is at issue if the discussion does not work. An atmosphere of mutual respect, trust and positive reinforcement is essential, but this is something that only develops over time.

In large groups in particular, it is a good idea to display the question visually as well as explaining it clearly. In a large class setting, we signal when time is up—a particular sound from a computer or smart phone application, for example, tells students that they need to stop working on the problem. Timing is critical. The timing allocated to exercises (e.g., during buzz groups) must be tight enough so that students don't wander from the task at hand. On the other hand, the timing allocated must be long enough to allow a serious attempt from most groups.

## Students' Notes

We ask students to read their notes, fill in the gaps and make sure they understand them. We request them to read their neighbors' notes and discuss any issues they may have with them. We ask students to write down questions on small sheets of paper that we hand out in advance and collect before the end of the lecture. We find this technique to be very helpful because it allows us to respond to the questions at the next lecture (or in an online forum or during an associated tutorial) and to gauge how the material is being received by the students. This technique is far less time-consuming than one might expect, because it is usually possible to group the questions into themes.

## Voting

We ask students to participate by raising their hands. For example, we ask them to answer a multiple-choice question by voting for a, b, c, etc. with a show of hands, and we include an option for 'don't know' (hopefully too many hands won't go up for this one!). Electronic voting systems (also known as audience response systems) are a more sophisticated way of recording student responses to such questions. As argued by Draper and Brown (2004), electronic voting systems have been shown to have benefits for formative assessment, particularly in numerate subjects. Salemi points out that the use of clickers in the teaching of economics 'allows the instructor to create two-way communication in a class of several hundred' (2009, p. 402). When deciding on the type of question to use for such exercises, it can be very useful to design questions similar to those that students might be faced with in their end-of-semester examination.

## E-learning

Over two consecutive years a number of years ago, grades in our first-year microeconomics module had been very low. In response, we introduced an e-learning (Aplia) component, which proved to be an effective incentive for students to engage in self-directed learning early in the module. At various intervals in the semester, students are requested to undertake an online test. Weekly practice tests are made available online, feedback is provided during lectures and students receive their individual marks on completion of the test. Because it is difficult for students to gauge the quality of their performance in large classes, quick feedback is critical. We still employ e-learning (which has been refined over time) in our module; feedback suggests that students find it beneficial.

## Online Forums

Online forums have huge potential as a way of engaging with students. Most students visit online chat environments, such as Facebook and Twitter, at least once a day. Such forums should not be seen as simply another means of getting through more module content but as a means of encouraging active and independent student engagement and learning. For online forums to be used effectively, instructors need to establish class participation guidelines that provide sufficient structure while also allowing for flexibility.

## Games

We have coached the teaching assistants of our intermediate economics module to play the Prisoners' Dilemma game with students in their tutorials that accompany the large class instruction. The game is played as a teaching tool to discuss the behavior of firms in an oligopolistic market structure. Despite the fact that the students were shocked to discover that they could play games in an economics module, feedback suggests that it is working well.

## Video/DVD

We use short video clips to help students to see real-life cases of microeconomic market structures. According to learning theorists, imagery is important for learning and remembering (Myers, 2004). For example, to illustrate the idea of duopoly (where two firms dominate a particular market), we show a five-minute video clip of the tea industry in Ireland, which is dominated by two firms. At the end of the clip, students begin to understand the underlying assumptions of such a market structure. We have found that clips can change the pace and dynamics within a lecture and increase students' attention spans. Short movie and television clips (usually three to five minutes in length) can be used to highlight particular economic principles, and students can be asked to write a brief paper that explains the economic content of the clip. As Sexton (2006) points out, even if the clips are not fully accurate, they can be useful springboards for discussion.

## Large Group Problem Solving

It is possible, even in very large groups, to set a collective task or challenge, ask everyone to get involved and then debrief and capture the learning that can ensue. Many teachers are accustomed to doing this in small groups, but we usually need to enlist additional courage and guidance before trying something similar in a large group setting. Large group tasks probably need to be simpler both to explain and conduct, but they can have a powerful impact by creating a shared reference point that all participants can draw on, and they can be strong demonstrators in the same collective space of some of the key principles of a business education. An activity that we have used often has been to ask the entire group to organize themselves into a line in order of age. The ensuing chaos and then the gradually emerging clarity followed by the attempted execution of this task tend to be extremely engaging and full of energy. Students express huge satisfaction when the task is completed successfully, and though very simple and linear, it contains the seeds of much reflection and discussion that can trigger students' ability to identify links between their own experience and links in the field. Who emerged as leaders of the task? How did people communicate? What devices did the group invent to get the task done? Were there people who remained passive and did not get involved? How successful was the final outcome? What lessons does this activity contain when reflecting on how we mobilize large groups of people to achieve the same collective outcome? Asking students to write about what the activity teaches them and how this activity relates to their understanding of the principles of organizational behavior also provides a nice assessment or reflection activity that enlists their critical thinking capacities and asks them to apply these to an experience that they have all shared.

## Feedback

It is notoriously difficult to establish the extent of impact that a particular teaching technique or classroom activity has on the learning of students. What we do know is that students who participate in classes that integrate some of the above activities express much higher levels of satisfaction, report working much harder in these modules and assess their own competence development more positively than those who operate in more exclusively didactic large group environments (Moore et al., 2007). Generally we witness much higher levels of student energy and engagement than might otherwise be likely, and we know that these are factors that sow the seeds for better learning, harder work and more commitment to the subjects in learners' curricula.

## CONCLUSION

Students are not passive learners who simply absorb knowledge. We have worked to create a far more interactive learning environment in our large group lectures, and evidence shows that this helps to eliminate that passive experience that students particularly associate with large class instruction. We encourage educators to experiment with the approaches we have outlined in this chapter. We are not for suggesting that large group lectures should involve the nonstop use of interactive exercises. On the contrary, we see the more traditional didactic lecturing approach as playing a central role in the classroom but believe that it needs to be applied in combination with the type of interactive approaches we suggest throughout this chapter. Interactive activities can be fun while also impacting substantially on the quality of the learning experience and outcomes. In an era of poor lecture attendance, of differing expectations among new cohorts of students and when large group teaching needs to justify its existence and add value more than ever before, we believe interactive activities in these settings are vital.

## REFERENCES

Barrett, T., & Moore, S. (2010). *New approaches to problem-based learning: Revitalizing your practice in higher education*. Abingdon: Taylor & Francis.

Bean, J. C. (2011). *Engaging ideas: The professors guide to integrating writing, critical thinking and active learning in the classroom* (2nd ed.). San Francisco: Jossey Bass.

Benzing, C., & Christ, P. (1997). A survey of teaching methods among economics faculty. *Journal of Economic Education*, 28(2), 182–188.

Borden, V., & Burton, K. (1999, May–June). The impact of class size on student performance in Introductory Courses, accepted for 39th annual conference of the Association for Institutional Research, Seattle, WA. http://www.eric.ed.gov/ERICWebPortal/search/detailmini.jsp?_nfpb=true&_&ERICExtSearch_SearchValue_0=ED433782&ERICExtSearch_SearchType_0=no&accno=ED433782

Carbone, E., & Greenberg, J. (1998). Teaching large classes: Unpacking the problem and responding creatively. In M. Kaplan (Ed.), *To improve the academy* (Vol. 17, pp. 311–326). Stillwater, OK: Professional and Organizational Development Network in Higher Education.

Cooper, J. L., & Robinson, P. (2000). The argument for making large classes seem small. *New Directions for Teaching and Learning*, 81(Spring), 5–16.

De Caprariis, P., Barman, C., & Magee, P. (2001). Monitoring the benefits of active learning exercises in introductory survey courses in science: An attempt to improve the education of prospective public school teachers. *Journal of Scholarship of Teaching and Learning*, 1(2), 1–11.

Draper, S. W., & Brown, M. I. (2004). Increasing interactivity in lectures using an electronic voting system. *Journal of Computer Assisted Learning*, 20, 81–94.

Edmonson, J. B., & Mulder, F. J. (1924). Size of class as a factor in university instruction. *Journal of Educational Research*, 9(1), 1–12.

Foreman, J. (2003). Next generation: Education technology versus the lecture. *Educause*, 38(4), 12–22.

Fransson, A. (1977). On qualitative differences in learning: Effects of intrinsic motivation and extrinsic test anxiety on process and outcome. *British Journal of Organizational Psychology*, 27(3), 244–257.

Harris, A. (2010). Active learning for the millennial generation. *Georgia Library Quarterly*, 47(4), 13–14.

McGlynn, A. P. (2005). Teaching millennials: Our newest cultural cohort. *Education Digest: Essential Readings Condensed for Quick Review*, 71(4), 12–16.

Moore, S., Armstrong, C., & Pearson, J. (2008). Lecture absenteeism among students in higher education: A valuable route to understanding student motivation. *Journal of Higher Education Policy and Management*, 30(1), 15–24.

Moore, S., & Kuol, N. (2005). Students evaluating teachers: Exploring the importance of faculty reaction to feedback on teaching. *Teaching in Higher Education*, 10(1), 57–73.

Moore, S., Walsh, G., & Risquez, A. (2007). *Teaching at college and university: Effective strategies and key principles*. Buckinghamshire: McGraw-Hill.

Murdoch, B., & Guy, P. W. (2002). Active learning in small and large classes. *Accounting Education*, 11(3), 271–282.

Myers, D. G. (2004). *Psychology* (7th ed.). New York: Worth.

Salemi, M. K. (2009). Clickenomics: Using a classroom response system to increase student engagement in a large-enrollment principles of economics course. *Journal of Economic Education*, 40(4), 385–404.

Sexton, R. L. (2006). Using short movie and television clips in the economics principles class. *Journal of Economic Education*, 37(4), 406–417.

Stanley, C., & Porter, E. (2002). *Engaging large classes: Strategies and techniques for college faculty*. Bolton, MA: Anker Publishing.

Stead, D. R. (2005). A review of the one-minute paper. *Active Learning in Higher Education, 6*(2), 118–131.

Urdan, J., & Schoenfelder, E. (2006). Classroom effects on student motivation: Goal structures, social relationships, and competence beliefs. *Journal of School Psychology, 44*(5), 331–349.

Watts, M., & Becker, W. E. (2008). A little more than chalk and talk: Results from a third national survey of teaching methods in undergraduate economics courses. *Journal of Economic Education, 39*(3), 273–286.

# 4 Engaging Large Groups of Individual Learners Through an Online Environment
## An Emerging i-Learner Generation?

*Fran Myers, Mike Phillips, Paul Raby and Carey Stephens*

INTRODUCTION

The Open University Business School (OUBS) has continually sought to integrate emergent online technologies within its curriculum as part of the Open University's core mission to be open to people, places, methods and ideas. Over the past 20 years, this has evolved from an emergent strategy stemming from individual academic interest in incorporating such technologies as a 'bolt on' to a traditional blended classroom and distance learning environment (Salmon, 2005) to a more deliberate learning design (OULDI, 2012), where the pedagogical approach embraces the digital environment and uses it to best fit student learning needs (particularly younger students) and to aid student retention.

During the last 5 years, the pace of development has accelerated in response to both internal stimuli such as academics and students tending to replicate familiar social and business online spaces in their learning environments (Lee, Danis, Miller & Jung, 2001) and external stimuli such as financial and social drivers. Many higher education institutions (HEIs) look at online solutions as a way of offering a quality, mass-customized experience at a perceived lower cost, in response to UK government policies and potential customer demand for flexible study at their own convenience (Laurillard, 2007).

This chapter seeks to provide a reflective overview of the authors' experiences of this continuing evolution in teaching innovation. It draws specifically on evidence gathered from a substantial ongoing study of the online behaviors of a cohort of 3,000 students on a Level 4 (first-year undergraduate) module. The chapter addresses four main themes in turn. Following a brief description of the Open University (OU) and its pedagogical approach, the chapter begins by exploring the evolution of learning platforms and spaces in the OU over the past decade. It describes how the previous emergent strategy of using 'safe' adaptations of social networking innovations, kept inside the university network, has evolved into a deliberate part of the learning design of modules over time, mirroring the evolution of social behavior online in wider society. Recent pedagogical work has pointed to the rise of a new generation of students, commonly referred to as the millennial generation. The second section of this chapter explores the traits associated with this millennial generation. The third section explores the posited effects of the rise of the millennial generation on curricula and pedagogical strategies, while the fourth section presents empirical research that explores the use of e-learning platforms and tools by the millennial generation. The analysis of a large amount of quantitative data allows for a critique of some of the theoretical assumptions made in the literature regarding the millennial generation. This both illuminates the shortcomings in our existing understanding of how the millennial generation engages in learning and acts as a clarion call for further research in this area.

## PEDAGOGICAL MODEL AND RESEARCH CONTEXT

The authors all occupy dual roles within OUBS as both as associate lecturers (ALs) teaching their own groups of students in the North West of England over the last 10 years and regional academics having line management responsibility for the delivery of the undergraduate program through a network of part-time associate lecturers, many of whom are also business practitioners.

Upon registration, students are allocated to a tutor (an associate lecturer in a local geographical region, in group sizes of around 20 to 25 students. Most Level 4 (first-year undergraduate) modules do have a face-to-face element, with up to four tutorials or day schools during the six-month duration of the module. For the most part, students work independently, with the primary mode of interaction with their AL and other students being through online media. In addition to marking assignments (tutor-marked assignments, or TMAs) and conducting end-of-module assessments (EMAs), the AL also facilitates an online tutor group forum (TGF) where students can actively participate in online collaborative work to support the learning process through a virtual learning environment (VLE) using the medium of a Moodle platform.

In line with the OU's mission of being open to people, places, methods and ideas, there are no entry criteria for OU students. This would present a pedagogic challenge in a conventional face-to-face campus-based higher education context, with a highly diverse student profile, but for the OU, this is complicated further by the dynamics of distance learning interaction and the developing use of online technologies as noted in the introduction.

An additional concern for the authors is the issue of student retention. The OUBS Business Studies undergraduate program grew from 2,750 students in the 2005–2006 academic year to 17,000 in the 2010–2011 academic year. As a large-scale provider of blended distance learning, the retention and progression of students is a major challenge for the OU. Student retention has become increasingly important, with funding for HEI in the UK undergoing seismic changes as the result of fundamental (and sometimes divergent) changes in government policies across the four Home Nations (Browne, 2010).

## EVOLUTION OF THE ONLINE CURRICULUM

OUBS currently provides a portfolio of online media tools to support students on its undergraduate modules. These have evolved over the past ten years to provide a variety of distinct functions that mirror the digital environments we inhabit elsewhere in our lives, albeit in an adapted 'safe' form within the university network.

The use of online tools in OUBS programs was pioneered by academics such as Gilly Salmon in the 1990s. Participants taking managerial courses were encouraged to explore areas such as differences in organizational culture through online discussion with another student. Laurillard (2008) discusses 'the context of the environment . . . learners inhabit'. In the OUBS context, the authors have found that online VLE spaces need to parallel the external media environment in order to remain popular and relevant to students. In contemporary times, the VLE encompasses a full portfolio of learning tools, from the 'conversational' dialogue (Laurillard, 2008) of the TGF providing structured learning, through to student cafes offering social space. Some examples of these tools are described in the following sections.

## THE TUTOR GROUP FORUM

The tutor group forum provides a safe, closed virtual classroom interaction space for dialogue between students and their personal tutor, typically on the basis of a 1:20 ratio, and is a continuing and key part of the OU's blended offering. Students are expected to engage with and contribute to the TGF, and they are assessed on their initial responses to questions set by the tutor, their interaction with other students and on a short précis they write reflecting on the ensuing debate. The role of the tutor here is to instigate and facilitate group discussion. Most interactions on these forums are conversational in nature and are course related, with typical postings from students having headings such as, 'Word count, what's included?' and 'Help with my assignment'.

This space is highly successful, with 90% of students in the study cohort participating in some form in their TGF. The mean number of postings per student is 16.5 (the 10% of students who are unable to contribute online, such as those in prison, are provided with an alternative learning experience using anonymous postings in paper format). Students who engaged more with the forum were typically more successful in their studies, with 75% of those gaining a pass grade making more than 10 posts to the forum, rising to 86% for those making more than 30 posts. However, it should be acknowledged that this may also be a reflection of the general effort put into their studies by more conscientious students.

## STUDENT CAFÉ

Student cafés across the OU are set out to provide a less formal, optional place for students to interact virtually. Signposting to students makes clear the distinction between these areas and the TGF. The student café for the cohort studied received 13,640 postings over the six-month period. Students typically posted a wider variety of messages than in the TGF, with many of the postings being social in nature or airing more general study concerns—with typical headings being 'did anyone see X on TV last night?', 'cannot believe we have nearly finished!' and 'what are you studying next?'. Many students recognized contributors from other cafes, with certain students building up reputations for being particularly helpful or knowledgeable in certain areas.

The cafés remain lightly moderated by the university in case of inappropriate behavior by students, such as inadvertently promoting plagiarism by sharing assignment work or 'trolling' (Donath, 1999). While this behavior is rare (typically one incident per cohort of students), the number of responses these postings provoke suggest how upsetting they are for other students. One such posting in the context of a recent student cohort garnered 11 responses in just over one hour before it was removed by the moderator.

## PERSONAL ONLINE SPACES

Students also have the ability to create their own shared areas, wikis and blogs within the network, which they can invite other students or academic staff to participate in. Communal areas such as Social Learn, which are again only lightly moderated, allow free sharing of information and resources across the whole university network. These tools allow students to build their own repositories and pathways throughout the environment, saving and sharing resources as they go.

Interestingly, the process of defining these areas has come about through emergent use by the whole learning community of both students and lecturers alike, reflecting the evolution of online media outside the university context. The TGF acts similarly to the physical and virtual professional networks that are inhabited through work, while the cafés provide a similar environment to social sites such as Facebook. In another mirror of the evolution of online environments, the OU flexible repository tool MyStuff has recently been removed, because, like its external counterpart,

MySpace (see Gillette, 2011, for a useful discussion on this area), its use diminished as participants moved on to use more dynamic media such as Social Learn.

The OU offers a growing proliferation of different online 'touch points' where students may feel engaged in their personal learning experience—not just the formal module requirements of the TGF but through informal/parallel (and nonassessed) online spaces. As an example of how these offering continue to expand and evolve, current institutional findings estimate that there are over a thousand Facebook user groups and pages about the OU (of which only two are official OU sites).

## THE MILLENNIAL GENERATION

The evolution of the online environment used by all OU students has happened in parallel with the engagement of the millennial generation with higher education, which many academics perceive as bringing fresh challenges to the evolution of online pedagogy. The rise of the millennial generation creates a variety of fundamental issues that must be wrestled with by educators at the start of the 21st century. In this section we elucidate a number of millennial generation traits. We explore these attributes with reference to the literature, our own educational experience and the research we have collected for this study.

Research on the perceived differentiating characteristics of the latest generation of students entering higher education was stimulated initially by the interest of professionals in HEIs worldwide (Keeling, 2003), drawing significantly on the work of Howe and Strauss (2000). The millennial generation (those born between 1982 and 2000) have been exposed to the accoutrements of information technology, such as computers and cell phones, from birth. On the basis that they now make up the majority of the student population at most traditional HEIs, the issue of potentially different generational perspectives has been further highlighted. Their arrival into the sector has also coincided with vast growth in the arena of technology-enhanced learning (TEL) (Laurillard, 2008), giving rise to speculation that this group of students may consequently have inherently different learning needs compared with previous generations, especially following exposure to such TEL through their learning experiences at second level. For example, the Melville (2009: 6) report states that: 'Present-day students are heavily influenced by school methods of delivery so that shifts in educational practice there can be expected to impact on expectations of approaches in higher education.' According to Black (2010: 95), millennials have an 'intuitive understanding of digital language' and use digital tools as 'an extension of their brains.' It is posited that these students may think and learn differently, whether because of these tools or because of other social factors, and evidence is beginning to emerge that they may have different dispositions toward learning. It has been suggested that millennials want to learn by working collaboratively; many of them enjoy the activity of teamwork.

This has far-reaching implications for future curriculum design, because it implies that, for millennials, the mode of learning is a process of information gathering and peer exchanges online (thus emulating social networking) rather than a reliance on the traditional design of assessment through subject knowledge and understanding created by academia. How students are interacting is changing the way they learn. Furthermore, McGlynn (2005: 15) states that the millennials 'have a preference to learn in their own time and on their own terms'. This echoes the rise of a 24/7 society where shopping and watching TV programs, for example, are no longer restricted to a predetermined time or set opening hours. Sarah Knight (2012) from Jisc writes that:

> Learners are already seeking both choice and control when it comes to the technology and are mixing and matching personal and institutional tools with skill. Technology, it seems, is central to their lives and therefore also to their studies, but increasingly the boundaries between study and other aspects of their lives are being eroded.

The desire for a personalized or 'self-service' student experience could be perceived as problematic for the OU traditional blended model that has been historically reliant on economies of scale. The need to deliver cost-effective distance learning education at scale and the desire for student retention challenge the individual need. The integration of technology and learning arguably reduces costs; however, the issue of individually tailored assessment could challenge the pedagogical integrity of courses. Many tutors report that, although younger students offer rich and varied references in their work, they are less critical about the validity of the sources they use on the web. This willingness to accept information accessed through the Internet as a source of knowledge reveals a need to stimulate critical thinking skills in students in a digital environment. While previous generations could assume that the filtering and organizing of cultural knowledge was largely done, millennials have to do much of it themselves. For these reasons educators need to facilitate processes that will equip students to do more than merely access information. This raises the question as to how universities should help millennials make the transition from the digital literacy of 'digital natives' (Black, 2010) to a more sophisticated 'digital maturity'; from informal knowledge gatherers to critically thinking academic learners, as described by Mingers (2000).

Significantly, younger students are not enamored with traditional textbook learning as they progress in the development of critical skills at Levels 5 and 6. Students offer comments such as 'ridiculous amount of reading involved', and 'shelf cracking books', and 'Previous to this I did B120 business studies which I thought was much better . . . designed'. These comments suggest a growing disenchantment with traditional learning tools. In sympathy with this view, Elam, Stratton and Gibson (2007: 22) suggest that 'the ease with which millennial students routinely engage in multitasking behaviors, enabled in part through the use of technology, has shortened their collective attention span'. Managing this potential evolution and the associated consequences will require continued monitoring and adaptation of program design to ensure that programs remain relevant to students while still retaining the key study skills necessary for employment that are currently embedded in HEI offerings.

The combination of underdeveloped critical thinking skills and disenchantment with traditional methods of teaching presents a major pedagogical challenge. Older learners will have been exposed to early learning primarily through textbooks and classroom environments that encouraged greater engagement and reflection. These processes encourage the development of critical facilities. In contrast, solitary online work lends itself to looking for quick answers. The question that arises is whether the latter, requiring only individual input, results in the acquisition of broad knowledge to the determent of the critical thinking skills traditionally acquired through classroom discussion and debate. Assessing and addressing this issue is a major challenge in the context of the millennial generation.

Specifically in the context of this study, OUBS has experienced changes to its undergraduate student cohort in terms of growth in both total numbers and constituency (with the proportion of students under 25 years of age growing significantly). The OU comes from a different starting position than most conventional HEIs, with a typical student population of older adult learners, often cited as having a 'second chance' outlook. However, younger students (fitting the profile of millennials) now typically make up 30% of OUBS student numbers. This large group of younger students has led some academics to postulate that part of the huge interest in learning through digital media might be due to the younger age profile of participants.

## EXPLORING THE MILLENNIAL GENERATION—RESEARCH AND FINDINGS

The previous sections have highlighted the rise of the millennial generation and elucidated some of the posited effects that the traits of this generation will have on the design of curricula and online learning moving into the future. In this section, we draw on the wealth of data available to the OU to explore some of these issues in more detail.

The authors took a case study approach by reviewing the dynamics of one core module, with B120, An Introduction to Business Studies module (year 1 undergraduate), chosen for the case study because it has consistently been the most populous and because it is a compulsory module in the BA Business Studies qualification. It has attracted many students new to higher education and has consistently received positive student feedback. The module's assessment strategy incorporates both written assignments and a small element of individual and collaborative online work.

A quantitative approach was used for the initial stages of the case study in order to identify key trends in online behavior which could then be subjected to further analysis such as by different age segments of the student cohort. Data were drawn from a recent cohort of B120 with more than 3,000 students, which included detailed analysis of 54,000 TGF online postings and cross-mapping with OU student record system entries made by tutors and learner support staff. The initial data set contained key information incorporating assignment and module results, personal profile data (including age and declared disability), number of individual student postings on forums and recorded tutor referrals or interventions for additional student support.

Assessment for B120 includes five sets of activities posted on the TGF by the tutor and four TMAs. These are spread evenly throughout the module, with each set of TGF postings comprising of three activities for the students.

Student engagement with the online element of modules has grown steadily over the past 10 years. A typical tutor group forum on a 60-point course (12 months duration) in 2002 received 191 posts, the average for a 30-point course (6 months duration) in 2009 was 620 (note that there were no direct comparable data, because OUBS offered its first 30-point course from 2006). Tutor engagement with students via the online forum has maintained a steady mean average around 10% of postings for a typical group, illustrating a consistent input for facilitation (although the input may have changed qualitatively over that time).

Previous perceptions of millennial generation behavior within the institution might have led to the assumption that this group of students would be the principal architects of this participation in online arenas, as the largest represented group (see the appendix). However, statistical analysis of the B120 case study cohort has revealed a different picture, with proportionally the most active group in online discussion being those aged between 36 and 45, who, despite comprising only 23% of the total cohort, were responsible for 28% of the 54,000-plus TGF postings. Younger students, aged under 25 (31% of this cohort), made only 25% of the total postings, while the group aged between 26 and 35 (36% of this cohort) made 34% of the postings.

The lower levels of online engagement displayed by the millennial group in this cohort perhaps also reflect the recent findings of Twenge, Campbell and Freeman (2012). The traits and behaviors they observed in their study indicated a 'Generation Me' with personal goals related to extrinsic values (money, image, fame) being more important than those related to intrinsic values (self-acceptance, affiliation, community) of a 'Generation We', which would be more engaged with the kind of collaborative working typified through a TGF environment.

The study also identifies the mechanistic engagement of all age groups with their TGF. Most students gain their online credit by the end of period

2 in the module, and subsequently postings decrease rapidly in period 3, with only the intrinsic learners keeping up the online dialogue. In contrast, activity rates in the social café space were unaffected by the life cycle of the module, showing the value for the students of this type of forum. Conversations between students changed at this point from social comments broadly around the module, such as 'who do you admire in business?' to looking beyond the module to 'what are we all doing next?', thus giving the institution insight into how communities can develop online and visibility on important issues for students.

The data set also highlights the correlation between engaged TGF contribution and success, which concurs with the Laing, Chao and Robinson (2005) study of nontraditional learners, which demonstrated a link between attendance and academic performance. This poses a pedagogical challenge for the OU in terms of learning design as to whether online engagement can be increased to ensure greater retention and enhanced student performance. However, it remains unclear whether the issue is about mode of learning or whether pedagogy can be developed to incorporate media used by learners in other aspects of their lives, even though its use may not necessarily increase academic achievement.

## CONCLUSIONS

Drawing on the initial outcomes from this study, several issues have been identified, particularly around the understanding of the dynamics of student engagement with online collaborative learning and some practical implications for the development of online/blended pedagogy.

Contrary to preconceptions (initially shared by the authors themselves), millennials show a lower-than-expected engagement with the online elements of blended learning and are not actually the main demographic segment currently engaging with online/forum interaction. Older age groups seem to have a proportionately greater engagement in terms of active postings and discussion, perhaps reflecting the shift in personal goals identified in millennials by Twenge et al. (2012), with less emphasis on community by 'Generation Me'. Although millennials may be considered to have a high level of digital literacy, the questions around digital maturity may be more important in driving future pedagogical initiatives as the learning context becomes more complex.

This study, along with others, may indicate the emergence of a new type of learner who demands personalized learning specific to the individual: a 'Generation Me', who could be termed an 'i-Learner'. There needs to be clarity about what learning we are actually designing for. As noted above, students may seek more personal or customized learning. Equally, academics may need to challenge their own preconceptions of what learners need versus what they want in an environment where the measurement of student satisfaction is increasingly a driver for HEIs and impacts on learning design, as noted by academics writing on the Times Higher Education website (2012). For example, the provision of social spaces online, while not necessarily directly contributing to learning, are important to students both in terms of community and to provide helpful institutional insight.

Institutions need to be more agile in the development and application of technology tools in higher education blended learning pedagogy. The pace of change in technology creates a tension between traditional academic administration and module development. The formal processes of validation, quality assurance and assessment administration are inherently bureaucratic, which can constrain academic responses to new technology and the social changes in its use. In addition, the ever-increasing diversity of the student body needs to be addressed by allowing flexibility in the design of online tools for interactive engagement with students. For the OU, facilitating such flexibility is a challenge. Too much emphasis can be attributed to technological intervention in supporting students. As suggested by Salmon (2005), success comes from a partnership with appropriate, well-supported and focused human intervention and pedagogical input and the sensitive handling of the sphere over time by trained online tutors.

## REFERENCES

Black, A. (2010). Gen Y: Who they are and how they learn. *Educational Horizons, 88*(2), 92–101.

Browne, J. (2010) *Securing a sustainable future for higher education: An independent review of higher education. Funding & Student Finance.* Retrieved from http://dera.ioe.ac.uk/11444/1/10-1208-securing-sustainable-higher-education-browne-report.pdf

Donath, J. (1999). Identity and deception in the virtual community, communities in cyberspace. In P. Kollock & M. Smith (Eds.), *Communities in cyberspace* (pp. 29–59). New York: Routledge.

Elam, C., Stratton, T., & Gibson, D.D. (2007). Welcoming a new generation to college: The millennial students. *Journal of College Admission, 195,* 20–25.

Gillette, F. (2011, June 22). The rise and inglorious fall of Myspace. *Bloomberg Businessweek Magazine.* Retrieved from http://www.businessweek.com/magazine/content/11_27/b4235053917570.htm

Howe, N., & Strauss, W. (2000). *Millennials rising: The next great generation.* New York: Vintage.

Keeling, S. (2003). Advising the millennial generation. *NACADA Journal, 23,* 30–36.

Knight, S. (2012) Academia tackles the future. *The Guardian.* Retrieved from http://www.guardian.co.uk/digitalstudent/academia

Laing, C., Chao, K-M., & Robinson, A. (2005). Managing the expectations of non-international students: A process of negotiation. *Journal of Further and Higher Education, 57*(2), 169–179.

Laurillard, D. (2007). Modeling benefits-oriented costs for technology enhanced learning. *Higher Education, 54*(1), 21–39.

Laurillard, D. (2008). Technology enhanced learning as a tool for pedagogical innovation. *Journal of Philosophy of Education, 42*(3–4), 521–533.

Lee, A., Danis, A.L.C., Miller, T., & Jung, Y. (2001). Fostering social interaction in online spaces. In *Human-computer interaction: INTERACT'01: IFIP TC. 13 International Conference on Human-Computer Interaction, 9th–13th July 2001, Tokyo, Japan* (p. 59–66). Ios Press.

McGlynn, A. (2005). Teaching millennials: Our newest cultural cohort. *Education Digest, 71*(4), 12–16.

Melville, D. (2009). *Higher education in a Web 2.0 world—Report of an independent committee of inquiry into the impact on higher education of students.* London: Joint Information Systems Committee.

Mingers, J. (2000). What is it to be critical? Teaching a critical approach to management undergraduates. *Management Learning, 31*(2), 219–237.

Open University Learn Design Initiative. (2012). Retrieved from http://www.open.ac.uk/blogs/OULDI/

Salmon, G. (2005). Flying not flapping: A strategic framework for e-learning and pedagogical innovation in higher education institutions. *Research in Learning Technology, 13*(3), 201–218.

Times Higher Education. (2012). Satisfaction and its discontents. Retrieved from http://www.timeshighereducation.co.uk/story.asp?sectioncode=26&storycode=419238&c=2&dm_i=12ZA,R1IV,5FMLPK,26MTG,1

Twenge, J.M., Campbell, W.K., & Freeman, E.C. (2012). Generational differences in young adults' life goals, concern for others, and civic orientation, 1966–2009. *Journal of Personality and Social Psychology, 102*(5), 1045–1062.

# 5 Prediction Markets in Management Courses
## Opportunities and Challenges

*Dorit Geifman and Daphne R. Raban*

INTRODUCTION

Online prediction markets, which use a financial market mechanism as an information aggregation and processing engine, are gaining a foothold within the corporate world, driving new management and business processes. A report in 2011 by McKinsey, a business analysis firm, states that 7% of 2,000 executives reported the use of prediction markets as part of their management tool kit (McKinsey, 2011). The integration of prediction markets into MBA curricula opens up new pedagogical *opportunities* and serves a dual purpose. It exposes students to innovative business methods and tools and at the same time facilitates the creation of an online experiential learning environment. The development of prediction markets that are appropriate in an educational context is challenging. The need to align the activity with pedagogical objectives requires that the educator possess a good understanding of the tool and its underlying concepts. The effective integration of prediction markers into the learning process calls for an iterative developmental approach. Several active learning modules and design considerations derived from their development process are presented here.

Prediction market is the general name for a family of tools that, by means of a market mechanism, leverage the collective intelligence and/or knowledge of a group of people to support a variety of processes—for example, forecasting, decision making, information aggregation, and problem solving. In these markets contracts are traded, where the underlying asset is a statement to be evaluated or an event to be forecast. The price of the contract reflects the market opinion as to the probability of the event occurring or the statement's chances of being correct. On the due date of the event, the market closes and the price of the contract that represents the actual outcome is fixed to the predefined amount, with all other contracts being nullified. The payoffs due to the traders are computed according to their holdings. The markets incorporate a monetary incentive, based on the performance of the trader, thus providing an inducement to disclose true private knowledge. In the public Internet sphere, markets are employed to predict the outcomes of, for example, political and current events (www.intrade.com) and movies' opening weekend box-office revenues (www.hsx.com). In the corporate environment, prediction markets are used for purposes such as sales forecasting (Chen & Plott, 2002), the prediction of operational indices (Guo, Fang, & Whinston, 2006; Remidez & Joslin, 2007) and innovation management (Dahan, Soukhoroukova, & Spann, 2010; LaComb, Barnett, & Pan, 2007). Due to antigambling regulations and budget limitations, most markets use virtual money as an incentive. Studies show that the use of virtual money does not diminish market accuracy (Servan-Schreiber, Wolfers, Pennock, & Galebach, 2004).

The number of students who engage in online and distance learning in the United States rose from 16% in 2003–2004 to 20% in 2007–2008 (National Center for Education Statistics, 2011). At the same time, social applications have penetrated many facets of life, blurring the borders between the personal domain, the workspace, and the learning environment. The ease of use and accessibility of wiki's, blogs, and other online collaborative tools facilitate the rapid deployment of new forms of cooperative learning. At the same time, computer-mediated learning environments touch on pedagogical paradigms such as collaborative and experiential learning and offer new opportunities for creative pedagogical initiatives.

In many MBA programs, educators appreciate and embrace the pedagogical effectiveness of experiential learning. Still, students and employees that take a more vocational perspective feel that the graduates recruited by organizations are often not adequately prepared to cope with real-world challenges. In a gathering of the deans of the major business schools to mark the 100th anniversary of the Harvard Business School, critics of MBA programs claimed that business education is too theoretical and detached from the real needs of corporate managers (Thompson, 2008). One way of reducing the gap between theory and practice in the field of management education is to incorporate computerized, networked tools such as business games, management simulations, and decision support tools as part of the curriculum (Rafaeli, Raban, Ravid, & Noy, 2003).

Efforts to address the criticisms leveled at business education have led to the introduction of new online teaching methods into the curriculum of business schools. The next section describes several implementations of prediction market–based learning activities, which complement the teaching of theory in business management and economics courses. The section that follows presents some design considerations that guided the development process.

## USING PREDICTION MARKETS IN CLASS

The active learning modules presented here follow two instructional approaches. The first approach is the use of a hands-on activity, based on simulated scenarios, to complement the lecture delivered in class. In a different design, the students trade remotely over an extended time and experience a more realistic use of prediction markets. The activities are developed and continuously refined at the School of Management at the University of Haifa. More details on the activities and their pedagogical benefits have been published previously (Raban & Geifman, 2009). When relevant, reports on two other educational deployments of prediction markets are referenced (Buckley, Garvey, & McGrath, 2011; Gangur & Martincik, 2011).

The first simulation-based module was developed as a classroom activity to complement the teaching of theories underlying the idea of collective intelligence. The Hidden Profile Task was used to illustrate how markets can serve as information aggregation mechanisms. The Hidden Profile Task is an assignment in which segments of partial information are distributed among several participants such that when all information is collected, a complete and certain picture is obtained (Stasser & Titus, 1985). Prediction markets are used to collect the partial information and combine the pieces into a unified specific outcome. This kind of market involves the collection of distributed information in order to solve a problem. This scenario can occur due to asymmetric information distribution among participants or from incomplete information, where people maintain only part of the required information (Page, 2007).

The students are presented with a crime scenario and details about six suspects, including the villain. A market is set up with six stocks, each representing a suspect. Each student receives private information, including an alibi for one or more of the suspects. The exercise is designed in a manner such that if all private information is combined, the guilty person can easily be identified. The students are instructed to buy the stocks of the suspects they believe might be guilty and sell stocks of suspects they believe are innocent. The market runs for 20 minutes, and during this time the students are not allowed to speak to one another. When the market closes, the stock representing the villain is expected to achieve the highest price. The incentive scheme consists of a modest prize (e.g., a book) for the student who achieves the highest account balance.

The activity took place in several classes. Only one group correctly identified the guilty suspect at the close of the market. In other cases, the correct answer was identified close to the beginning of trading but then drifted and the final outcome was not the correct one (see Figure 5.1). Analysis of the problem suggested that several students based their trading decisions on stereotypes instead of objective information—the suspect's alibi in this case. This led to the redesign of the assignment and the use of an unambiguous, synthetic scenario.

The new design uses problem-solving markets that process individual solutions to a problem into a collective solution, which is represented by the market price (Meloso, Copic, & Bossaerts, 2009). For open-ended problems, the participants post the possible solutions as contracts in the market.

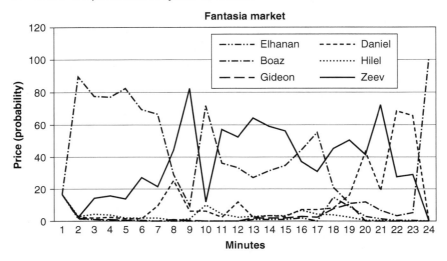

*Figure 5.1* Hidden Profile Task Trading Patterns

When the exhaustive set of possible solutions is known in advance, they are configured at market set-up.

Collective problem solving was simulated by using the Knapsack Problem. The Knapsack Problem represents a family of computationally complex problems studied in the fields of computer science and operational research. No one-size-fit-all algorithm solves these problems, and heuristics must be applied to solve specific cases; therefore, it is particularly suited as a collective intelligence task. In this activity, the Knapsack Problem was framed as the Burglar Problem:

> A burglar broke into a house and filled his sacks with loot. Each sack weighs differently and contains different worth of goods. Alas! When trying to leave the house, the burglar could not carry all the sacks because the burden was too heavy. Help the burglar choose the sacks that he can carry while maximizing his profit.

The students receive a list of weight and price values corresponding to individual sacks and a total weight constraint (see left side of Figure 5.2). They have 2 minutes to select the subset of sacks that maximize the total value under the given weight constraint. Most of the students will not reach the correct solution within this time frame but will familiarize themselves with the problem. After 2 minutes, the marketplace opens for trading, with each sack represented by one stock (see right side of Figure 5.2). The students are instructed to buy the stocks of sacks that they

**Max. weight: 14kg.**

| | Value | Weight | Item |
|---|---|---|---|
| ☑ | 2 | 3 | A-305 |
| ☐ | 3 | 4 | B-305 |
| ☐ | 4 | 6 | C-305 |
| ☐ | 5 | 3 | D-305 |
| ☐ | 6 | 5 | E-305 |
| ☑ | 9 | 13 | F-305 |
| ☐ | 8 | 6 | G-305 |
| ☐ | 7 | 9 | H-305 |
| ☑ | 6 | 2 | I-305 |
| ☐ | 5 | 4 | J-305 |
| ☐ | 8 | 7 | K-305 |
| ☐ | 9 | 7 | L-305 |
| | 17 | 18 | Total |

**Q305-1 – What is the solution to the burglar's problem?**

| Worth | # stocks | Change | Price | Item |
|---|---|---|---|---|
| $261.16 | 20 | $0.91↑ | $13.52 | A-305 quick trade |
| | | $0.20↑ | $10.20 | B-305 quick trade |
| | | $0.57↑ | $10.57 | C-305 quick trade |
| | | $0.22↑ | $13.06 | D-305 quick trade |
| | | $-0.40↓ | $10.95 | E-305 quick trade |
| $207.59 | 20 | $0.76↑ | $10.76 | F-305 quick trade |
| | | $0.95↑ | $10.95 | G-305 quick trade |
| | | ------ | $10.00 | H-305 quick trade |
| $256.66 | 20 | $1.32↑ | $13.29 | I-305 quick trade |
| | | ------ | $12.40 | J-305 quick trade |
| | | ------ | $10.00 | K-305 quick trade |
| | | ------ | $10.00 | L-305 quick trade |

*Figure 5.2* The Knapsack Problem Screens

believe are part of the solution and sell the stocks of sacks that are not. While the market runs for 6 minutes, the students are not allowed to speak to one another. When the market closes, the stocks of the sacks that comprise the correct solution are expected to gain the highest price. The incentive scheme consists of a modest prize for the student who achieves the highest account balance.

Overall, 35 markets were run in 24 undergraduate and graduate classes. In all classes, a small number of individual students identified the correct solution. The markets as a whole identified the correct solution in 17 cases.

Prediction markets can be used for the types of activities that can be suitably adapted for market uses in real-world settings. For example, prediction markets can forecast future uncertain events (Wolfers & Zitzewitz, 2004). In this case, the outcome of the event can be affected by unknown actions or events that have not yet occurred. This type of market was introduced as a complementary, voluntary activity in a business simulation game course that took an entire term on the MBA program. In this business game, students were charged with managing firms competing in a virtual world. The students worked in competing teams, each responsible for operating one firm for several game 'years', and the team that achieved the highest shareholder value by the end of the last year won the game. The business game was characterized by intense activity and competition.

A prediction market was set up to predict the winning team and the firms' performance indices. The markets were open during the last four 'years' of the game until a few hours before the final game results were published. The students, who were players and concurrently prediction markets traders, traded under conditions where they had a certain perceived sense of influence on the outcome.

Every week supplementary events that influenced the intermediate results of the game as well as events that related to general current events were introduced maintain interest and increase activity level. The incentive scheme consisted of a small prize for the student who achieved the highest account balance when the markets closed. A participation reward of two grade points was awarded to students who executed at least three trades.

The markets were run in three MBA classes. Thirty-eight out of 114 students participated in trading, representing 18 of the 20 competing firms. Two out of the three markets identified the game winner correctly.

The focus of the learning tools previously described is the teaching of social computing concepts. Other schools use prediction markets to enhance the teaching of economic and financial theories. Buckley et al. (2011) used prediction markets to apply the material delivered in risk management courses to real-world events. An insurance loss market was set up to predict insurance losses that occurred during a specific time period in three particular states in the United States. They demonstrated that over the duration of the course, and as students gained more trading experience, their decision-making skills improved. Gangur and Martincik (2011) report the ongoing use of prediction markets as a supplementary activity in courses on finance and capital markets analysis. In this case, students trade securities in four areas: politics, sports, economics, and entertainment. Sophisticated incentive schemes are used to internalize the knowledge that was delivered in class.

The next section will highlight some of the more significant observations that resulted from our experience in the development of prediction markets–based active learning activities.

## REFLECTION ON CONSIDERATIONS AND LESSONS LEARNED

The development of prediction markets activities at our school is an ongoing process. Initially, the work was based on theory and insights available in academic and business literature (Luckner, 2008; Spann & Skiera, 2003). The accumulated knowledge and understanding of the tool was recorded in an online wiki (http://pm.haifa.ac.il), which developed into a structured taxonomy of prediction markets (Geifman, Raban, & Sheizaf, 2011). The performance of the markets and the activities in all classes are monitored and evaluated. Problems and observations that are encountered during the lessons are analyzed and integrated into subsequent versions of the activity. Some of the findings are described in the following sections.

## Trading Topics

The most critical and difficult challenge that the lecturer faces is the formulation of a suitable scenario that will result in an enjoyable activity that addresses the objectives of the course and is realized in a well-functioning market. Such a scenario should promote high levels of participation, generate market liquidity, and allow for timely and effective resolution of the market. The short duration of in-class activities imposes constraints on the design of the scenario. It inhibits trading on the basis of real-world events and calls for the use of simulation-based scenarios. This led to the use of the Mystery Puzzle, which was based on the Hidden Profile Task. It was simple and appealing to the students, and did not require the use of external information. However, the ambiguous nature of the problem and its components caused problems in this scenario. In some cases, a wrong interpretation by the students of the statements fed into their stereotype perceptions and affected their trading patterns. An attempt to rephrase the problematic statements yielded no better results and led to the redesign of the activity. The second design used a computational problem, the Knapsack Problem.

In prediction markets scenarios, real-world events should be aligned with the objectives of the course. To generate market activity and interest, they should be nontrivial but not too complex, and reasonably dynamic. The actual outcome of the event must be unambiguous to allow for timely deterministic market resolution. Nondeterministic scenarios, which are used for idea management and opinion elicitation, require a different set of design considerations and are discussed elsewhere (Raban & Geifman, 2009).

## Training

The concepts underlying prediction markets are grounded in economic theories of efficient markets, and the trading process is similar to that in financial trading. It is therefore reasonable to expect that students who do not possess a background in economics or finance may encounter difficulty in understanding the underlying concepts and in coping with trading procedures. This is especially critical in in-class activities, as students are given a limited time to familiarize themselves with the system and the activity. Consequently, for each different activity using prediction markets, a detailed training kit was developed, and a training market, similar in structure to the main activity market, was set up. The students receive a presentation and an opportunity to practice with the training markets before they proceed to the main exercise. To learn whether students' background affects their performance,

14 problem-solving markets administered in the business programs were compared to 21 markets that were run in information management courses. While there was no statistically significant difference ($p > .05$) in the number of students that correctly solved the problem individually in each of the markets, 79% of the markets in the business-oriented classes identified the correct solution compared to 29% in the other markets. This outcome indicates that students' background and prior knowledge must be considered and further emphasizes the importance of training for a successful deployment.

## Incentives

Incentive schemes have a significant effect on the level of participation and market liquidity, which in turn affect both the market outcome and the involvement of the students in the educational activity. In a classroom setting, the short trading period and the creation of a competitive atmosphere in class are sufficient to create high trading volumes. In this case, a modest performance-based prize, granted to the student with the highest account balance after market resolution, is sufficient. In the business simulation market, which runs for a period of several weeks, additional measures to increase motivation were required. General current events that were, at the time, the focus of public attention were added to the game-related topics to increase student motivation and interest. In addition, a participation-based prize of a two grade bonus was given to students who executed at least three transactions. The participation prize turned out not to be sufficient. Some of the students did not find the reward attractive enough to start trading, while others only traded the minimum required number of transactions. A more complex participation incentive scheme that is tied to the financial concepts that are being studied in the course is possible (Gangur & Martincik, 2011). In this case, final market credits are exchangeable with course credits, and an inflation mechanism is applied to the students' virtual cash to encourage them to make the best use of their money.

## Markets Outcome

When running prediction markets, one should assume that not all markets will demonstrate the expected behavior. Students should be aware of the meaning of market price. A price of $79 reflects a 79% probability of the event occurring, but also a 21% probability of it not happening. Analyzing the trading patterns (see Figure 5.1) of unsuccessful markets can stimulate an interesting class discussion. Most of the markets in the Hidden Profile Task did not identify the villain, and many of the markets in the Burglar Problem did not arrive at the correct solution. In the discussion that followed, some well-known decision-making flaws emerged and were evident from trading patterns. One is the cascading effect, a known effect in market bubbles (Shiller, 2002) whereby past price increases feed back into the

*Table 5.1* Results of Postactivity Questionnaire

|  | Mean | Standard Deviation |
|---|---|---|
| Trading improved my confidence in my opinion | 4.02 | 1.75 |
| My trading was motivated by the willingness to solve the problem | 4.24 | 1.764 |
| My trading was motivated by the willingness to win the game | 5.42 | 1.424 |
| I had difficulty in coping with the system | 3.27 | 1.718 |
| I found the activity to be interesting | 5.84 | 1.257 |
| Prediction markets can be used as an effective decision support tool | 4.94 | 1.586 |

*Note*: 1 = do not agree; 7 = agree; N = 80.

market as a signal for further demand that boosts additional price increases. The other is the negativity bias, where individuals find negative information more influential in forming their impression than positive information (Skowronski & Carlston, 1989). In the Hidden Profile Task activity, stereotype matching and filtering of information were evidence that students maintained their preexisting stereotypic belief despite disconfirming information (Johnston, 1996; Stewart, 1998).

## Students' Feedback

As part of the Hidden Profile Task, the students were asked to complete questionnaires regarding their impressions of the effectiveness of the tool and the difficulty in performing the activity on a scale from 1 to 7. The results, presented in Table 5.1, indicate that not all students perceived the tool as effective in assisting them with their own decision-making or problem-solving processes. Yet the students understood the potential of the tool for decision making and found the activity interesting. In contrast to the normative expectation that the students would be motivated by their desire to reach a correct decision, most students were motivated by their willingness to play and win the game.

## CONCLUSION

This chapter presents the fruits of the development of several experiential learning activities that are multifaceted and have many applications. The versatility of prediction markets, exhibited by the variability of function and deployment options, enables the development of in-class activities that efficiently scale to large classes and introduce experiential learning to online, distance learning environments. These examples demonstrate how market-based activities can help students to internalize theoretical concepts and transform knowledge into real-world skills. They expose students to state-of-the-art management tools and contribute to an interesting and exciting learning atmosphere.

Prediction markets are new, and their effectiveness as a forecasting and decision support tool is being still studied by the academic and business communities. The students were aware that they were experimenting with new instruments and concepts. They appreciated the fact that while the outcome of the markets was not always as expected, they could still gain personal insights and hands-on experience with regard to information processing and decision-making patterns, and how individual behavior affects the collective outcome of the group.

Beyond the teaching and learning goals achieved, these activities contribute to the research agenda of the School of Management. The opportunity to run multiple markets in different configurations provides the school's researchers with a good platform for experimental research.

The availability of the Internet platform and the abundance of off-the-shelf applications offer new opportunities to enhance theoretical teaching with practical experience. It is now easier to introduce new methods for changing and improving the instruction process, and the use of technology-based activities rooted in social applications is well aligned with the lifestyle of the millennial generation, who constitute the majority of the student body.

## ACKNOWLEDGMENT

The authors wish to thank Inklingmarkets.com for its continued support of the prediction markets activity in our school.

## REFERENCES

Buckley, P., Garvey, J., & McGrath, F. (2011). A case study on using prediction markets as a rich environment for active learning. *Computers & Education*, 56(2), 418–428.

Chen, K. Y., & Plott, C. R. (2002). Information aggregation mechanisms: Concept, design and implementation for a sales forecasting problem. Working paper, Lee Center Workshop, Caltech, California.

Dahan, E., Soukhoroukova, A., & Spann, M. (2010). New product development 2.0: Preference markets—How scalable securities markets identify winning product concepts and attributes. *Journal of Product Innovation Management*, 27(7), 937–954.

Gangur, M., & Martincik, D. (2011, July). A prediction market in education and market liquidity. In *Recent Researches in Educational Technologies*. Paper presented at the Proceedings of the 8th WSEAS International Conference on Engineering Education, Corfu, Greece (pp. 32–36). Athens, Greece: WSEAS Press, 32–36.

Geifman, D., Raban, D. R., & Sheizaf, R. (2011). P-MART: Towards a classification of online prediction markets. *First Monday, 16*(7).

Guo, Z., Fang, F., & Whinston, A. B. (2006). Supply chain information sharing in a macro prediction market. *Decision Support Systems, 42*(3), 1944–1958.

Johnston, L. (1996). Resisting change: Information-seeking and stereotype change. *European Journal of Social Psychology, 26*, 799–825.

LaComb, C. A., Barnett, J. A., & Pan, Q. (2007). The imagination market. *Information Systems Frontiers, 9*(2), 245–256.

Luckner, S. (2008). Prediction markets: Fundamentals, key design elements, and applications. Paper presented at the 21st Bled eConference eCollaboration: Overcoming Boundaries through Multi-Channel Interaction, June, Bled, Slovenia, 236–247.

McKinsey. 2011. Business and Web 2.0: An interactive feature. Last modified November 11. Retrieved from https://www.mckinseyquarterly.com/Business_and_Web_20_An_interactive_feature_2431

Meloso, D., Copic, J., & Bossaerts, P. (2009). Promoting intellectual discovery: Patents versus markets. *Science, 323*(5919), 1335.

National Center for Education Statistics. (2011). Fast facts. Last modified August 12. Retrieved from http://nces.ed.gov/fastfacts/display.asp?id=80

Page, S. E. (2007). *The difference: How the power of diversity creates better groups, firms, schools, and societies*. Princeton, NJ: Princeton University Press.

Raban, D. R., & Geifman, D. (2009). Designing online information aggregation and prediction markets for MBA courses. *Interdisciplinary Journal of E-Learning and Learning Objects, 5*, 247–262.

Rafaeli, S., Raban, D.R., Ravid, G., & Noy, A. (2003). Online simulations in management education about information and its uses. C. Wankel & R. DeFillipp (Eds.). InEducating managers with tomorrow's technologies (pp. 53–80). Greenwich, CT: Information Age Publishing Inc.

Remidez Jr., H., & Joslin, C. (2007, December). *Using prediction markets to support IT project management*. Paper presented at the 2nd International Research Workshop for IT Project Management, Montreal, Canada.

Servan-Schreiber, E., Wolfers, J., Pennock, D. M., & Galebach, B. (2004). Prediction Markets: Does Money Matter? *Electronic Markets, 14*(3), 243–251.

Shiller, R. J. (2002). Bubbles, human judgment, and expert opinion. *Financial Analysts Journal, 58*(3), 18.

Skowronski, J. J., & Carlston, D. E. (1989). Negativity and extremity biases in impression formation: A review of explanations. *Psychological Bulletin, 105*(1), 131–142.

Spann, M., & Skiera, B. (2003). Internet-based virtual stock markets for business forecasting. *Management Science, 49*(10), 1310–1326.

Stasser, G., & Titus, W. (1985). Pooling of unshared information in group decision making: Biased information sampling during discussion. *Journal of Personality and Social Psychology, 48*(6), 1467–1478.

Stewart, D. D. (1998). Stereotypes, negativity bias, and the discussion of unshared information in decision-making groups. *Small Group Research, 29*(6), 643.

Thompson, R. (2008). *Harvard Business School discusses future of MBA*. Retrieved from http://hbswk.hbs.edu/item/6053.html

Wolfers, J., & Zitzewitz, E. (2004). Prediction markets. *Journal of Economic Perspectives, 18*(2), 107–126.

# Part II
# Dynamic Learning Environments

# 6 Introduction to Dynamic Learning Environments

*Conor Carroll*

As educators we endeavor to create learning environments that are engaging, aligned with learning outcomes and, above all, dynamic. As outlined in the introduction, the millennial generation has posed numerous pedagogical challenges for educators. For them, the traditional mode of 'chalk and talk' teaching may be seen as outdated and not fit for purpose—these students can, after all, access encyclopedic information instantaneously. Changing learning styles and the technological revolution have led to fundamental changes in how students learn, and their levels of engagement differ from earlier generations. Students can now access learning material for free, remotely and at their own discretion through the web.

However, access to information doesn't necessarily translate into more knowledgeable or skillful students. To educate the millennial generation effectively, educators may need to fundamentally reconfigure how they approach teaching and create a real value-added learning experience for students. To this end, educators have developed pedagogic interventions such as blended learning, problem-based learning, the case method, experiential learning, reflective learning, research-based learning, action-based learning and self-directed learning, among other approaches. For example, the notion of the 'flipped classroom' is gaining increased traction. Here, basic information transfer in the form of traditional lectures is delivered through online video. This frees up time in the classroom for in-depth immersion in the business topic, with the focus being on interaction, debate, development of deeper understanding, problem solving and critical analysis. Educators must face up to the inherent educational challenges but also leverage the exciting opportunities that now exist.

Real value-add experiences must now take place within classroom settings. For this to occur educators need to move away from asymmetric communication, instead fostering an environment that enables symmetrical two-way dialogue between the educator and the student. The creation of dynamic learning environments does not necessarily mean that we must leverage emerging technologies within the classroom but rather that we focus on the basic mechanics of delivery. New technologies, aids, applications, networks and platforms will continually emerge, but placing a renewed focus on delivering an inspiring educational experience that is memorable, insightful, and arouses the intellectual curiosity of our students should be our central aim.

This section of the book explores how international business educators are deploying innovative pedagogical tools within their classes. In chapter 8, Daly describes a modern take on the traditional case study method within business education. The rationale behind using the case study method as the primary pedagogic device is strong. Case studies have been used widely for decades in disciplines such as business, law and medicine. The case study method of teaching has a particularly long and rich history within business schools, being used at leading universities such as Harvard for over 50 years (Gomes & Knowles, 2000). Daly's chapter on 'The Live Case Study Approach in Business Education' explores how the case method can be revitalized and radically retuned for the current generation of business students. His approach focuses on adding realism to the learning experience, fostering group collaboration, allowing for interdisciplinary opportunities and enhancing critical thinking. Through the use of live cases, students are better able to apply, analyze, synthesize and evaluate information, which helps them make informed decisions. Live cases allow students the opportunity to assess situations and sort out and organize key information and prompt them to ask the right questions, define opportunities and problems, identify and evaluate alternative courses of action, analyze and interpret data, evaluate the results of past strategies, develop and defend new strategies, interact with other decision makers and make decisions under conditions of uncertainty (Lamb & Baker, 1993). In particular, cases ask the fundamental question of students, 'what would you do in a situation?' (Jackson, 2011). The distinguishing features of live cases, such as participation, subject/context accessibility and relevance, make this format even more appropriate for the new generation of business students. The case study method has evolved from the Socratic method of dissecting a past situation or problem with the academic instructor questioning/interrogating students' reasoning and analysis. The evolved live case study method brings the real world into the classroom, yet does so in a way that is both structured and maximizes the learning opportunities for students.

In chapter 10, Teckman discusses how the 'Future Leaders' Experience' in an executive education program enhances the realism of the educational experience. Typically academics strive to create safe and comfortable learning environments in which their students can flourish. Teckman's chapter provides an interesting counterpoint, suggesting that we must emotionally engage with students by creating realistic simulations that are far removed from the artificial and staid environment of lecture theaters. These simulations allow for hugely beneficial reflective learning opportunities when faced with challenging critical incidences, challenging personality types and realistic, high-pressure situations. Problem-based learning, experiential learning, and simulations are now dominating many pedagogic delivery strategies in business schools. Exponents of these strategies espouse the axiom of 'learning by doing'. Yet they are rarely reflective of critical incidents that happen in industry. Students need to understand that they cannot act on pure logic, devoid of emotion and empathy. Business decision makers are heavily influenced by their environmental circumstances and their interactions with people. As Schumann, Scott and Anderson (2006) suggest, simulations need to be more qualitative and should incorporate the human dimensions of managing a business, rather than being only quantitatively based and formulaic. Indeed, by embedding emotional components within the learning context, students are more likely to remember the learning experience (Kuhn, 1998). Teckman's chapter represents an example of how this can be achieved.

The author also makes the interesting assertion that, as academics, we fetishize over postlearning evaluations and avoid creating high-pressure learning situations that may damage immediate postevaluation feedback. Anderson and Lawton (2008) posit that few academics are willing to risk poor student evaluations when tenure or promotion is on the line. The real value of the learning experience comes considerably after the event, when students reflect on their experience and rationalize the true value of the learning experience, which tests their knowledge and newly acquired skill sets and pushes them emotionally.

McCarthy examines the key issues of assessment and the delivery of feedback to students. Learning is a holistic experience, not just an isolated process in the classroom. For effective knowledge acquisition to occur, students need to process and reflect on their own performance within assessments. Here the author reclassifies the lecturer's role as a 'learning coach'. Indeed the vernacular of the term *pedagogy* is derived from helping children to learn, whereas *andragogy*, in contrast, focuses on how adults learn (Knowles, Swanson & Holton, 2005) and requires a very different approach. The chapter emphasizes the importance of developing assessments that are relevant to the target audience. This increases student engagement and enhances students' motivation to learn. A key component is that of students taking on some of the traditional roles of the teacher, through self-assessment and student-created codes of conduct. By engaging in these activities, students are enhancing their self-awareness skills and learning from reflecting on their performance. Integral to developing these skills is the delivery of timely, constructive feedback, or rather 'feed-forward'.

In chapter 7, Maiksteniene describes how she deploys the innovative and highly original 'ten-sentence case' format. Here the author develops a new format of case delivery aligned to the learning style of the millennial generation. The traditional case can typically involve 5 to 20 pages of detailed case material, where students have to decipher the text material to form congruent analysis. The format of the ten-sentence case' allows students to use technology to further research a topic and improves their critical questioning skills, which in turn improves their sense-making of a context. In an era when students can drown in a deluge of information on subject areas, protagonists, companies and industries, less is more. The instructor's role in this approach is to craft a case that prompts the students to start asking the right questions. This is closely attuned to Garvin's (2003) call for cases to develop a spirit of inquiry and foster debate. In doing so, it forces students to proactively engage, gamifies the learning experience and, above all, creates an active learning environment that is dynamic and has several nonlinear learning trajectories for students.

## REFERENCES

Anderson, P. H., & Lawton, L. (2009). Business simulations and cognitive learning. *Simulation & Gaming, 40*(2), 193–216.

Garvin, D. A. (2003). Making the case: Professional education for the world of practice. *Harvard Magazine, 106*(1): 56–75.

Gomes, R., & Knowles, P. A. (2000). A trust-building strategy to reduce adversarial tension and increase learning in case pedagogy. *Marketing Education Review, 10*(2), 49–58.

Jackson, G. (2011). Rethinking the case method. *Journal of Management Policy & Practice, 12*(5), 142–164.

Knowles, M. S., Swanson, R. A., & Holton III, E. F. (2005). *The adult learner: The definitive classic in adult education and human resource development* (6th ed.). Boston, MA: Elsevier.

Kuhn, J. W. (1998). Emotion as well as reason: Getting students beyond 'interpersonal accountability'. *Journal of Business Ethics, 17*(3), 295–308.

Lamb Jr., C. W. and Baker, J. (1993). The case method of instruction: Student-led presentations and videotaping. *Marketing Education Review, 3*(1), 44–50.

Schumann, P. L., Scott, T. W., & Anderson, P. H. (2006). Designing and introducing ethical dilemmas into computer-based business simulations. *Journal of Management Education, 30*(1), 195–219.

# 7 Encouraging Enquiry-Based Learning
## A Ten-Sentence Case That Expands Itself

*Kristina Maiksteniene*

> But . . . in real life, we do not solve business problems where events are laid down in chronological order and the amount of available information is fixed!
>
> —A student who hasn't prepared for a case discussion class

## INTRODUCTION

Let me start by acknowledging that discussing comprehensive Harvard-style business cases has been one of my favorite instructional techniques in the context of graduate marketing courses for more than a decade. Until a couple of years ago, the quotation above, by a student who had clear millennial-like traits, cast serious doubts as to whether our case discussion classes should continue as they used to. It also encouraged deeper reflection on the reasons why students came unprepared for case discussions, especially when case texts exceeded ten pages. Through in-class and out-of-class observations and discussions, several insights came to the surface. Most of these were related to the changing knowledge acquisition and problem-solving processes of students with learning styles associated with the so-called millennial generation. First, students showed an increasing aversion to chronological or linear storytelling. Many were not reading the case from the beginning to the end, but jumping backward and forward between various subchapters, thus skipping important pieces of information altogether. Second, when reading a long, written case, millennial students were tempted to replace an entire fragment of text with their findings on the Internet or with subjective observations from elsewhere. Third, during the class, they were inclined to share their up-to-date knowledge of a particular business situation's outcomes post factum, and base arguments upon them. Even worse, sometimes it was evident that students had access to case solutions or teaching notes sourced from the Internet. All these factors lead to our traditional case discussion classes becoming increasingly jeopardized.

As with many new things, the method I will discuss in this chapter was born of necessity. A couple of years ago I was preparing a class for a group of young executives from the Netherlands. Due to changes to the agenda, on the morning of the class, the program coordinator called asking if I could think of some material to be taught for an extra two hours. Yes, I replied, I have a perfect business case to illustrate the given topic. However, it was too late to ask students to read it! What I did—and it worked perfectly well—was to teach what will be referred to as a *ten-sentence case*.

In brief, the idea of the method is as follows: provide students with only minimum case facts (I suggest ten bullet-pointed sentences) at the beginning of the class, and then organize for the full case picture to be *reconstructed* in a highly interactive class process. One can think about each of these initial ten sentences as puzzle pieces. The students' task is to assemble these pieces into the full case and gather the missing pieces so that the problem can be subsequently solved—and to do all this within a limited amount of time. To be specific, after reading the ten sentences, student teams each have to create and prioritize their own clarifying questions and gather missing information during an active questioning round, in isolation from other teams. Multiple solutions to the case emerge, because different student teams have gathered different information on the subject and so most likely have come up with very different solutions. Technology-enabled learning environments add further possibilities to this method, such as letting students work online, via interacting and knowledge sharing in social networks, videoconferencing with case protagonists and so on. Although technology seems to help maintain high levels of energy in millennial classes, teaching millennials does not necessarily have to be the prerogative of technology-savvy instructors.

## MILLENNIAL LEARNERS AND THE CASE METHOD: A NEED TO LOOK FOR NEW SOLUTIONS

The portrait of the *millennial* or *digital native* generation was first sketched by Howe and Strauss (2000; 2003) and Prensky (2001a; 2001b). It has been argued that due to their lifelong state of permanent technological immersion, people of this generation, born roughly after the year 1982, are processing and managing information in fundamentally different ways to previous generations. However, some authors have challenged the notion of a 'fundamentally different generation' in their critique of the digital native discourse (e.g., Selwyn, 2009; Hesel & May, 2007), and some have even likened such discussions to an 'academic form of a moral panic' (Bennett, Maton & Kervin, 2008, p. 775). However, even the critics have acknowledged that there is a clear need to remain mindful of the changing information needs of young people (Selwyn, 2009). Following the premise that birth year and place in history are a major factor in how a person's brain is wired to learn, Prensky (2001a) claims that today's students are no longer the people our educational system was designed to teach.

For more than a hundred years, the traditional case method of instruction has been considered best practice in effective business education. By 'traditional' case method we mean in-class discussions of cases of five to twenty pages in length, which students prepare in advance and where the instructor's role is that of the sole moderator of the case. In contrast to traditional lecturing, the case method seemed to better accommodate the traits associated with learners of the past decades, such as a desire for interactivity, involvement, self-dependent decision making and some manifestation of *edutainment*. Thus, mastering the skills required to choreograph a case class became very important for those who were teaching younger generations.

However, as already mentioned in the introduction, there are signs that the traditional way of organizing case discussions is facing certain difficulties in millennial classes. Traditional case discussion methods rest on several premises that may be less relevant to both how millennial generation students learn and how business people actually make their decisions. Consider the following quotations from a popular case study handbook by Ellet (2007):

> The art of the case method instructor is to ask the right question at the right time, provide feedback on answers, and sustain a discussion that opens up meanings of the case. (p. 11)
>
> If they [students] don't come to class well prepared, the case method will fail because the people responsible for making meaning from the case are not equipped to do so. (p. 12)
>
> A case must have an adequate fact base to make possible reasonable conclusions (sufficient information on which to base conclusions). (p. 13)

These three quotations reflect the three assumptions that the traditional case method is based upon. First, the traditional case method appears to assume that the instructor is the only one with the right to pose questions. But let's face it: when the instructor alone moderates, or 'choreographs' (Rangan, 1995) a written case discussion, more often than not, students hear questions before they start identifying information domains to be investigated. Questions posed by an instructor can often kill potentially more meaningful questions that students may have. Additionally, it goes without saying that in real life business situations, no instructor is around the corner prepared to pose all the 'right' questions to the decision maker.

Second, the traditional case method assumes that the class is well prepared. However, it is especially difficult to motivate students to prepare, or even to read the case. According to Prensky (2001a), digital natives prefer random (nonlinear) access to information, have a preference for image over text-based content and are impatient with slower and more structured means of acquiring information and knowledge. Prensky (1998, p. 02.17) also observes that 'unbridled hyperlinking may make it more difficult for them [digital natives] to follow a linear train of thought'. Finally, the traditional case method discussion assures by design that everyone in class is on an equal footing with regard to knowledge of the general facts of the case, and no new information appears over the course of the problem-solving process. In fact, many instructors require that no additional information should be actively sought when preparing for the case, and some instructors get nervous when a student announces unknown facts in the course of a discussion. However, this implies that the case fact base is finite—which naturally cannot be true in today's learning and business environments. In the real world, there is usually no 'boss' who would write and present all available information in a form of a structured case text for a particular manager to solve.

To summarize, based on the numerous debates about the intergenerational differences between students and instructors (the so-called digital native–digital immigrant divide), there are plenty of reasons to assume that information acquisition and learning needs have changed dramatically for students and instructors alike. There is no doubt that this leads to a need for innovations in case learning and teaching.

## AIM AND OBJECTIVES OF PROPOSED TECHNIQUE

The proposed *ten-sentence case* technique aims to increase teaching effectiveness for millennial students. It does so by recognizing the previously mentioned challenges that traditional business case discussion methods pose in teaching this particular cohort. With regard to these challenges and taking into account some of the general theoretical considerations for effective learning activity design (Beetham & Sharpe, 2007), the three primary objectives of the technique are:

1. To keep students motivated and engaged.
2. To challenge students appropriately.
3. To bring existing capabilities of students into play.

Motivation and engagement come primarily from creating authentic learning experiences, as students choose the depth and the breadth of the problems to be explored, depending on their prior knowledge, interest in the subject and their interests and strengths in particular management areas. Students are expected to be appropriately challenged by acting not only as task solvers but also as task formulators during a case session. Finally, millennial students' capabilities are best brought to bear by letting them access information on their own terms and to process it in a randomized or networked pattern.

## DETAILS OF THE COURSE IN WHICH THE TEACHING TECHNIQUE HAS BEEN DEPLOYED

For more than two years, the *ten-sentence case* technique has been actively practiced by the author in MBA-level classes as well as in executive training programs at the ISM University of Management and Economics in Vilnius, Lithuania. Student profiles have, so far, consisted of managers with a minimum of four years of business experience in MBA-level classes or managers with varying experience levels in open and in-company executive training. The geographical distribution of students ranges from relatively homogeneous groups of local (Lithuanian) students to international groups with diverse cultural backgrounds, such as visiting executive students from other European countries. Class sizes vary from 12 to 48 people. The disciplinary areas covered are marketing strategy, management and international business. People born after 1982 constitute slightly more than half of the student body (this proportion is gradually increasing over the semesters). Therefore, the technique has been applied to mixed groups in terms of digital technology fluency.

## COMPREHENSIVE DESCRIPTION OF THE TEACHING TECHNIQUE

The realization of the *ten-sentence case* technique may take a variety of forms, depending on course goals, time frame or the profile of student group. What follows is a description of the suggested general sequence of steps, classified into two stages: case preparation (steps 1 to 3) and case discussion (steps 4 to 9).

### Step 1 Selecting a Source Case for Analysis

The first step is to find a suitable case that can be summarized in ten sentences. It could be a business case from public sources, a textbook case or just a good story from the instructor's own business or consulting practice. I also use cases that our executive students have previously written about their own business situations as part of their coursework. The ideal business case is one that the instructor is very familiar with. There are no particular requirements for the subject content of the case. I have successfully used both heavily quantitative cases and cases that focus on organizational and behavioral aspects of marketing.

### Step 2 Prioritizing the Business Issues to Focus On

After selecting a source case, the instructor should prioritize business issues to focus on the ten-sentence case to be constructed. The unique feature of a ten-sentence case is that different, sometimes unforeseen, business issues are revealed during the course of a discussion, as student groups uncover more and more information during their questioning rounds. However, for the discussion to be more focused, intended priorities (or topics) should somehow reflect either in the title of the case or in the ten-sentence content itself.

## Step 3 Constructing a Ten-Sentence Case

Here, the goal is to produce ten sentences that will briefly acquaint students with the main facts or events of the case. The ten sentences have to be succinct enough to fit on a single PowerPoint slide. Writers of traditional cases ask themselves, 'How much information do students need to have in order to be able to solve the problem?' When constructing a ten-sentence case, the corresponding question is: 'How can I give students an appetite for gathering more information and motivate them to grapple with the emergent issues?'

There are several alternatives for structuring a ten-sentence case.

- *Chronological events*. One of the ways is to tell it as a story. The ten bullet points could reflect key events that make up the case's *story time line*, as they relate to one another in a pattern or a sequence, possibly through cause and effect. The ten sentences also may be used to re-create traditional elements of a plot line, such as the exposition, the rising action, the climax and the falling action (with the resolution element left for the case solvers).
- *Key facts*. A second approach is to deliver the most important factual information, focusing on numbers. Such a ten-sentence slide could look like an excerpt from an executive summary of a set of financial statements or a market research report. It could also resemble a sequence of important but seemingly random facts overheard in a company's corridors.
- *Strategic summary*. Another way is to bullet-point the most important strategic facts of a particular company's situation. For example, these could be answers to the following questions: *What is the company's product or service?* (briefly describe what it sells); *What is the company's market?* (briefly discuss who it is selling the product or service to); *What is the company's revenue model?* (discuss how the company expects to make money); *Who is behind the company?* (the background and achievements of the company team); *Who is the competition?* (briefly discuss who they are and what they have accomplished); *What is the company's competitive advantage?* (discuss how this company is different and why it has an advantage over the competition).
- *Opinion potpourri*. An interesting alternative way to construct a ten-sentence case is by listing various contradictory opinions and attitudes toward the question under discussion by the case protagonist and the

key decision makers. There should be a proper balance of opinions and counteropinions included, so students become eager to discover inherent biases, resolve the manifested conflicts and to seek the best, 'unbiased' solution.
- *Chapter headlines.* If one is lucky enough to have a well-structured and well-written case to start from, it may be sufficient just to take the headlines of case chapters and list them as ten bullet points on a slide.
- *Elevator speech.* Finally, you can approach this task by constructing a concise, carefully planned 'elevator speech'—in other words, a description of the business situation that a new acquaintance should be able to understand in the time it would take to ride in an elevator.

With traditional, long, written cases, students complain that there is a lack of information to make a decision (Hawes, 2004). The idea of a ten-sentence case is to make this deficit of information deliberate.

## Step 4 Assigning Students to the Groups

Before starting a discussion, student groups of the usual size (four to six people) should be formed, following any process that the instructor has used in the past. It is useful to consider whether to form groups based on a balanced distribution of students with various functional expertise or industry experience, as this will eventually influence the extent to which the groups' solutions to the case differ.

## Step 5 Acquainting Students with the Case

A ten-sentence case could be presented on one PowerPoint slide to the entire class at the same time. Alternatively, it could be printed on a sheet of paper and distributed to everyone in class, so students can make notes during the solution process. In any case, it is important that the instructor provides no additional comments about the case content or issues at this stage.

## Step 6 Prioritization of Clarifying Questions by the Students

Naguib Mahfouz, an Egyptian writer and Nobel Prize winner said: 'You can tell whether a man is clever by his answers. You can tell whether a man is wise by his questions.' In business, the ability to prioritize issues and identify additional information requirements is key to managerial success. After acquainting themselves with the ten-sentence case, every student group, in isolation from one another, should be given some time to come up with a list of prioritized questions that they would ask the instructor. These questions should be information-seeking questions, which is to say they should clarify the facts, numbers, names, business practice descriptions and so on. Questions should be answerable in one or two words; open questions asking for any explanation, opinion, or issue elaboration are disqualified.

## Step 7 Questioning Round

For the questioning round, the instructor should arrange a quiet place to spend some time with each group. I simply go outside of the classroom to an isolated place with four to six chairs around me. Any group that feels they are ready for the *questioning round* goes outside the classroom to meet the instructor for five minutes in isolation from other groups. The other groups may continue their question prioritization during that time. Timekeeping should be very strict. The instructor has the right to decline to answer some of the questions if the facts are not known or, as in case of consulting cases, particular answers are considered confidential.

## Step 8 Solution and Discussion Rounds

The groups that have finished their questioning rounds come back to the class to discuss and solve the case based on the new information they have gathered. Group presentations and discussion can be organized in various formats. Each student group may solve a case and substantiate its solution in a very different way, depending on what questions they asked the instructor. That is why the technique of the *ten-sentence case* is in the true spirit of co-creation, with students co-designing learning experiences personalized to individual needs and preferences. The *aha* moment comes when student groups hear each other's presentations and see how different their conclusions or recommendations have been based on the additional information they have gathered. In the end, this is 'learning based on collectively seeking, sieving, and synthesizing experiences rather than individually locating and absorbing information from a single best source' (Dede, 2005, p. 7).

## Step 9 Case Debrief

The instructor may conclude the entire case session with a traditional debriefing session asking *What are the lessons?* or *What actually happened?* I also find it instructional to mention case facts that didn't come to the surface (i.e., those that were not discovered by any of the case groups during the questioning round). If class time allows, I may organize an additional discussion round, pooling all the cumulative information that participants have gathered in their respective groups. This usually leads to the most dynamic discussion, which comes from the fact that people discuss a case that they actively *re-created* themselves!

## STUDENT FEEDBACK ABOUT THE TEN-SENTENCE CASE

A questionnaire has been constructed to evaluate how the ten-sentence technique performs against the formulated objectives. It has been administered to 94 students and participants of management training programs (only those born after 1982) who have taken classes involving the ten-sentence case technique at the ISM University of Management and Economics. The questionnaire asked for levels of agreement with each of seven statements corresponding to the learning activity design factors by Beetham and Sharpe (2007) as well as two additional statements on perceived learning effectiveness of the ten-sentence and more traditional case methods. Student responses were recorded using a seven-point Likert scale in which 1 = *fully disagree* and 7 = *fully agree*. The results of the survey are provided in Table 7.1.

On average, the students surveyed agreed or fully agreed with all nine items of the survey. With regard to the process measures (questions 1 to 7), they most strongly agreed with 'I have been active' (6.43), 'I have been motivated and engaged' (6.33), and 'My existing capabilities were brought into play' (6.22). This is not unexpected, as most of these items represent the intended learning objectives of the method. Looking further, it was also encouraging that students had strong positive views about the ten-sentence case method's potential to lead to effective learning outcomes (6.36). In general, since case studies are fairly often considered by students to be effective, the additional question, 'Overall, any case method discussions lead to very

*Table 7.1* Student Evaluation of the Ten-Sentence Case Process and Learning Outcomes

|   | Please rate to what extent you agree or disagree with the following statements regarding your recent ten-sentence case discussion session: | Mean rating (N = 94) | Standard deviation |
|---|---|---|---|
| 1 | I have been motivated and engaged. | 6.33 | 0.98 |
| 2 | I was appropriately challenged. | 6.16 | 1.25 |
| 3 | My existing capabilities were brought into play. | 6.22 | 1.08 |
| 4 | I have been active. | 6.43 | 0.82 |
| 5 | I had opportunities for dialogue. | 6.02 | 1.13 |
| 6 | I received intrinsic feedback. | 5.91 | 1.33 |
| 7 | I had opportunities for consolidation and integration of material. | 6.01 | 1.27 |
| 8 | The ten-sentence case method led to very effective learning outcomes for me. | 6.36 | 0.87 |
| 9 | Overall, any case method discussions lead to very effective learning outcomes for me. | 6.01 | 1.14 |

effective learning outcomes for me' (6.01), highlighted the somewhat higher relative effectiveness of the ten-sentence method.

## CONCLUDING REMARKS AND SUGGESTIONS FOR THE METHOD'S FURTHER USE

There are many ways in which instructors could improve upon the *ten-sentence case* procedure that has been described above. Some tried-and-tested approaches include:

- *Using students as case informants.* Some students may be in a good position to provide extra information about the case (e.g., if they worked in the industry or country where the case action takes place or have familiarized themselves with this case from public sources). The instructor could employ them as informants during the questioning round to answer other groups' questions. However, the instructor must ensure that no information distortion takes place and that all the facts are cited from reliable sources.
- *Organizing online information gathering.* A second round of questioning could be organized, where students spend a set period of time accessing information from anywhere on- or offline. Millennial students are used to doing such research, are happy to apply concepts from their work situations and post online frequently and eloquently (Winsted, 2010); also, students get highly involved and often carry the debate and discussion onto Skype conference calls.
- *Gamification elements.* Students teams could be allocated some fictitious currency, which they could spend according to their choice (e.g., having a number of minutes to browse the Internet, to call friends, to chat with a business expert, or to 'buy' additional clarifying questions from the instructor).

According to Strebel and Keys (2005), great conversations require three central skills: the ability to ask, the ability to listen and the ability to redirect on the fly. Traditional case discussion classes do not seem to develop all three abilities equally well. As per my favorite saying, the questions worth asking are usually not those found in the end of the case. For millennial students, 'the end of the case' doesn't even exist, because they can extend a case infinitely by accessing the digital world at their fingertips. That is why I believe the ten-sentence case method is a more natural way for millennials to learn. Hopefully, other instructors will find this technique effective. They will never need to worry about a lack of active learning within a millennial classroom.

# REFERENCES

Beetham, H., & Sharpe, R. (2007). *Rethinking Pedagogy for a Digital Age: Designing and Delivering E-Learning*. London: Routledge.

Bennett, S., Maton, K., & Kervin, L. (2008). The 'Digital Natives' Debate. *British Journal of Educational Technology*, 39(5), 775–786.

Dede, C. (2005). Planning for Neomillennial Learning Styles. *Educause Quarterly*, 28(1), 7–12.

Ellet, W. (2007). *The Case Study Handbook: How to Read, Discuss, and Write Persuasively About Cases*. Boston: Harvard Business Review Press.

Hawes, J. M. (2004). Teaching Is Not Telling: The Case Method as a Form of Interactive Learning. *Journal for Advancement of Marketing Education*, 5(4), 47–54.

Hesel, R. A., & May, S. B. (2007). Dispelling the Millennial Myth. *Currents*, 33(2), 16–22.

Howe, N., & Strauss, W. (2000). *Millennials Rising: The Next Great Generation*. New York: Vintage Books.

Howe, N., & Strauss, W. (2003). *Millennials Go to College*. Washington, DC: American Association of Collegiate Registrars and Admissions Officers.

Prensky, M. (1998). *Twitch Speed: Keeping up with Young Workers*. Retrieved February 15, 2012, from http://www.twitchspeed.com/site/article.html

Prensky, M. (2001a). Digital Natives, Digital Immigrants. *On the Horizon*, 9(5), 1–6.

Prensky, M. (2001b). Digital Natives, Digital Immigrants, Part II: Do They Really Think Differently? *On the Horizon*, 9(6), 1–6.

Rangan, V. K. (1995). *Choreographing a Case Class*. Boston: Harvard Business School Publishing.

Selwyn, N. (2009). The Digital Native—Myth and Reality. *ASLIB Proceedings: New Information Perspectives*, 61(4), 364–379.

Strebel, P., & Keys, T., Eds. (2005). *Mastering Executive Education: How to Combine Content with Context and Emotion, the IMD Guide*. London: Financial Times/Prentice Hall.

Winsted, K. F. (2010). Marketing Debates: In the Classroom and Online. *Marketing Education Review*, 20(1), 77–82.

# 8 The Live Case Study Approach in Business Education

*Peter Daly*

## INTRODUCTION

A report by the Association of American Colleges and Universities (AACU) on college learning for the new global century suggests that we are living in a time of great change which is only set to intensify. More specifically, the report states that 'the context in which today's students will make choices and compose lives is one of disruption rather than certainty, and of interdependence rather than insularity' (AACU, 2007, p. 2). Because future graduates are also expected to work in very complex and uncertain environments, which are both messy and interdisciplinary (AACU, 2010), there is an onus on business educators to employ product-based pedagogies that engage students in learning knowledge and skills through an extended inquiry process that is structured around complex and authentic questions and carefully designed products and tasks. According to the Association to Advance Collegiate Schools of Business (AACSB), business schools should ensure that 'interactive experiences are available in all courses and all major learning experiences of the program' (AACSB, 2012, p. 39), whereby various student groups have the opportunity to learn from each other, and the school's programs should involve collaboration and cooperation among participants in the educational process. This is a clear advocacy of the enhancement of experiential learning (Kolb, 1984; Kolb & Kolb, 2005) in higher education. This chapter outlines one of a series of options within the domain of experiential learning methods: the live case study (henceforth LCS), which offers real and complex questions to students and which espouses cross- and interdisciplinary knowledge and the development of alliances with significant others beyond the business school to enrich the educational experience. The chapter is structured as follows. First, the LCS as opposed to a traditional case study (hereafter TCS) will be defined; second, the advantages and disadvantages of the LCS method will be reviewed; third, an LCS as part of a business communication workshop within a career development module at a French business school will be outlined; finally, some advice and recommendations will be provided to those intending to integrate an LCS method into a teaching module.

## LIVE CASES IN BUSINESS EDUCATION

The case study method is rooted in the Socratic method and is historically linked to the teaching of law at Harvard Law School by Professor Christopher Columbus Langdell in 1870 (Shulman, 1986) and at the beginning of the 20th century at Harvard Business School (in 1919). The current dean of Harvard Business School, Nitin Norhia, still advocates the use of the case method and says 'The case method has enabled us to be closer to how business evolves. I think the winning business school will be closest to how that [developments in business practice] unfolds' (Bradshaw, 2011). Indeed, it is difficult to imagine a business education without the use of the case study method either in its TCS format or as a LCS. Duane Hoover (1977) makes an interesting classification between TCS, which he terms as a 'cognitive case, i.e., cases that deal with facts or information in a report or written format' (p. 161) as opposed to an LCS, which 'in addition to cognitive aspects of the learning event, the individual is also involved emotionally and behaviorally, because he is engaged in a set of behaviors and experiences' (p. 161). This distinction nicely captures the experiential learning dimension of an LCS that impacts the student more, who has, as a result, a more emotional behavioral commitment to the case study. Markulis (1985, p. 169) has reviewed some of the objections against TCS and notes that they are impersonal and sterile, not real, overly simplistic, outdated once they are written, replete with student and instructor bias, and lacking rigorous quantitative analysis. In contrast, live cases have three distinguishing features:

1. Personal participation by key decision makers during the case presentation and discussion;
2. The immediate accessibility of the company for the students;
3. The company situation or strategic decision is one that has just recently been made or is about to be made.

Burns (1990) puts it simply when he states that the key ingredient in an LCS is realism. Whereas in a TCS, students are restricted to the role of analyst and hence passive observers responding to facts and events provided by a distant outside party (Bailey, Sass, Swiercz, Seal & Kayes, 2005), in an LCS, they must play the role of consultant, interacting with a real complex and messy situation in order to provide a solution to a current problem. The current and relevant nature of the problems in an LCS means that students must gain an overall 'whole' image of the company and develop a systems perspective to see the big picture quickly. So, rather than being disconnected from the realities and complexities of an organizational environment, its culture, and other salient decision factors in a competitive classroom environment, the LCS projects the student into a cooperative environment, which is conducive to learning and where every student and all solutions proposed are valued by the client. The LCS can be defined as:

> A case analysis, that involves a current problem or issue, that a company is investigating, in which the company provides information regarding the problem/issue to the instructor and students. The problem or issue has not been resolved and the company is seeking input from the students to assist them in making a management decision. In other words, everything is happening *now*. Students can be viewed as consultants (loosely speaking; not literally) for the firm and at the end of the live case analysis, students present their recommendations to the firm. (Simkins, 2001, p. 2)

Therefore, there are three main stakeholders in the learning event: the client (or company who has the problem); the instructor (who structures the LCS within the teaching objectives and module) and the students (who act as 'consultants' to work through the case and provide recommendations).

LCS have been used extensively in business education in a number of disciplines, mainly in marketing (Kennedy, Lawton & Walker, 2001; Elam & Spotts, 2004; Maher & Shaw Hughner, 2005; Camarero, Rodríguez & San José, 2009; Parsons & Lepkowska-White, 2009); but also in entrepreneurship (Read & Sarmiento, 2006), strategy (Simkins, 2001; Roth & Smith, 2009), mathematical statistics (Särkkä & Sagitov, 2008), organizational theory and management (Weir, 1978), project management (Kramer, Sankar & Hingorani, 1995), business policy (Markulis, 1985); accounting (Barkman, 1998) and ethics (McWilliams & Nahavandi, 2006; Laditka & Houck, 2006).

In the literature, two main types of pedagogies have developed in the LCS approach. The first is where the student teams conduct mini-consulting projects for a company, which works closely with business school faculty to develop an interesting live case experience that is linked to a particular module or course. Rashford and Neiva de Figueiredo (2011) define this LCS approach as the *live case intervention method*, which involves the CEO entering the classroom to outline an unsolved problem that he or she is grappling with. The second approach, the *student authored case method* (Lincoln, 2006), is a hybrid method of case instruction using the TCS and an LCS. With this method, students collect, process and analyze information as well as conceptualize and lay out information in a manner to set a decision-making foundation. They must write a case study and case solution and assume various roles such as researcher, petitioner, interviewer, negotiator, writer, editor and team member.

## LEARNING AND THE LCS APPROACH

Gentry (1990) classifies the live case study pedagogy as being very high in experiential learning potential because it meets the criteria he sets out as the 10 critical components of experiential learning: (1) related to business curriculum; (2) applied by having the expected educational outcomes articulated and related to the curriculum; (3) participative, as students are actively involved in the process; (4) interactive, as one moves beyond the instructor/student dyad to include the client; (5) having a whole-person emphasis to incorporate the behavioral and affective dimensions as well as the cognitive dimension; (6) involving contact with the environment (either real-world or real-world-like contact); (7) encompassing variability and uncertainty; (8) being a structured exercise; (9) including student evaluation of the experience; and (10) incorporating feedback with equal amounts of process and outcome feedback. In the next section, we will outline the various advantages and disadvantages of this type of pedagogy.

## ADVANTAGES OF LCS APPROACH

There are many advantages to using an LCS method from the perspective of the student, the client and the instructor. Regarding the student perspective, Rashford and Neiva de Figueiredo (2011) see this experiential approach as building on previously acquired knowledge and moving away from the silo, discipline-based focus typical of the TCS method to a more global, cross-disciplinary approach that enables students 'to think 'like a leader'; that is, the ability to intuitively incorporate the existence of various stakeholders, to understand how to effect lasting change that needs to be at least acceptable and hopefully beneficial to all stakeholders and to communicate proposals and decisions in a very clear way' (2011, p. 642). Apart from the fact that the LCS incorporates hands-on real projects into different courses (Titus & Petroshius, 1993; Simkins, 2001) and bridges theory and practice by relating real business concepts to real-world application (McWilliams & Nahavandi, 2006; Simkins, 2001; Hayes Godar, 2000; Weir 1978, among others), students are also held accountable for their positions and opinions, which they must defend in front of the client (McWilliams & Nahavandi, 2006; Read & Sarmiento, 2006). The students are also seen to build self-confidence when applying their knowledge in the company (Camarero et al., 2009), and this requires them to be sure of themselves in front of the client. The LCS helps students to develop soft skills such as analytical skills (Titus & Petroshius, 1993); synthesis of key information in a protean corporate environment (Read & Sarmiento, 2006); critical thinking and increased awareness of complexity (McWilliams & Nahavandi, 2006); people skills (Barkman, 1998); and written and oral business communication skills (Kramer, Sankar & Hingorani, 1995; Elam & Spotts, 2004) to name just a few.

As far as the instructor is concerned, the LCS is an experiential learning method that bridges theory, practice and the real world, which is seen to support a significant increase in understanding of and confidence in harder skills (Culpin & Scott, 2012) and the application of theoretical concepts (McWilliams & Nahavandi, 2006).

From the point of view of the client, it receives faculty-supervised consulting work (Hayes Godar, 2000) and gets students to work on and provide novel solutions to problems it is encountering in its business. The client also has the opportunity to interact with the local higher educational establishment or business school and can develop other synergies such as getting involved in research projects; becoming more visible to students for potential recruitment opportunities; bringing its practical experience to the classroom and becoming more relevant on the marketplace.

## DISADVANTAGES OF LCS APPROACH

From a student perspective, one of the main disadvantages is the ambiguity inherent in this type of method, including comprehending the new role of their professor, working with a client on a real problem and the messy nature of the information provided (Kennedy et al. 2001). Weir (1978, p. 233) points to the issue of complexity in the LCS: 'experience has shown that some students cannot handle the complexity of learning about concepts and about the organization at the same time. They tend to neglect one or the other.' This suggests that an LCS must be contextualized within an overall program of study that includes strong theoretical concepts and principles. Camarero et al. (2009) emphasize another drawback: student motivation, as this type of project requires extra effort. They also discuss the danger of having too much realism because this may hinder and interfere with learning. They look at the necessity of defining the assignment well and stress the participation of the company, representatives of which must be present and must provide the appropriate information to the students.

As far as the instructor is concerned, using an LCS is very time-intensive (Simkins, 2001, Kennedy et al., 2001), and there is a lack of recognition from the business school for innovating with this type of pedagogy (Elam & Spotts, 2004). There is also a necessity for the chosen case to illustrate the concepts that the professor wants to focus on in a specific course (Weir, 1978). There can also be a great uncertainty regarding what the student will produce, and the instructor must have a high level of trust and confidence in students' knowledge and maturity to deal with the client. If the live case is being used for assessment, it must match the content perfectly, which requires major negotiation with the client. If the instructors want to publish a case study, they may have to wait until the company has implemented the project to preserve the client confidentiality. This issue of confidentiality is crucial in the LCS because it is difficult to ensure complete confidentiality if critical analysis of the subject is to be discussed in class. The client must therefore be made aware of the risk of this critical analysis and discussion by students and instructors. Markulis (1985) outlined four major problems with the LCS method: (1) the reluctance of some companies to divulge sufficient information about their company, especially financial information; (2) the majority of companies wanting to get involved in live cases are small and medium-sized enterprises (SMEs), which limits the generalizations one can make; (3) student intimidation when presenting in front of managers and the danger that they may not be that critical of the firm's current strategy; (4) the availability of managers and employees of a company to attend presentations during the day. For an LCS to be a success, then, the client must open up the company to student inspection and make staff resources available to help students complete the task, and the students must not be afraid to take a position and express their opinions. In my experience, students engage more with the LCS and produce impressive work for the clients and are more interested and prepared to discuss the issues being studied intelligently if the company representatives are in the room during the presentation of findings. In the next section, we report on an LCS carried out at EDHEC Business School, including the different phases of the method.

## LIVE CASE APPROACH AT EDHEC BUSINESS SCHOOL

The live case: Awak'iT—Shaping the Next Generation of Learning Academy (Daly, 2012) was used as a key part of a business communication workshop within an obligatory career development module for all MSc students at EDHEC Business School. The students were studying various MSc programs in business management (arts and NGO management; entrepreneurship; law and tax management; marketing management; and strategy and organization consultancy). In this section, we will outline the five stages of the workshop methodology: (1) the preplanning of the live case, (2) the development of the material, (3) the director's presentation to the students, (4) student teamwork and presentation and (5) the plenary debriefing session.

### 1. Preplanning of the Live Case

Six months prior to the workshop, the company Awak'iT (http://www.awakit-groupe.com/), a digital communications group with headquarters in Paris, was contacted to see if it would like to work with our MSc students. Awak'iT is a young, dynamic, entrepreneurial SME that develops knowledge containers and contents for other companies. In the past few years, it has noticed two major trends in its business: the importance of a culture of learning to advance one's career and the integration of generation Y into the workplace. Awak'iT studied both the traditional and the online learning markets and noticed that graduates learn differently and want to not only learn but also share their knowledge and competence and co-construct knowledge with their peers. While it had many ideas about the type of learning required, the company felt it necessary to consult young graduates to reflect on this issue for two reasons: (1) they are its target population for future prospects, and (2) they are in the best position to bring fresh ideas to the question. Awak'iT posed two macro-questions: How should the next generation of learning academies be shaped? and What is *the* value-added learning provider for their clients? In addition, Awak'iT sought answers to the following questions:

1. Which business model is most appropriate? Analyze the existing business models of corporate universities/academies and propose a sustainable business model for Awak'iT to enable them to be competitive in this market.
2. Who are the main global competitors? Analyze the main global competitors to ascertain how they provide learning solutions. What are the market niches that are not being filled? How can Awak'iT create a value proposition for its clients to address this new need for training, and how can it differentiate itself from its competitors?
3. What are the legal issues concerning intellectual property (IP) in France that Awak'iT needs to consider? Analyze the French IP legal issues and provide detailed information on what aspects must be considered carefully.

## 2. Development of Material

Together with the associates of the company, a case brief was developed to include some of the following issues: the company profile; historical overview with key milestones; management structure of the company; the company's concept; a SWOT analysis with detailed information on existing and future prospects; and a list of major competitors and Awak'iT's differentiation strategy. As well as this case study, other key information about the company was compiled such as corporate documentation, annual reports, information on company strategy, video material and interviews. Once the instructors and the associate directors were satisfied with the amount of information available, it was posted on our business school learning platform (Blackboard®) one month prior to the associate directors' presentation to all MSc students.

## 3. Director's Presentation to Students

The associate directors of Awak'iT came to present to all MSc students their company and the strategic problem they are facing. This is a mandatory presentation of the company and forms part of the career development workshop curriculum. They clarified the already distributed material, explained the corporate culture and strategy and answered various questions posed by the students on the material and the project they were about to embark on. The interaction with the associate directors of the company is crucial to clarify logistics, to ensure that the students understand the challenges facing the company and for the company to express its particular business needs. This interaction is videotaped, and the video file is made available on the learning platform for students to watch later on to clarify any points they may have missed.

## 4. Student Teamwork and Presentation

The students then have two weeks to work in teams of four on the case study. Professors within the business school are available to answer questions regarding strategic or managerial issues. The company professionals make themselves available and provide students with contact information for various key people to answer any particular corporate queries that arise, to provide additional information or just to bounce ideas around. The groups then present their findings to two people: a business communication instructor and an associate director. The business communication instructor provides immediate constructive feedback on presentation form, and the associate director of the company assesses content. The students must hand in a copy of their slides and an executive summary of their main findings. The jury debriefs each presentation immediately, and students leave with a written evaluation of their presentation skills and content as well as a written peer evaluation of communication skills.

## 5. Plenary Debriefing

When all students have presented, the associate directors and the business communication instructors debrief prior to a plenary debriefing with all MSc students. The main objectives of the debriefing are to provide the students with detailed feedback on the presentations, appraise the communicative competence of students on a strategic issue and give the floor to the company to ascertain the feasibility and viability of the solutions put forward by the students.

### ADVICE FOR THOSE CONSIDERING THE LCS METHOD

Those who would like to integrate an LCS into their teaching should consider the following issues:

## 1. Preplanning and Selection

Negotiation with the company getting involved in an LCS experience starts at least one semester in advance. The company is selected according to how the concepts the professor intends to teach are illustrated and how this integrates into the course objectives. It is also advisable for instructors to document everything and not to forget to plan an extensive debrief of the case study by the client with the students. To assess the suitability of the company, instructors should ask the following questions: Does the company already have a strong relationship with the educational institution? How well known is the company to your students? How interesting is the sector/product/company?

## 2. Involvement and Commitment of the Company to the LCS

The company must be 100 percent committed. To ensure complete commitment, it is best to approach the CEO of the company, because this individual can mobilize the staff resources required and give the students the opportunity to 'think like a leader'. The CEO and company representatives must have the time to prepare the case, deal with student questions, attend student presentations, provide process and outcome feedback to students and offer some kind of prize for the best ideas.

## 3. Relevant Information and Current Problems

The LCS problem must be current and one that the company is grappling with at the moment and not an issue that it has already been working on for some time. The company must also find the right balance between too much information and not enough; too much impedes student creativity (they just regurgitate the already given information), and too little will frustrate the students and result in perceived failure to carry out the brief.

## 4. Confidentiality

It is important to ascertain what information can be shared and discussed with students and what must remain confidential. Working with top management enables instructors to deal with confidentiality more effectively.

## 5. In-built Flexibility

As planning the case with the client begins, the problem identified initially may already have been solved or may no longer be relevant to the company once the CEO meets the students. Therefore, the professor should start by creating a general brief on the company and ensure that flexibility is built into the work process, because the project can change radically.

## 6. Structured LCS with Detailed Feedback

The LCS must be as structured as possible and time must be made available for both process and outcome feedback. Students expect both and want to ensure that their extra effort is rewarded by the instructor and corporate follow-up and detailed feedback on their recommendations.

### CONCLUSION

This chapter presented the live case study theoretically as a business education teaching method with high experiential learning potential. The various advantages of this approach were outlined to include the possibility of building on prior knowledge, the development of various soft skills, the linking of theory and practice, increased student motivation and engagement and the opportunity for students to be held accountable for their positions and opinions. Some of the disadvantages of this approach include its time-intensive nature for the instructors and the client, the issue of confidentiality and the availability of managers to commit themselves to such an endeavor. An LCS process as part of a business communication workshop was described in five stages: (1) preplanning, (2) material development, (3) CEO presentation, (4) student teamwork and (5) debrief. For those considering this type of case study method, six pieces of advice were given regarding: (1) preplanning and company selection, (2) corporate involvement, (3) the problem chosen and information available, (4) confidentiality, (5) the in-built flexibility, and (6) the structuring of the LCS and the feedback.

## REFERENCES

Association of American Colleges and Universities. (2007). *College learning for the new global century: A report from the National Leadership Council for Liberal Education and America's Promise*. Washington, DC: Author.

Association of American Colleges and Universities. (2010). *Raising the bar: Employers' views on college learning in the wake of the economic downturn*. Washington, DC: Author. Retrieved from http://www.aacu.org/leap/documents/2009_EmployersSurvey.pdf

Association to Advance Collegiate Schools of Business International. (2012). *Eligibility procedures and accreditations for business accreditation*. Tampa, FL: Author. Retrieved from http://www.aacsb.edu/accreditation/standards-busn-jan2012.pdf

Bailey, J., Sass, M., Swiercz, P. M., Seal, C., & Kayes, D. C. (2005). Teaching with and through teams: Student written, instructor facilitated case writing and the signatory code. *Journal of Management Education*, 29(1), 39–59.

Barkman, A. I. (1998). The use of live cases in the accounting information systems course. *Journal of Accounting Education*, 16(3/4), 517–524.

Bradshaw, D. (2011, January 24). Navigating a route for the 21st century. *Financial Times*. Retrieved from http://www.ft.com/intl/cms/s/2/ab936364-257e-11e0-8258-00144feab49a.html#axzz1p6kqSgSA

Burns, A. C. (1990). The use of live cases in business education: Pros, cons and guidelines. In J. W. Gentry (Ed.), *Guide to business gaming and experiential learning* (pp. 201–215). London: Kogan Press.

Camarero, C., Rodríguez, J., & San José, R. (2009). A comparison of the learning effectiveness of live cases and class projects. *International Journal of Management Education*, 8(3), 83–94.

Culpin, V., & Scott, H. (2012). The effectiveness of a live case study approach: Increasing knowledge and understanding of 'hard' versus 'soft' skills in executive education. *Management Learning*, 43(5), 565–577.

Daly, P. (2012). The live case: Awak'iT—Shaping the next generation of learning academy. Lille campus, France: EDHEC Business School.

Duane Hoover, J. (1977). A 'live case' approach to the business and society course. *New Horizons in Simulation Games and Experiential Learning*, 4, 159–165.

Elam, E. L. R., & Spotts, H. E. (2004). Achieving marketing curriculum integration: A live case study approach. *Journal of Marketing Education*, 26(1), 50–65.

Gentry, J. W. (1990). What is experiential learning? In J. W. Gentry (Ed.), *Guide to business gaming and experiential learning* (pp. 9–20). London: Kogan Press.

Hayes Godar, S. (2000). Live cases: Service learning consulting projects in business courses. *Michigan Journal of Community Service Learning, 7*(1), 126–132.

Kennedy, E. L, Lawton, L., & Walker, E. (2001). The case for using cases: Shifting the paradigm in marketing education. *Journal of Marketing Education, 23*(2), 141–151.

Kolb D. A. (1984). *Experiential learning: Experience as the source of learning and development*. Englewood Cliffs, NJ: Prentice Hall.

Kolb, A. Y., & Kolb, D. A. (2005). Learning styles and learning spaces: Enhancing experiential learning in higher education. *Academy of Management Learning & Education, 4*(5), 192–212.

Kramer, S. W., Sankar, C. S., & Hingorani, K. (1995). Teaching project management issues through live cases from construction sites. *Journal of Professional Issues in Engineering Education and Practice, 121*(4), 250–255.

Laditka, S. B., & Houck, M. M. (2006). Student-developed case studies: An experiential approach to teaching ethics in management. *Journal of Business Ethics, 64*(2), 157–167.

Lincoln, D. J. (2006). Student authored cases: Combining benefits of tradition and live case methods of instruction. *Marketing Education Review, 16*(1), 1–7.

Maher, J. K., & Shaw Hughner, R. (2005). Experiential marketing projects: Student perceptions of live case and simulation methods. *Journal of Advancement in Marketing Education, 7*, 1–10.

Markulis, P. M. (1985). The live case study: Filling the gap between the case study and the experiential experience. *Developments in Business Simulation and Experiential Exercise, 12*, 168–171.

McWilliams, V., & Nahavandi, A. (2006). Using live cases to teach ethics. *Journal of Business Ethics, 67*(4), 421–433.

Parsons, A. L., & Lepkowska-White, E. (2009). Group projects using clients versus not using clients: Do students perceive any differences? *Journal of Marketing Education, 31*(2), 154–159.

Rashford, N. S., & Neiva de Figueiredo, J. (2011). The live in-class CEO intervention: A capstone experiential technique for leadership development. *Journal of Management Education, 35*, 620–647.

Read, E., & Sarmiento, T. (2006). *The benefits of using 'live' case studies in entrepreneurship education*. Coventry University Research Paper, Coventry, England.

Roth, K. J., & Smith, C. (2009). Live case analysis: Pedagogical problems and prospects in management education. *American Journal of Business Education, 2*(9), 59–66.

Särkka, A., & Sagitov, S. (2008). *Live case studies in a new course on statistical consulting*. Retrieved from http://www.math.chalmers.se/-serik/Papers/ailaserik.pdf

Shulman, Lee S. (1986). Those who understand: Knowledge growth in teaching. *Educational Researcher, 15*(2), 4–14.

Simkins, B. J. (2001). *An innovative approach to teaching finance: Using live cases in the case course*. Working paper, Oklahoma State University, Stillwater, OK.

Titus, P., & Petroshius, S. (1993). Bringing consumer behavior to the workbench: An experiential approach. *Journal of Marketing Education, 22*(Spring), 20–30.

Weir, J. (1978). The use of live cases in teaching organizational theory and management principles to graduate students. *Journal of Experiential Learning and Simulation, 1*, 227–234.

# 9 Authentic Assessment—Key to Learning

*Grace McCarthy*

## INTRODUCTION

One of the distinctive characteristics of the millennial generation is the desire for continuous feedback on their performance (Meister & Willyerd, 2010). As Wilson and Gerber (2008) note, millennial students have grown up with video games from which they constantly receive feedback and rewards for achievement, and they continue to seek feedback both in their studies and in the workplace. However, Wilson and Gerber also note that many of these students are prone to overestimate their own performance. They need guidance to help them accurately self-assess. This chapter explores the issues of assessment and feedback and proposes approaches that can be used effectively with a wide range of adult learners. The chapter begins with a discussion of our aims and objectives, which is followed by a description of the context in which the example assessment tasks are used. The chapter then discusses the approaches we have found useful in both the design and conduct of assessment and feedback and includes a discussion of student feedback on assessment and feedback. The chapter concludes with a discussion of the applicability of the approaches outlined to other discipline areas.

## AIMS AND OBJECTIVES

The aim of this chapter is to illustrate how the use of authentic assessment can both engage millennial students in the learning process and assure that learning has taken place. Feedback is an integral part of assessment and will also be discussed. The specific objectives of this chapter are:

- To explore the role of authentic assessment in creating a dynamic learning environment in a business school context
- To illustrate a variety of authentic linked assignments
- To outline good practice in feedback
- To show how authentic assignments and good feedback are valued by students

## CLASS PROFILE

Sydney Business School (University of Wollongong, Australia) has offered a master of business coaching degree since 2008. Class sizes are typically 15 to 20 students to ensure adequate time for skills development. Students include full-time external coaches, internal coaches and managers. MBA students also take coaching subjects as electives. They are usually the younger students in the class, although all have work experience and meet the same entry criteria as students taking the coaching masters itself, including attending a selection interview. Students in this program learn about coaching theory and develop coaching skills through a variety of activities and authentic assessments. Lecturers utilize coaching skills such as active listening, powerful questioning and constructive feedback in their interactions with students. In fact, students have suggested renaming the role of lecturer 'learning coach'.

The delivery format is based on intensive face-to-face workshops, typically two days at a time, from Friday to Saturday. The intensive format allows time to explore topics in depth but has an even greater benefit in allowing time for informal peer learning, with students sharing their insights and expertise as well as developing rapport. Between face-to-face workshops, students practice and reflect on their skills, read and prepare assignments, and have 24-hour access to a wide range of resources on an e-learning platform. The spaced format helps reinforce learning, encourages reflection and highlights the link between theory and practice as well as allowing time for trust, relationships and respect to develop.

## APPROACH

### Link with Adult Learning Theories

Underpinning all coaching theory is the theory of adult learning, according to Cox, Bachkirova and Clutterbuck (2010). In particular, they highlight the relevance of andragogy (Knowles, Swanson & Holton, 2005), transformative learning (Mezirow, 1991) and experiential learning (Kolb, 1984). McCarthy (2010a) also includes reflective learning, based on Schoen (1983). There is congruence between the content of the course and the way we deliver the course. In respecting our students as adults, we seek to design assessment tasks that challenge and motivate them, bearing in mind Price, Carroll, O'Donovan and Rust's (2011) principle that assessment is central to the learning experience, and, indeed, for many students, assessment guides the focus of their learning.

## ASSESSMENT DESIGN

Our assessments are designed to not only assess students' learning but encourage student learning. In other words, assessments are not only intended to assess the standard that students have reached but form an integral part of the curriculum and learning experience. We do this by creating assignments that are relevant to both the course content and the workplace. We incorporate reflection in each assignment to ensure that students engage critically with the theory and understand how it applies in their own practice. Flint and Johnson (2011, p. 74) note that 'if students do not see the relevance of a task, they get frustrated and annoyed.'

In keeping with the philosophy of coaching, lecturers encourage students to take ownership of their own learning and to use each assignment to develop and grow. Students conclude assignments with an action plan with three to five SMART (specific, measurable, attainable, relevant and time-based) goals, specifying which areas of their skills the students plan to improve, how they will do this, by when and, crucially, how they will know they have achieved this. For example, if a student has a goal to improve her listening skills, how will she know that she has indeed achieved that goal? This requires students to consider in-depth what exactly they mean by 'good listening skills'. These assignments are rigorous in academic terms, requiring students to review peer-reviewed academic research as well as explore professional competency frameworks. They require critical analysis as well as reflective writing. Importantly, they constantly challenge the students to consider the relevance of what they have learned for their own personal and professional growth.

## AUTHENTIC ASSIGNMENTS

An authentic assignment is one that is similar to a task in the real world. In this sense, the most obvious assessment task for a business coach is to be assessed on their coaching. This is something that students both fear and relish. One of the graduates noted that it was far more confronting than an exam, because normally no one sees how we coach. Another assignment asks students to coach each other using an online medium of their choice, whether an e-learning platform such as Blackboard, by e-mail, telephone, videoconferencing/Skype or even SMS. This enables students to experience firsthand the challenges of virtual coaching mentioned in the literature (McCarthy, 2010b). It also heightens their self-awareness as they reflect in their assignment on the impact of, for example, not being able to see body language if they are coaching by e-mail or telephone.

In another assignment, students adopt the role of a coach, giving a sales presentation to potential clients. This allows students to demonstrate their ability to articulate the nature of coaching to nonspecialist audiences. The ability to adapt their communication skills to different audiences and purposes is an important skill, because coaching is an emerging profession and graduates need to be able to explain what it is, whether within their own organization or to other organizations.

Rather than a lecturer explaining everything to the class, students facilitate the rest of the class in learning about a coaching-related topic—for instance, how to calculate the return on investment of coaching or how to coach people from different generations or cultures. The students work in groups and put huge effort into their workshops, often dressing up, using props and even giving promotional gifts to the audience. It is said that we learn best when we teach others, and certainly the students learn a great deal when they do these assignments, not only about the topic itself but also about how to work in a group and how to facilitate a group session. The students later reflect on the processes they have used, and this helps consolidate their learning and prompts them to consider how they would improve the process if doing something similar again. The variety of approaches in these workshops is greater than most individual lecturers could adopt, and this is always a memorable aspect of the course.

Rather than an essay on codes of conduct, the assignment in our course requires students to identify common elements in codes for business coaches, and then to create their own code with examples of how they would use it. This requires the students to develop research and analytical skills so that they can synthesize and assess the value of what they find in the academic and professional literature, reflective skills so that they can decide what applies in their own context, creative skills to develop something original that they themselves can use and ethical reasoning so that they can illustrate their code with examples of how they would apply it. This intertwining of academic skills and real-world contexts that leads to the production of something the students can use in their professional lives is an example of how assignments can be worthwhile and motivating, not merely something required to pass a subject. This is particularly important for the millennials, who value real and relevant communication in all aspects of their lives (Partridge & Hallam, 2006).

The key to designing authentic assessment tasks is a thorough understanding of the work context in which our students operate and to constantly update ourselves on what is happening in their world. The assignments we set enable students to develop and demonstrate higher-order thinking skills, as they relate what they have learned to specific contexts (Gartenlaub, 1999) rather than writing only about generic theory. An added advantage of authentic assessments is that many are conducted in class, which creates a dynamic social learning environment, where students learn from each other, again responding to the millennials' desire for social interaction and entertainment (Partridge & Hallam, 2006). An added bonus is that there is no question about who has actually completed the assignment, unlike essays, which can be purchased by unethical students.

## SELF-ASSESSMENT AND REFLECTION

In completing authentic assessment tasks, students learn to see the relevance of research to their work, and they learn how to evaluate the quality of their own work and that of the research they are reading. Boud and Falchikov (2007) argue that self-assessment is a vital first step in students identifying the gap between their current knowledge and skills and their goal. They note that being able to assess one's own work accurately is not only a cognitive skill but also requires reflexivity and commitment. This commitment is fostered through relevant assignments. Nicol and MacFarlane-Dick (2006) suggest that when students self-assess, they are, in effect, giving themselves feedback. Crisp (2011) sees diagnostic assessments as a way of promoting an attitude of self-regulation in students, noting that such assessments could be done through self- or peer assessment. Learners who are self-regulated are more effective learners, according to Nicol and MacFarlane-Dick (2006).

## FEEDBACK

Timely constructive feedback to and from peers and lecturers helps keep people motivated and improves their self-awareness. Formative feedback is given at draft and practice stages, so that students build both competence and confidence. As students go through the process of becoming 'conscious competent' or 'reflective competent', feedback is important to help them calibrate their own judgment and gain confidence in their self-assessments. However, the literature suggests that students often do not find feedback helpful or motivating, while staff are frustrated when students seem to ignore the feedback they have received (Burke, 2009; Price, Handley, Millar & O'Donovan, 2010). The type of feedback students do find useful includes being told where they had not met the requirements and suggestions of what to work on for the future (Walker, 2009).

Our experience is different from this typical experience, perhaps because feedback is an integral part of the coaching process. In the admissions interview, all students are asked about their conception of feedback and about their experience of giving and receiving feedback. They come to the course with an expectation of giving and receiving feedback, and of being expected to reflect on feedback and how to address it. In the assessment on identifying good practice in listening mentioned above, the students' actual listening is not assessed by the lecturer. However, students receive feedback from their peers, which they reflect upon and compare with their self-assessment before deciding on how they plan to improve. This assignment is the first of a series of linked tasks the students undertake before being assessed conducting a coaching session. Later tasks include the following:

- Students coach someone outside the class for a minimum of five sessions and are assessed on their reflections.
- Students observe professional coaches in action, compare what they see with what they have learned from the theory and reflect on how they can apply what they have learned to their own practice.

In each of these assignments, students reflect on what they have learned and update their learning and skills development plans. By developing their own set of evidence-based standards for good practice, students create an assessment framework that they own and that is powerful because they have developed it themselves, based on their review of the academic and professional literature. By coaching people outside the class (after doing some practice sessions in class), they have an opportunity to discover their own natural coaching approach before they observe others coaching or before they are assessed demonstrating their coaching skills directly. The linking of assignments is recommended by Meyers and Nulty (2009) and Boyle and Mitchell (2011), not least because when feedback from one assignment is relevant to the next assignment, that relevance motivates students to learn from the feedback.

Another example of linked assignments is the students' research project, which all students complete as part of their program. Rather than having only one report to submit at the end of the subject, students submit three pieces of work:

- A research proposal incorporating a literature review and proposed methodology and including an application for ethics approval. This proposal is presented in class for peer feedback as well as for feedback by the lecturer. Marks are given two days later than the feedback comments to encourage a focus on learning rather than marks.
- A presentation of draft findings to peers and a panel of academics.
- A final research report, including a closing ethics report.

All the topics are related to coaching, but students choose a topic they feel passionate about. They help each other define their research questions, piloting questionnaires and practicing interview skills. They share resources and give feedback to each other on their research proposals and draft findings. This mutually supportive environment using coaching skills such as listening and questioning is far from the solitary journey experienced by many research students. Although new to research, by helping other students to understand what is required, students become more competent at defining their own questions and choosing and defending their methodology. Feedback on each of these tasks informs the next stage and also gives the students confidence that they are on the right track. Monaco and Martin (2007) suggest that feedback helps millennials to construct their sense of self by indicating where they are academically. Carless (2009) suggests that incorporating self-assessment helps students understand the feedback they receive. It also helps them develop confidence in their own judgment. The final assessment task is not a huge dissertation but rather the length of many journal articles, equivalent to 5,000 words. Students are encouraged to submit their work for publication in journals or conference proceedings, and several have done so. The project also equips students with the skills to conduct ethical research postgraduation and allows them to see the value in doing research and sharing their findings. Some have also enrolled in research degrees.

The constructive use of peer feedback contributes to a supportive interactive learning environment, where students learn from observing others. Feedback helps students make sense of their experience, and this in turn engages students in their learning (Duane Hoover, Giambatista, Sorenson & Bommer, 2010). Prior to our students giving each other feedback, we collectively review good practice in feedback as outlined in the coaching literature and highlight the connections between coaching and education. For example, the principle that feedback should be about behaviors, not comments about the person, is both a tenet of coaching feedback as defined by Parsloe and Leedham (2009) and also one of the conditions for assessment to support learning identified by Gibbs and Simpson (2004). Having developed a shared understanding of feedback, and framing the giving and receiving of feedback within the context of course learning outcomes, students are well positioned to give specific and constructive feedback. Feedback helps identify blind spots and heightens awareness, the starting point for students to improve their performance. Students value the feedback they receive from peers because it is given in a positive spirit, with their interests at heart.

The timing of feedback is important, especially where assignments build on what has been learned in previous assignments. This is only possible when students receive feedback in time to use it in their next assignment. This also encourages the lecturer to give 'feed-forward'—suggestions that will help the student improve his performance in the future rather than criticism of what he has already done. This future focus is in keeping with a coaching approach (McDowall & Millward, 2010).

We define detailed grading guidelines or rubrics for each assessment task, spelling out key elements such as what is meant by an original contribution or critical analysis or what we are looking for in a demonstration of coaching skills. These rubrics help us articulate what we are looking for and help the students understand our expectations. For example, a high distinction for the critical analysis criterion of an assignment on codes of conduct requires the student to demonstrate a deep understanding of the purpose and types of codes of conduct, identify appropriate elements of a code of conduct for a business coach, justify the selection with reference to theory and experience, carefully and thoroughly evaluate information from all relevant perspectives and include an insightful conclusion that is clearly linked to concepts developed in the paper. In another assignment, a high distinction is earned for the criterion of research depth if students support their arguments throughout with evidence from relevant recent references, including journal articles from a wide range of sources, cite all references correctly in text using the Harvard system of referencing and correctly in the list of references and, overall, demonstrate outstanding insight and understanding in applying the relevant academic research to their personal reflection. Sharing an understanding between lecturer and student of what is expected makes it easier for the students to address and easier for them to understand the feedback when they receive it. Using the same or similar rubrics when the same criterion is used in different assignments helps students develop their understanding of what is needed and to learn from the feedback; in other words, not only are the assignments linked but the rubrics are also. As Boyle and Mitchell (2011) note, unless students understand the rubrics, they will not be able to write assignments to match the rubrics, nor will they be able to understand the feedback referencing those same rubrics.

## STUDENT FEEDBACK

Since our course began, we have been gathering data at the end of each course and following up with students who have graduated. All surveys are anonymous. End-of-subject surveys are conducted by the university centrally, and we believe they are positively affected by the students' enjoyment of the transformative learning experience (i.e., the scores are typically very high). We therefore also use postgraduation surveys on SurveyMonkey, sending a link to all graduates. The response rate for the 2012 postgraduation survey was 51.2%, $N = 22$. Key findings relating to assessments are summarized in Table 9.1.

*Table 9.1* Responses to Questions Relating to Assessment

| Survey topic | Responses |
| --- | --- |
| Usefulness of assessments | Students rated a variety of different assignments as useful, with the top-rated assignments being those related to individual coaching skills, coaching sessions, reports, observation of coaching sessions, reflective components in assignments and presentations. |
| Most important outcomes of assessments | Highest ratings were given to the following outcomes:<br>• Something I can use in real life<br>• Helps me reflect and grow<br>• Encourages me to explore topics in depth, encourages me to explore a wider variety of information sources<br>• Gives me the opportunity to work with my fellow students<br>• Gives me the opportunity to develop my coaching skills<br>• Gives me the opportunity to develop my academic skills<br>• Gives me confidence that I am doing well |
| Attributes of effective assignments | Students rated the following attributes as most important:<br>• Assessment task is meaningful, similar to a real-world task and has clear task instructions.<br>• Marking criteria are communicated in advance.<br>• Feedback is specific, constructive and timely. |

As can be seen from the first question, about the usefulness of the assessments, students value a variety of assignments, but they particularly value relevant and practical assessments where they can see for themselves how their skills are developing and where they still have room to improve. Tying in theory with reflection helps students see the value of theory, and they valued reflective components in their assignments more than purely reflective journals. Traditional forms of assessments such as exams were valued by some students but not to the same extent as more authentic assessments. This was confirmed by the responses to the second question, about the most important outcomes of assessments, where students particularly valued assessments related to real life, which helped them reflect and grow. Similarly, in question 3, which asked students to rate the attributes of effective assignments, students rated as most meaningful assessment tasks similar to real-world tasks, with clear instructions and marking criteria communicated in advance. Timely, specific and constructive feedback was also important. A later question asked students to rate the usefulness of the skills and knowledge gained in the course on a scale of 1 to 10, where 1 is 'I do not use any of the skills or knowledge I gained on the course', and 10 is 'I use all the skills and knowledge I gained on this course.' Ninety percent of the students responded 8, 9, or 10, with the remaining 10% responding 5. This indicates a good match between the aims of the course in developing skills and knowledge and the outcomes achieved by students (i.e., the real-world relevance), which we strive to achieve both in in-class activities and assessment tasks does indeed result in the students gaining knowledge and skills they can apply in real life.

## CONCLUSION

A similar approach could be applied in many management disciplines where there are skills as well as theory to be learned (e.g., strategy, marketing, and human resource management). The relatively recent focus on graduate attributes or transferable generic skills has highlighted the need for students to develop employment-relevant skills such as communication or teamwork as well as to learn about discipline-specific theory and functional or technical skills such as how to write a business plan, draft a budget or select staff for an overseas assignment. Assigning aspects of the course for students to present ensures that students have a deep understanding of that element, because people learn more when they teach others. As noted, the different styles of the presenting students and the effort they put in to presenting results in an engaging learning experience for everyone. Involving practitioners in deciding on the skills to be assessed as well as on the assessment panel also increases the relevance of the curriculum and the motivation of the students. Examples range from entrepreneurship students making proposals to venture capitalists to accountants presenting expert witness testimony in court to MBA students facing up to stakeholders following revelations of an environmental disaster or the use of child labor in their supply chain. Encouraging self-assessment, reflection and peer feedback and taking responsibility for one's own learning are applicable in all business school contexts.

Unfortunately, many university courses have become divorced from skills development or have concentrated primarily on academic skills (Bennis & O'Toole, 2005). Balancing theory with practice helps students understand theory better as they see how it can be applied, which in turn motivates them to learn more. Furthermore, skills development is expected by business school accreditation bodies such as the Association to Advance Collegiate Schools of Business (AACSB) and Equis. AACSB advises that graduates need to be equipped with problem-solving, cooperative and functional skills and that they are prepared for lifelong learning (AACSB, 2012). Similarly, Equis (EFMD, 2012) expects graduates to develop general skills such as communication and critical analysis and management skills such as teamwork, project management and presentation skills.

Relevance helps students' engagement and motivation to learn. Including not only analytical and evaluation skills but self-assessment and reflection skills ensures that students graduate as reflective practitioners, equipped for continuing professional development. Boud and Falchikov (2005) argue that contributing to lifelong learning is often seen as an elusive goal for universities. Integrating learning activities and developing assessment tasks that foster skills development as well as acquisition of knowledge are key to achieving this goal. Authentic tasks also increase motivation, engagement and retention, creating an interactive learning environment where students learn from each other as well as from their lecturer and readings. To ensure such assessments are also rigorous in academic terms and consistently and fairly evaluated requires the lecturer to articulate clearly what is required at different levels of performance and to ensure students understand these requirements. Linking assessment tasks so that feedback can be used in later assignments is valuable in ensuring that students pay attention to feedback, particularly where the feedback is specific, constructive and timely. While it may not yet be common to hear students say that they enjoyed an assessment task or found a task worthwhile, that is often the experience of students in our course.

## REFERENCES

Association to Advance Collegiate Schools of Business (AACSB). (2012). *AACSB business standards 2012*. Retrieved from http://www.aacsb.edu/accreditation/standards/

Bennis, W. G., & O'Toole, J. (2005). How business schools lost their way. *Harvard Business Review*, 83(5), 96–104.

Boud, D., & Falchikov, N. (2005, July). *Redesigning assessment for learning beyond higher education*. Paper presented at HERDSA Annual Conference, Sydney, Australia.

Boud, D., & Falchikov, N. (2007). Developing assessment for informing judgement. In D. Boud and N. Falchikov (Eds.), *Rethinking assessment in higher education* (pp. 181–197). London: Routledge.

Boyle, B., & Mitchell R. (2011, December). *When is feedback helpful to student learning?* Paper presented at ANZAM annual conference, Wellington, New Zealand.

Burke, D. (2009). Strategies for using feedback students bring to higher education. *Assessment and Evaluation in Higher Education, 34*(1), 41–50.

Carless, D. (2009). Trust, distrust and their impact on assessment reform. *Assessment and Evaluation in Higher Education, 34*(1), 79–89.

Cox, E., Bachkirova, T., & Clutterbuck, D. (Eds.). (2010). *The complete handbook of coaching*. London: Sage.

Crisp, G. T. (2011). Integrative assessment: Reframing assessment practice for current and future learning. *Assessment and Evaluation in Higher Education, 37*(1), 33–43.

Duane Hoover, J., Giambatista, R. C., Sorenson, R. L., & Bommer, W. H. (2010). Assessing the effectiveness of whole person learning pedagogy in skill acquisition. *Academy of Management Learning and Education, 9*(2), 192–203.

EFMD. (2012). *Equis standards and criteria 2012*. Retrieved from http://www.efmd.org/index.php/accreditation-main/equis/equis-guides

Flint, N. R. A., & Johnson, B. (2011). *Towards fairer university assessment: Recognizing students' concerns*. Abingdon, England: Routledge.

Gartenlaub, M. N. (1999, May). *Authentic student assessments and how they are used for developing the workforce skills of tomorrow*. Paper presented at the ASQ Quality Congress, Anaheim, CA.

Gibbs, G., & Simpson C. (2004). Conditions under which assessment supports students' learning. *Learning and Teaching in Higher Education, 1*, 3–31.

Knowles, M. S., Swanson, R. A., & Holton III, E. F. (2005). *The adult learner*. San Diego: Elsevier.

Kolb, D. (1984). *Experiential learning*. New York: Prentice Hall.

McCarthy, G. (2010a). Approaches to the postgraduate education of business coaches. *Australian Journal of Adult Learning, 50*(2), 323–357.

McCarthy, G. (2010b, June). *Virtual teams, eLearning and developing coaches*. Paper presented at the 4th Australian Conference on Evidence-Based Coaching, Sydney, Australia.

McDowall, A., & Millward, L. (2010). Feeding back, feeding forward and setting goals. In S. Palmer and A. McDowall (Eds.), *The coaching relationship: Putting people first* (pp. 55–78). Hove, England: Routledge.

Meister, J. C., & Willyerd, K. (2010). Mentoring millennials. *Harvard Business Review, 88*(5), 68–72.

Meyers, N. M., & Nulty, D. D. (2009). How to use (five) curriculum design principles to align authentic learning environments, assessment, students' approaches to thinking and learning outcomes. *Assessment and Evaluation in Higher Education, 34*(5), 565–577.

Mezirow, J. (1991). *Transformative dimensions of adult learning*. San Francisco: Jossey-Bass.

Monaco, M., & Martin, M. (2007). The millennial student: A new generation of learners. *Athletic Training Education Journal, 2*(April–June), 42–46.

Nicol, D. J., & MacFarlane-Dick, D. (2006). Formative assessment and self-regulated learning: A model and seven principles of good feedback practice. *Studies in Higher Education, 31*(2), 199–218.

Parsloe, E., & Leedham, M. (2009). *Coaching and mentoring, practical conversations to improve learning*. London: Kogan Page.

Partridge, H., & Hallam, G. (2006). Educating the millennial generation for evidence based information practice. *Library Hi Tech, 24*(3), 400–419.

Price, M., Carroll, J., O'Donovan, B., & Rust, C. (2011). If I was going there I wouldn't start from here: A critical commentary on current assessment practice. *Assessment and Evaluation in Higher Education, 36*(4), 479–492.

Price, M., Handley, K., Millar, J., & O'Donovan B. (2010). Feedback: All that effort, but what is the effect? *Assessment and Evaluation in Higher Education, 35*(3), 277–289.

Schoen, D. (1983). *The reflective practitioner: How professionals think in practice.* Aldershot, England: Ashgate.

Walker, M. (2009). An investigation into written comments on assignments: Do students find them usable? *Assessment and Evaluation in Higher Education, 34*(1), 67–78.

Wilson, M., & Gerber, L. E. (2008). How generational theory can improve teaching: Strategies for working with the millennials. *Currents in Teaching and Learning, 1*(1), 29–44.

# 10 The Worst Day of My Life
## The Future Leaders' Experience

*Jon Teckman*

> Bart (handcuffed naked to a lamppost): This is the worst day of my life!
> Homer: No, son, this is the worst day of your life *so far*!
> —*The Simpsons Movie,* 20th Century Fox, 2007

## INTRODUCTION

What has been the worst day of your life so far? That is an easy—if painful—question for me to answer. The worst day of my life so far was December 6, 1989—the day my big brother, Mike, was killed in a car crash. More than twenty years ago now, but I can still remember every heartbreaking moment, every terrible detail. Perhaps you've suffered the death of a beloved family member or close friend or experienced the deep pain and misery of the break-up of an important personal relationship. Even something as apparently mundane as moving house has been shown to be one of the most stressful, traumatic and upsetting things that we go through in life. If you are just 35 years old as you are reading this, then you have already enjoyed and endured more than 12,750 days of triumph and disaster, joy and despair. So for one day to stand out as the very worst day? That really has to have been 24 hours that made an impact at a deep and emotional level.

With this in mind, imagine receiving feedback from a participant on a leadership development program that read: this was 'the worst day of my entire life'. Not 'one of the worst days' or 'this was a really tough day', but 'the worst day of my entire life'. I might have seriously considered whether leadership development was, in fact, the right field of endeavor for me to be in, had the next sentence not read: 'But I wouldn't have missed it for the world.'

What kind of program could bring out such a visceral reaction in this participant (and also be hailed by his fellow participants as being simultaneously both 'bloody awful' and 'amazing')? This chapter describes The Leadership Experience, the immersive and challenging simulation developed at Ashridge Business School that generated this feedback. The chapter describes the rationale behind the program and the ground-breaking research that underpinned its design and development and concludes with some thoughts about why the program has been, and continues to be, highly successful in educating effective leaders.

## AIMS AND OBJECTIVES OF THE PROGRAM

One of the major challenges we face when trying to create effective leadership development programs is how to put the participants' feet to the fire and hold them there until the skin begins to crackle—but within a safe and controlled environment, in which good learning can take place. Too many management programs still focus excessively on the science of management rather than the true emotional core of the challenges involved in trying to get people to do things because they *want* to do them rather than because their leader wants them to. As Adcroft and Dhaliwal put it, 'When management as an activity has been made scientific, its weakness has always been its lack of emotion and humanity . . . If the activity is a blend of the rational and irrational, scientific and emotional, individual and collective, it is not unreasonable to expect management research [and, one might add, development] to reflect this' (2009, p. 65). Evidence suggests that the learning experience is made significantly more effective when students are engaged at an emotional level rather than simply through an intellectual or theoretical approach—'the more emotionally engaged a learner is, the more likely he or she is to learn' (Palombo-Weiss, 2000, cited by Reitz, 2009, p. 13).

It is within this context that the Ashridge simulation described in this chapter was conceived and designed. It began life as the Future Leaders Experience but is now generally referred to simply as The Leadership Experience (TLE). The aim of the simulation is to re-create the real pressures of the workplace as far as is possible within an artificial learning environment. The goal is to develop 'muscle memory' within the participant's limbic system so that if, in their future managerial career, they face similar situations, they will feel that they already have some experience and knowledge lodged in their subconscious which might provide them with some insight in determining how to deal with them.

The Leadership Experience was originally designed by Ashridge faculty members Eve Poole and Melissa Carr. Poole and Carr (2005) interviewed more than 300 leaders about the events that had had the greatest impact on their leadership style and practice. From the responses received, they produced a long list of the critical incidents that had been identified as having the most significant bearing on the leaders' development. These incidents were grouped into themes including:

- Managing Self
- Managing Change
- Dealing with Staff
- Dealing with Peers
- Delivering Bad News

The results were then further analyzed to produce a final list of critical incidents which were incorporated into the simulation to achieve the most effective possible approximation of the real-life events that had the deepest and longest-lasting impact on the leaders interviewed. TLE has been carefully designed, therefore, to replicate the real pressures of organizational leadership in situations designed to be as close to real life as they possibly can be. Furthermore, in response to the finding that the single most important facet that leaders wished they'd possessed earlier in their careers was greater self-knowledge (Poole & Carr, 2005), the program designers added elements to ensure participants would end the process knowing significantly more about themselves and the way they responded to difficult situations than when they began.

## THE LEADERSHIP EXPERIENCE

The simulation can be run over one to three days and is structured around a series of critical incidents that happen to a group of participants working together as a senior management team. The participants are briefed that the team has been called together to sort out some fundamental issues affecting the future of their organization. They are given detailed information about the organization and asked to process this as a group, making initial decisions about what are the most important aspects of the scenario presented to them. Although there is an organizational structure already in place, there is no established hierarchy, and the participants are free to organize themselves as they wish to enable them to carry out their assignment—for example, in terms of creating new management tiers or responsibilities. Conflict can arise at this early stage as some participants seek to assert themselves and control the direction that the group takes. Unhelpful alpha-male behaviors are often seen at this stage—and not necessarily always from the men in the group! While not deliberately fomented or encouraged in either the program design or the way the simulation is facilitated, the presence of genuine role ambiguity and conflict is an important part of the experience and one of the central aspects of TLE that helps it approximate more accurately real work situations.

Significant efforts are made to ensure that the simulation is as realistic as possible. All briefing documents used are designed to be authentic and internally consistent (except where some ambiguity is actually beneficial to the process). It can distract the participants from both the task and the real learning of the exercise if they are worrying about perceived discrepancies in the documentation. It is also important that the faculty team is able to observe the participants' conduct without getting involved in the situation other than to introduce new elements to the scenario according to a tried-and-tested plan. However, participants are able to step out of the exercise at any time and speak to one of the facilitators if they are feeling overwhelmed by the experience or wish to reflect on anything that has happened up to that point. In an intense experience such as this, the duty of care exercised by the facilitators is imperative.

As the group proceeds with the task, the facilitators introduce a series of surprises and challenges that force the participants into confronting difficult and unexpected situations. These may appear to be random, and in some cases hugely annoying from the participants' point of view, because they distract attention away from the main focus of the group. However, they are all based on Poole and Carr's (2005) original research into the critical leadership incidents and are designed to help the participants develop strategies for dealing with such incidents should they encounter similar situations later in their careers. The specific nature of the incidents involved is a closely guarded secret (participants pledge to keep the details confidential at the end of the program), but they are usually cited as having been the most powerful and useful part of the simulation. It is this layering of multiple events, forcing the group to reorganize and reprioritize as they go along, that makes the simulation so realistic, so demanding and, we believe, leads to the long-term, deep learning achieved by the process.

This is reinforced by giving the participants as much information as possible about their behaviors, performance and impact during the simulation. Typically several types of feedback will be built into the program, including: one-to-one feedback with a member of faculty; a structured group discussion in which the participants give each other direct comments on how they perceived each other during the exercise; and the opportunity to pair up with another participant for an in-depth discussion about the key learning points and how they might be applied within their specific work context. Many aspects of the simulation—including all the critical incidents—are videotaped, and the participants are given a copy of the DVD to take with them for subsequent reflection on their performance and impact.

Whatever the length of the simulation, it is vital that adequate time—generally at least a full day—is available for structured reflection and review after the event, both to help cement the learning and to deal with any emotional aftereffects of what can be an intense and grueling process. The one-to-one coaching session, during which each participant is given detailed personal feedback by a member of the facilitating team who has been paying particular attention to them during the exercise, is of particular importance and value.

## THE IMPACT AND LONG-TERM RESULTS OF TLE

In 2009, TLE was used as the second module of a four-module program designed for leaders in creative industries (specifically advertising, design and commercial music). The immediate feedback on the module was not altogether positive—low scores and poor evaluative comments were received from several members of the group. Fortunately, for this program feedback was received on *four* separate occasions:

1. Evaluation forms received immediately after the delivery of the module;
2. Evaluation forms received within the month following the delivery of the module;
3. An evaluation of the program as a whole (some three months after the delivery of the TLE module); and
4. An independent evaluation carried out by the Arts Council of England (the program's sponsor) some three months after the end of the entire program (six months after the simulation element).

This multiplicity of evaluations enabled us to identify a striking trend, as the real, longer-term impact of this deep and visceral experience emerged, strongly suggesting a growing level of internalization and self-realization had taken place within the group over time. It also enables us to make some observations about the effectiveness of immediate post-program evaluation.

We initially asked for feedback on three aspects of the program:

- How well the program met its stated *objectives*;
- The extent of the *value* of the program to the individual; and
- Whether the participant would *recommend* the program to a colleague.

The first two metrics were scored on a scale of one to five and the third on a scale of one to ten.

The immediate responses on this particular program were 3.2 out of 5 (64%) for the *objectives* and *value* scores and a *recommend* score of 6.3 out of 10 (63%). These are very low—embarrassingly low—scores. To put them in context, the corresponding scores for the first module of this same program had been 80% and 84%, respectively, for *objectives* and *value* (no score for *recommend* had been collected at the end of that module). To rub further salt into the wounds, these below-par scores were accompanied by comments such as:

'Didn't engage or enjoy as much as I would have liked.'
'False environment.'
'Very frustrating. Not sure how valuable it really was.'
'[The simulation was] quite good though felt a bit rushed.'

Based on these quantitative results and qualitative comments, the initial assessment of the module had to be that it had failed. But then—just as in all the best Hollywood movies—the story began to change. Being creative types, the group had interpreted our instruction to them to complete their feedback forms and hand them in immediately, as 'any time before the next module will do'. Over the next few weeks, more forms arrived, all neatly typed up and with well-thought-through comments. They presented a much more positive account of the respondents' experiences:

> 'An excellent exercise!'
> 'Very clever, very insightful, very well managed.'
> 'Excellent. Stimulating verging on thrilling.'
> 'The simulation [was] a very useful exercise in reminding me of the importance of . . . self-awareness and assessing blind spots.'
> 'Bloody hell! This was a great exercise.'

The quantitative evaluations backed up these comments. The *objectives*, *value* and *recommend* scores were almost exactly 50% higher (at 96%, 94% and 95%, respectively) than those received immediately after the event. From significantly underperforming the levels of satisfaction expected of Ashridge programs, the module was now exceeding expectations. Overall, this module scored the highest satisfaction scores of any of the modules on the program, despite the fact that the initial, lower scores brought the overall average down.

This trend—of the simulation having greater learning impact as more time passed after the end of the program—was further evidenced by the feedback received at the end of the whole program (three months after the module) and through the Arts Council of England's independent evaluation carried out some six months after the simulation had taken place. In both of these exercises, the simulation was easily the most talked about and valued of the 'taught' sessions (the talks by guest speakers, most of whom were exceedingly eminent and respected in their creative fields, were the only sessions to score higher). The language used to describe the simulation still reflected the visceral, almost shocking emotional experience the participants had been through, but the value delivered by the simulation was also even more clearly appreciated:

> 'The simulation exercise [was] bloody awful, but really good.'
> 'Post the simulation exercise, because we'd been through something quite horrible, it actually joined us, joined us as a team.'
> '[The simulation] was amazing. It was such a great effort from every side . . . And I think we all enjoyed it greatly.'

Significantly, the two participants who had given the lowest scores initially later praised this module as having been the most valuable ('Most useful session: the awful simulation exercise; awful but good learning experience'). An independent evaluator of the program, noted that 'Several elements of the program's content . . . were highly praised by the [participants]. In particular, module two—the Simulation was cited as having a significant impact on participants individually.'

This change in students' evaluations over time, I believe, has a wider significance than just within the context of this program or this technique. To paraphrase Adcroft and Dhaliwal, leadership is about 'poets not census takers'; by fetishizing the instant, semiformed opinions delivered through the immediate post-program evaluation forms, business schools risk promoting the safe and easy over the risky but transformative. With TLE, the challenge for both facilitators and participants is that the learning outcomes are not written up on a flip chart or highlighted in a PowerPoint slide for everyone to copy down. They are individual and personal and may emerge months or even years after the program.

This also has significant implications for the faculty facilitating the program or similar simulations. As Poole and Carr observed (2005, p. 50): 'In an industry where much evaluation is carried out via exit poll style "happy sheets"' it was a big risk for the tutors to place participants in a tense and highly pressurized situation where disquiet and unease were as likely as 'light bulb moments' of intense realization. 'We self-consciously took the decision that we would rather participants found the event uncomfortable but learned from it, than that they enjoyed it but went away empty-handed' (2005, p. 50). This was a courageous decision and one which meant that the facilitators themselves modeled the 'resilience and bravery that are key elements of good leadership' (2005, p. 50).

But the final word in this section must go to the supplier of the title of this chapter whose identity, like the detailed content of the simulation, must remain a secret. His assessment of the exercise began with him describing it as the worst day of his entire life; then he added that he wouldn't have missed it for the world. He elaborated:

> There isn't another day when I've learnt more about myself. It really has changed my thinking and my perception of myself quite substantially. And all of it is for the better . . . I felt I totally drowned but with hindsight that's a good thing.

## DISCUSSION AND CONCLUSIONS

One thing about feelings, son: don't expect them always to tickle.
—Dr. Tyrone Berger (Judd Hirsch) (*Ordinary People*, Paramount, 1981)

Megan Reitz (2009) drew on several years' experience of running TLE to explore the effectiveness of the simulation in producing long-term benefits for participants. What emerged from her research was that it was often the emotional impact of the program that resonated long after the event. After all, leadership is relational and relationships are emotional. To be effective, therefore, leadership training must embrace rather than shy away from emotions. Many alumni of TLE described their experience of the program as an 'emotional roller-coaster', using terms like *fun*, *frustrating* and *anxiety-provoking* to describe how it felt to be put through such a challenging and immersive experience. Reitz cites a substantial body of research evidence to support her view that the most important impact of the TLE is to engage participants' emotions at least as much as their cognitive or practical skills. To quote from Reitz (2009, p. 11):

> Brewer claims that in order for events to be well recalled, they need to be unique, consequential, unexpected and emotion-provoking (1986). Rubin and Kozin . . . found that vividness of memories correlated with their rated importance, degree of surprise and emotionality (1984). Emotionality seems to be a key element in recall. LeDoux [2000] [states that] explicit memories . . . with emotional content differ from those without such content. The former tend to be longer lasting and more vivid.

In other words, not only does the highly emotive content of the simulation help to make it more realistic and relevant to the participants' actual working lives, it also helps the long-term recall of the experience, massively increasing its usefulness as a development tool. Furthermore, as behavioral economist Nick Powdthavee notes in his 2010 book *The Happiness Equation*, it is generally better for people not to:

> rely completely on emotions in situations where they have little or no prior experience. The explanation is simple: in these circumstances, the emotional part of our brain will not have had enough chances to adapt and learn from our past experiences, which will inevitably make it impossible for it to distinguish which decision is better for us. (Powdthavee, 2010, p. 7)

By exposing them to a variety of situations in which they have to react emotionally rather than by following established procedures or a rule book, TLE enables participants to engage at this deeper level and—albeit within a sheltered training environment—to practice (and receive feedback on) appropriate responses, which can then be assimilated into their 'muscle memory' and called on if a similar situation arises back in the real world.

The objective of all providers of leadership and management training must surely be to help their clients develop the skills they will need to fulfill their roles more effectively in their future careers. This means developing training experiences that can impersonate, as closely as possible, the reality of high-pressure leadership jobs. By traditionally focusing on the scientific or technical aspects of management, many universities and business schools have become adept at developing participants' ability to improve their performance in carrying out the routine aspects of their roles, but they have not developed their emotional capacity for dealing with the really tough aspects of the job. The Ashridge Leadership Experience immersive simulation is based on research into the most critical incidents that senior leaders have faced in rising to their senior positions. By simulating these key moments—many of which impact at an emotional rather than a technical or logical level—and applying real pressure to the participants, TLE has proved very successful in replicating the conditions they will face when they step up to bigger jobs in the future.

Just as the sports training ground can never fully replicate the match-day atmosphere of the packed stadium, nor military drills the do-or-die reality of the battlefield, the management school classroom can never truly deliver the genuine emotional tensions of the workplace. However, by making the experience as grounded as possible in the real emotions that face managers in a variety of situations, we have developed a simulation that, like good sporting or military training, can prepare the participants within the safety of a controlled, professionally facilitated environment for the very real battles they will face when they step back into the real world. In this way, we can provide managers with a realistic opportunity to test their responses to critical incidents in a controlled environment and help them practice the responses they can employ when faced with similar situations at work. We have created a process that can simultaneously deliver 'the worst day of my entire life' and fundamentally change the way people approach their future managerial careers.

## REFERENCES

Adcroft, A., & Dhaliwal, S. (2009). Disconnections in Management Theory and Practice: Poetry, Numbers and Post-Modernism. *Philosophy of Management*, 7(3), 61–69.

Brewer, W.F. (1986). What Is Autobiographical Memory? In D.C. Rubin (Ed.), *Autobiographical Memory* (pp. 25–49). Cambridge: Cambridge University Press.

LeDoux, J. (2000). Emotion Circuits in the Brain. *Annual Review of Neuroscience*, 23, 155–184.

Palombo-Weiss, R. (2000). Emotion and Learning: Implications of New Neurological Research for Training Techniques. *Training and Development*, 54(11), 44–49.

Poole, E., & Carr, M. (2005). If I Knew Then What I Know Now! 360° *The Ashridge Journal* (Spring), 46–50.

Powdthavee, N. (2010). *The Happiness Equation*. London: Icon Books.

Reitz, M. (2009). Experiencing Leadership. 360° *The Ashridge Journal* (Winter), 10–13.

Rubin, D.C., & Kozin, M. (1984). Vivid Memories. *Cognition*, 16(1), 81–95.

# Part III
# Critical Thinking

# 11 Introduction to Critical Thinking

*Patrick Buckley*

The ideal of critical thinking is the wellspring at the root of Western civilization. The dialogic methods Socrates used to explore the confused meanings, mixed metaphors and illogical beliefs that can confound the human cognitive process are, in many ways, the elemental source of Western intellectual thought. Despite, and perhaps because of, its central place in the discourse on the nature of human thought and the intellect, critical thinking lacks a universally agreed-upon definition. Definitions that do exist can be divided into two broad types (Patrick, 1986). Limited definitions, or what Paul (1984) refers to as weak definitions, focus on specific cognitive skills, such as evaluation, appraisal or the use of criteria to make warranted judgments. In contrast, strong definitions tend to equate critical thinking with higher-order cognitive functions such as decision making or problem solving. From this perspective, specific cognitive skills, such as evaluation or inference, are considered necessary but are not sufficient to ensure critical thinking.

Glaser (1941) suggested that the ability to think critically has three main components. First, it requires a positive effect on behalf of the individual toward evaluating and critiquing their own thought processes. As reported by Halpern (1999), thinking critically involves the deliberate use of cognitive skills and strategies to evaluate the outcome of thought processes. Second, Glaser writes that the critical thinker must possess a range of specific cognitive skills. Such skills include interpretation, analysis, evaluation, inference, explanation and self-regulation (Facione, 1990). Finally, the ability to think critically requires skill and experience in applying the aforementioned cognitive skills across a range of domains.

Critical thinking has been ascribed as an attribute of great leaders and philosophers throughout human history. However, far from being the preserve of the elite, the ability to think clearly, rationally and critically is something that all individuals should strive toward. Modern democracies are founded on the assumption of an informed and rational citizenry able to participate intelligently in society. Indeed, the development of critical thinking faculties in children and young adults is more pressing than ever before. Changes in the ways we work, live and structure our society mean that the ability to think critically is more important than ever. Contemporary workforce participants, particularly in white-collar professions, need to be flexible, knowledgeable and information literate. The concept of lifelong learning is becoming embedded in the workplace. The assumption that one can know enough at a point in time to be sufficiently educated for an entire career is rapidly becoming an anachronism.

The ubiquity of technology and the ever-increasing speed of technological development add weight to the requirement that individuals can think critically. Due to the information technology revolution, global telecommunications networks and technologies such as the Internet, citizens and workers today have more access to information than at any point in human history. However, the efficient utilization of these immense information flows is still a major challenge facing both individuals and organizations. While technical solutions—for example, improved search engine technology and the semantic web—can ameliorate some of the challenges in this regard, this information deluge also serves to heighten the importance of critical thinking skills. Now more than ever, individuals need to be able to search for, analyze, evaluate and interpret information effectively and efficiently.

The importance of being able to think critically is also highlighted by the recent economic turmoil that has enveloped many parts of the world. The global financial crisis was caused, at least in part, by the blind acceptance of financial instruments whose inherent risk was not appropriately considered. The interconnected nature of the modern world means that a sustainable future for individuals and societies requires a more critical and holistic perspective on business practices.

Pedagogical design is crucial to developing critical thinking. According to Bean (2011), the educator who seeks to develop critical thinking skills in his or her charges has three main tasks. First, the teacher must design problems to prompt critical thinking. These problems should have a number of attributes. They should be interesting and should both motivate and engage the student. Problems that develop critical thinking skills should not have a right answer, but instead cause students to engage in a dialogic process, either internally or with a facilitator and their peers, and prompt the evaluation of competing solutions. Second is the creation of an educational environment that encourages inquiry, exploration, discussion and debate. Such an environment should place a premium on valuing the dignity and contribution of all students and encourage contributions from everyone. The final responsibility of the educator who seeks to inculcate the skills of critical thinking is to provide a critique of students' habits and thinking processes. Constructive criticism is vital in assisting students to identify errors in the cognitive processes, but just as importantly, it emphasizes to the students the importance of critically self-reflecting on their decision-making processes and so plays a key role in developing the reflective skills that Glaser (1941) identifies as being a core element of critical thinking (Bean, 2011).

In this book, our contributors have identified a number of innovative ways that educational processes prompting and developing critical thinking faculties in students can be embedded into the curriculum. Blackshields and McCarthy begin this section by describing how they develop students' critical thinking skills in the context of a module in economics. Of particular note is their use of an almost archetypical character to frame the learning, in the form of Sherlock Holmes. This conceit offers them the opportunity to draw on examples and narratives from the source books as well as other media representations of the 'great detective'. Their approach is structured, moving from introductory work through to guided work and onto 'culminating performances', where students attempt to solve a problem using the methods and techniques of critical thinking, as represented by Sherlock Holmes. The chapter describes how Blackshields and McCarthy's approach can be used in a module on economics, but their unique and captivating approach could be deployed across the social sciences as a framework that would allow students to develop their critical thinking skills in any domain.

Zupan et al.'s chapter introduces design thinking, an innovative methodology which they report as being increasingly important across a range of disciplines, including entrepreneurship. Their key insight is that product design and development are not linear processes. Instead, the creation of prototypes inevitably leads to 'the testing phase provid[ing] additional insights which may lead to another ideation session, modified prototypes and sometimes even to a redefinition of an actual problem'. This 'messy' and iterative process prompts students to continually reevaluate the mental models and criteria they are using to make their decisions and plans and prompts the kind of self-reflection associated with critical thinking. As with Blackshields and McCarthy's approach, while this chapter presents the relevant methodology applied in a specific context, the authors provide sufficient detail and insights into its operation to allow other practitioners to integrate this approach easily into their own modules.

Finally, Adcroft provides a detailed description of a feedback mechanism that prompts students to take responsibility for their own learning. By providing a series of interlocking mechanisms such as structured marking schemes, generic feedback forms and exemplars of excellence, students are given a variety of feedback which they can use to evaluate the decision-making processes they use when critically evaluating an information source (in this case, an article from the *Harvard Business Review*). Students are expected to reflect on the feedback and identify where they can improve. Crucially, students are then expected to develop action plans that detail exactly how they will progress their work in future. Following Bean's (2011) recognition of the importance of academic guidance to students at this stage of the learning process, the development of these action plans is undertaken in conjunction with their peers and academic staff. Students are expected to drive this process, however, which serves to emphasize to them the importance of taking responsibility for their own learning experience.

Critical thinking is a crucial facility for all individuals. The nature of the postindustrial workforce, the pervasiveness of information resources and the requirement that a healthy society be composed of independent thinkers who can evaluate and, where necessary, criticize existing norms and structures all serve to emphasize this point. Developing and honing the critical thinking skills of the students in their charge is a crucial responsibility of the modern academic. This section describes a number of innovative approaches that can be integrated into modules across the range of disciplines that comprise the study of business. By drawing on the insights and experiences of the authors presented here, educators are provided with some valuable tools that they can use to meet this responsibility.

## REFERENCES

Bean, J.C. (2011). *Engaging Ideas: The Professor's Guide to Integrating Writing, Critical Thinking, and Active Learning in the Classroom.* London: John Wiley & Sons.

Facione, P.A. (1990). *Critical Thinking: A Statement of Expert Consensus for Purposes of Educational Assessment and Instruction. Research Findings and Recommendations.* Retrieved from http://www.eric.ed.gov/ERICWebPortal/detail?accno=ED315423.

Glaser, E.M. (1941). *An Experiment in the Development of Critical Thinking.* New York: Columbia University, Teacher's College.

Halpern, D.F. (1999). Teaching for Critical Thinking: Helping College Students Develop the Skills and Dispositions of a Critical Thinker. *New Directions for Teaching and Learning,* 80(Winter), 69–74.

Patrick, J.J. (1986). Critical Thinking in the Social Studies. ERIC Digest No. 30. Retrieved from http://www.eric.ed.gov/ERICWebPortal/detail?accno=ED272432

Paul, R.W. (1984). Critical Thinking: Fundamental to Education for a Free Society. *Educational Leadership,* 42(1), 4–14.

# 12 'The Game Is Afoot!'—Playing the Sleuth in Creative Problem-Solving Performances by Business Economics Students

*Daniel Blackshields and Marian McCarthy*

### ACT I: THE PROBLEM WITH PROBLEM SOLVING

#### Scene I: The Nature of Problem Solving

Economic problems are often complex and ambiguous, reflective of uncertain internal and external business environments. Therefore, problem solving with economics requires the use of judgment, particularly when one cannot reference prototypical cases (Jonassen, 1997). Judgment requires the ability to think *with*, not merely *about*, economics.

Problem solving involves Bloom's higher-order cognitive skills of investigation, reflection, analysis, synthesis and evaluation (Brickell, Harper & Ferry, 2002). Van Sickle (1992) distinguishes novice from expert problem solvers in economics, identifying two types of knowledge needed for expert problem solving: domain-specific knowledge and metacognitive knowledge. The latter enables conscious processing of a problem representation, problem comprehension, shifting strategies when necessary and monitoring solutions (McNamara, 1994; Mumford, Reiter-Palmon & Redmond, 1994; Jauŝovec, 1994 and Davidson & Sternberg, 1998). Novices tend not to be metacognitively aware when problem solving. As a result, they tend not to engage in general analysis of problems' contexts or provide support or evaluation of solutions (Van Sickle, 1992, p. 57). Echoing Bloom's challenge that 'most students can excel if they learn under appropriate conditions' (as cited in Moore, O'Neill & Barrett, 2008, p. 51), Van Sickle argues that 'Students must be guided explicitly in applying and adapting these general cognitive skills in economics if more than a few are to succeed' (Perkins & Salomon, 1989, as cited in Van Sickle, 1992, p. 61). He argues that not consciously supporting students' metacognitive knowledge leaves a gap in students' ability to reason effectively with economics.

We address this gap through the pedagogical use of the fictional consulting detective Sherlock Holmes as a metacognitive model of expert problem solving. The Sherlock Holmes Investigative Model (SHIM) is designed to explicitly scaffold the development of economics students' metacognitive knowledge.

## ACT II: THE QUEST FOR A SOLUTION

### Scene I: The Economist as Detective in Economics Education

Breit and Elzinga (2002) use the detective as a metaphor to illustrate the economic way of thinking in a series of novels under the pseudonym Marshall Jevons (*Murder at the Margin*, 1993; *The Fatal Equilibrium*, 1986 and *A Deadly Indifference*, 1998), wherein a professional economist and amateur sleuth, Professor Henry Spearman, uses economics to solve crimes.

The milieu Spearman inhabits is the classic detective story with its puzzle-detection-explanation structure. Such stories are writerly texts (Barthes, 1975, p. 4, as cited in Scaggs, 2005, p. 38) in that they 'encourage [readers] . . . to imitate the detective and to retrace the causative steps from effects back to causes' (Caprettini, 1983, p. 135). The plot of such stories opens with a 'plethora of potential clues' (Horsely, 2005, p. 26). Explanations are temporal in nature with evidence being classified and reclassified as the story is unveiled. Fiction is potent as a simulation (Oatley, 1999). In this vein the classic detective story acts as a problem-solving simulation by enabling readers to enter 'empathetically into another's [the detective's] life being' (Witherell, Tan Tran & Othus, 1995, pp. 40–41), facilitating deep learning as beliefs and assumptions that guide people's actions are revealed.

The Spearman mysteries focus on illustrating the use of economics. Opportunity cost, demand, supply and marginal analysis are used in unfamiliar contexts to illuminate their interpretative potency. Spearman's metacognitive knowledge is often only hinted at in the stories. We supplement the pedagogical use of the Spearman mysteries by modeling Sherlock Holmes's investigative process to scaffold students' understanding of the metacognitive knowledge needed for expert problem solving.

### Scene II: The Sherlock Holmes Investigative Model

Holmes, as with all scientific problem solvers, subscribes to the rule that his investigative process should be public: 'It has always been my habit to hide none of my methods either from my friend, Watson or from anyone who might take an intelligent interest in them' (Doyle, 2006, p. 751, *The Reigate Squires*). His conversations with Dr. Watson are a form of Socratic dialogue in which the expert mentors the novice toward the correct process to solve the case (Caprettini, 1983, p. 151). For Holmes, the exemplar detective requires the powers of observation and knowledge as well as deduction. This form of reasoning, abductive reasoning, attempts to account for the most plausible explanation for 'surprising observations'. Its key tenets are pattern recognition and plausible reasoning. It is formally expressed as:

| | |
|---|---|
| Result (observation) (P1): | This man is bleeding. |
| Rule (P2): | Knife wounds causes bleeding. |
| Case (inference) (P1 = P2): | This man's bleeding was caused by a knife wound. |

This hypothesis is a working hypothesis, plausible but not deductively valid. Similarly, Frank urges economics students to view their answers as 'intelligent hypothesis suitable for further refinement and testing' (2008, p. 13).

Abductive reasoning is a means of reasoning in our everyday experience (Johnson-Laird, 2008). It is an important form of reasoning where there is incomplete information and uncertainty, and it enables the formation of hypotheses and the development of new perspectives on phenomena (Patokorpi, 2007). Abductive reasoning is important for business (Dew, 2007) because 'Many new strategies start with an abductive leap . . . which explains a change in data about the environment . . . the quality of your abductive reasoning processes can determine the quality of your design alternatives, and therefore the quality of your strategic choices' (Dew, 2007, p. 43).

Abductive reasoning often occurs unconsciously, because 'human beings . . . are superb pattern recognizers and adept at dealing with imperfect and partial knowledge, they tend to abduct quite readily' (Dew, 2007, p. 39). At times people hypothesize too quickly, making inappropriate 'leaps of abstraction' (Senge, 1990). Expert problem solvers in general and in business in particular, must therefore focus on the qualities required to develop intelligent hypotheses. These qualities are embodied by SHIM (see Figure 12.1).

Holmes, like all experts, perceives phenomena differently from novices (Didierjean & Gobet, 2008). Three attributes enable Holmes to perceive differently from Dr. Watson and Scotland Yard: his masteries of observation,

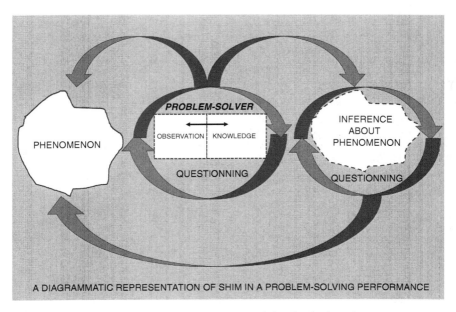

*Figure 12.1* A Diagrammatic Representation of the Sherlock Holmes Investigative Model in a Problem-Solving Performance

knowledge and inference development (Truzzi, 1983). These qualities are bound by his mastery of asking the right question (Sintonen, 2004). These masteries enable Holmes to consciously manage and evaluate his problem-solving process.

*The Mastery of Observation:* The necessity of facts to solve cases is foremost in Holmes's methodological reflections. 'It is a capital mistake to theorize before you have all of the evidence. It biases the judgment' (Doyle, 2006, p. 27, *A Study in Scarlet*). Holmes faults Scotland Yard for developing hypotheses to fit a few outstanding facts, ignoring little details and refusing to consider evidence not supporting their original hypothesis. He is mindful of the confirmation bias. The importance of the criterion of comprehensiveness of observation when hypothesizing is implied in statements such as 'You know my method. It is founded on the observation of trifles' (Doyle, 2006, p. 500, *The Boscombe Valley Mystery*). He cautions against quick evaluative impressionism: 'never trust general impressions, but concentrate . . . on details' (Doyle, 2006, p. 477, *A Case of Identity*) and overlooking the importance of the absence of facts. In *The Silver Blaze*, it is Holmes's decision to accept the 'non-fact' of the non-barking dog that solves the case.

*The Mastery of Knowledge:* Holmes's second mastery, one inexorably linked to the mastery of observation, is that of knowledge. Holmes realizes that facts are appreciated through hypothetically posited rules. It is this rule that generates the intelligibility of the observed fact (Harrowitz, 1983, p. 190). 'It is my business to know things. Perhaps I have trained myself to see what others overlook' (Doyle, 2006, p. 471, *A Case of Identity*). Holmes proclaims that 'one's ideas must be as broad as nature if they are to interpret nature' (Doyle, 2006, p. 38, *A Study in Scarlet*), suggesting the importance for him of developing broad and deep knowledge to enable quantitatively and qualitatively more rules to be called upon in his investigations.

Expert problem solvers are aware of what they know and its relevance and applicability to solving particular problems, as failure to manage one's cognitive resources effectively may lead to a failure to access knowledge or a failure of awareness of applicable knowledge. Experts' long-term memory organization sets them apart from novices (Didierjean & Gobet, 2008). Holmes recognizes the importance of memory for his work: 'My mind is like a crowded box-room with packets of all sorts stowed away therein' (Doyle, 2006, p. 1368, *The Lion's Mane*).

*The Mastery of Inference Development:* While Holmes's masteries of observation and knowledge enable him to develop hypotheses from what seem like disparate and unconnected facts, it is his attention to how he forms hypotheses, the mastery of inference development, that enables him to assess his hypotheses. He realizes the provisional nature of any hypothesis. Holmes's hypotheses 'obey an imperative of simplicity and plausibility according to logical and empirical criteria firmly accepted by society and obey a complementary ban—"never guess!"' (Bonfantini & Proni, 1983, p. 128):

'I will give my process of thought. . . . That process . . . starts upon the supposition that when you have eliminated all which is impossible, that whatever remains, however improbable, must be the truth' (Doyle, 2006, p. 1268, *The Blanched Soldier*). Holmes's process for eliminating hypotheses echoes Popper's falsification principle (Caprettini, 1983, pp. 135–53): 'One should always look for a possible alternative and provide against it. It is the first rule of criminal investigation' (Doyle, 2006, p. 957, *The Black Peter*).

*The Mastery of Asking the Right Question:* The glue binding these three masteries is Holmes's mastery of asking the right question of both the phenomenon and his own investigative process. Here there are parallels between detective and scientist both engaged in a model-based discovery game, subjecting sources of information to a series of strategically organized questions (Hintikka & Hintikka, 1983, p. 159). A successful game is dependent on choosing questions that ensure that relevant information is elicited (Hintikka & Hintikka, 1983, p. 157). As Holmes says, 'all day I turned these facts over in my mind, endeavoring to hit upon some theory which could reconcile them all, and to find that line of least resistance' (Doyle, 2006, p. 851, *The Empty House*).

These masteries can be actively explored with students by decoding Holmes's observations on his investigative process. Thus, students can decode the metacognitive knowledge of an expert problem solver.

## ACT III: THE GAME IS AFOOT: USING SHIM IN ECONOMICS EDUCATION

### Scene I: Using SHIM in the Economics Classroom

SHIM is embedded into economics classrooms through the teaching for understanding (TfU) framework. The TfU framework evolved from Harvard's Graduate School of Education research on what it means 'to understand' It defined understanding as 'flexible performance capability'; the ability to go beyond information, to create new knowledge, to use knowledge and skills in diverse situations (Perkins, 1998, p. 39). Through performance, students 'reshape, expand on, extrapolate from, and apply what they already know challeng[ing] misconceptions, stereotypes and tendencies towards rigid thinking' (Blythe, 1998, p. 62). TfU is appropriate for cognitive apprenticeship pedagogies as students are invited into the knowledge construction process and enabled to situate and transform their learning from their own experiences through guided practice.

The unit of courses using SHIM is called The Economist as Detective (EconDec). It is a 12-week unit (2 hours per week) for students studying introductory economics. EconDec is exclusively designed to develop students' metacognitive knowledge for problem solving with economics. TfU's four integrated parts are used to design EconDec (see Figure 12.2).

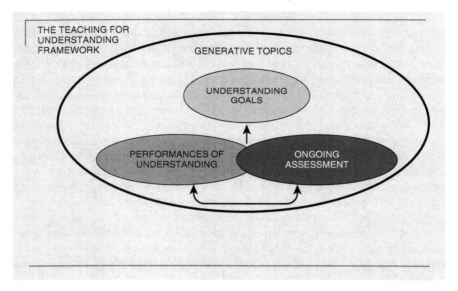

*Figure 12.2* The Teaching for Understanding Framework

Courses using EconDec have the following overarching understanding goals (throughlines):

1. Students will develop their understanding of what constitutes expert scientific problem solving.
2. Students will develop their understanding of informal reasoning skills for problem solving with economics.

EconDec has a series of student understanding goals:

1. Recognize and formulate appropriate questions that are amenable to economic analysis.
2. Identify and interpret relevant evidence with relation to these questions.
3. Justify a solution to these questions, given the evidence interpreted.
4. Communicate solutions to problems in a scientific manner to a nonexpert audience.

Using the generative topic of economics and art and the understanding goals, a series of performances of understanding are designed so students can reflectively engage in problem solving. TfU recommends a sequencing of performances with increasing complexity and student self-reliance:

1. Introductory performances explore the ideas and processes of a unit and students' levels of understanding. In EconDec, this is entitled 'Our First Case: Solving the Problems of Robin Hood'.

2. Guided performances develop understanding of a unit's goals, building on the experiences of introductory performances. In EconDec, this is entitled 'Watching the Detective'.
3. Culminating performances demonstrate students' deepened understanding of the unit's understanding goals. In EconDec, this is entitled 'From Dr. Watson to Mr. Holmes'.

Each performance has ongoing assessment, consisting of self-, peer and teacher reflections, designed in line with transformative learning principles (Kegan, 1994), so students can diagnostically reflect on their developing problem-solving processes (see Figure 12.3).

## Scene II: The Introductory Performance—The First Case

This performance introduces students to problem solving with economics, to the economist as a detective metaphor and to reflecting on their own problem-solving processes. We adapted the teaching case 'Robin Hood' (Lampel, 1991) for this performance.

### *The Plot*
Robin Hood is concerned about the current state and future prospects of his Merrymen. They have increased in number, but food and resources are becoming scarce. He feels that there are internal difficulties in the band and, externally, the Sheriff of Nottingham is becoming more powerful. Robin has identified a number of possible solutions to his problems.

It is a short narrative, rich in imagery. It allows students to use economics in an unusual setting, enabling them to appreciate economics as a way of thinking about phenomena. Because it is an ill-structured problem, students can use any economic concepts that they believe helps them to identify and solve Robin Hood's problem(s).

### *Scene II.I: The Performance Design*
This is a 3-week team-based role-playing performance designed to encourage teamwork and peer scaffolding of learning. Depending on class size, students are randomly allocated to either (1) an economic consultancy agency which consists of three agencies of five or six members each; (2) Robin Hood's Business Advisory Group (five or six members) or (3) the Merrymen (and -women).

Agencies and the advisors appoint leaders and scribes to guide and record discussions respectively. Students are thus encouraged to maintain chains of evidence and make their investigations public. This evidence is used in the guided performance to reflect on this performance using SHIM. The Merrymen and -women act as Adam Smith's 'impartial spectators', assessing the performances of the agencies and advisors.

116  *Daniel Blackshields and Marian McCarthy*

| Overarching Understanding Goals (Throughlines) |
|---|
| i) Students will develop their understanding of what constitutes expert scientific problem-solving
ii) Students will develop their understanding of informal reasoning skills for problem solving with Economics |

| Generative Topic: Economics and Art |
|---|
| Unit: *The Economist as Detective*. (Understanding Goals (UG))
Students will understand how to:
i) *Recognise and formulate appropriate questions that are amendable to economic analysis.*
ii) *Identify and interpret relevant evidence with relation to these questions.*
iii) *Justify a solution to these questions, given the evidence interpreted.*
iv) *Communicate solutions to problems in a scientific manner to a non-expert audience.* |

| | UGs | Understanding Performances | Ongoing Assessment |
|---|---|---|---|
| Introductory Performance *Our First Case: Solving Robin's Problems* (3 weeks) | #1 #2 #3 #4 | Acting as consultants, business advisors, impartial spectators identifying the problem(s) and offering strategic economic recommendations to Robin Hood | **Feedback:** Informal and oral by students and teacher. **Criteria:** Display the use of a problemsolving process in a problem-solving performance. |
| Guided Performance(s) *Watching the Detective* (6 weeks) | #1 #2 #3 #4 | Role playing as Dr. Watson decoding Sherlock Holmes' investigative process in *The Adventure of the Six Napoleons* and transferring the use of SHIM to decode Prof. Spearman's investigative process in *Murder at the Margin* and their own performances in the introductory performance | **Feedback:** Informal and oral by students and teacher. **Criteria:** Display an increasingly sophisticated understanding of a problem-solving process and an ability to reflect on their problem-solving performances. |
| Culminating Performance(s) *From Dr. Watson to Mr Holmes* (3 weeks) | #1 #2 #3 #4 | Role-playing as Sherlock Holmes in his first economics case: *The Government's Response to the Housing Crisis* wherein using SHIM and economics students identify the problems in the housing market and offer strategic economic recommendations to the British government | **Feedback:** Informal and oral by students and teacher. Written reflections by students via the reflective journal also assessed with feedback from teacher. **Criteria:** Display an awareness and use of an expert's problemsolving process in a problem-solving performance. |

*Figure 12.3* A Teaching for Understanding Graphic Organizer for the Economist as Detective

## Scene II.II: Performance Enactment

Each group is given role-specific instructions. Agencies have a week to deliberate on the case and are asked to address the following:

1. What you believe are the key problem(s) of Robin Hood and his organization of Merrymen and to be able to put forward evidence from the case notes as to why you believe this.
2. Possible solutions to the problem(s) identified.

In week 2, each agency makes a 15-minute presentation to the advisors and the impartial spectators based on these questions. These presentations are filmed for feedback purposes.

The advisors then deliberate and in week 3 make a 15-minute presentation to the agencies and impartial spectators addressing the following:

1. Consider your representation of the 'problem'.
2. Given the problem as you see it, what criteria would you look for in terms of assessing the analysis/recommendations of each team?
3. Deliberate on each consultancy team's analysis and decide on a winning agency.

A series of debriefing performances follows this presentation. First, the impartial spectators publicly reflect on the problem representation(s) and solution(s) of the agencies and the advisors using the following considerations to guide them:

1. Consider the teams' representations of Robin's problem in relation to your own initial thoughts. Are there differences? If so, what are they? Why do you think the teams have represented the problem differently?
2. Consider the teams' solution to Robin's problem in relation to your own initial thoughts. Are there differences? If so, what are they? Why do you think this has occurred?

The class views the films of the presentations using the following questions to guide reflection on their own and the other teams' problem-solving processes:

1. Consider your representation of Robin's problem in relation to the other agencies and/or the business advisors' representation. Are there differences? If so, what are they? Why do you think the teams have represented the problem differently?
2. Consider your solution to Robin's problem in relation to the other agencies and/or the business advisors' decision on the winner. Are there differences? If so, what are they? Why do you think this has occurred?

Finally, students engage in the following reflection:

1. Consider this problem-solving exercise. What specific approaches did you take to solving the problem? What did you find easy, and what did you find difficult? What are your feelings toward the exercise? What have you learned about problem solving from this exercise? Does your experience in this exercise connect with any other experiences that you have had?

These debriefings are recorded on whiteboards, filmed and put on Blackboard for students to reflect upon throughout EconDec.

This performance affords students the opportunity to immerse themselves in problem-based learning. It implicitly introduces students to SHIM, explicitly developed thereafter in the guided performance. This performance encourages the investigation of their own problem-solving processes and acts as a novice-led conversation for teachers to identify gaps in students' problem-solving processes.

## Scene III: The Guided Performance—Watching the Detective

SHIM is embedded into a 6-week role-playing, team-based guided performance. Agencies and advisory groups are retained, and the Merrymen are allocated randomly into teams of five or six members to form their own agencies. Each student is given The Sherlock Holmes Investigative Model Workbook (Blackshields, 2011), which is designed to scaffold reflections on Holmes's investigative process and subsequent use of SHIM to decode Professor Spearman's investigative process in *Murder at the Margin* and students' own introductory problem-solving performances.

The design and enactment of this performance follows a narrative format (Egan, 1995). Narratives help students to understand the intuition behind the economic way of thinking (Frank, 2008, p. 10). We use the original story and Granada TV's (2007) faithful adaptation of the Sherlock Holmes adventure, *The Six Napoleons* (SIXN). SIXN is one of the best stories for illustrating Holmes's investigative process juxtaposed against that of Dr. Watson and Inspector Lestrade (see Chapter Appendix). We use film as well as text given the increasing recognition of the importance of visual encoding of information for learning (Myers, 2004).

### *Scene III.I: Performance Design*
Role-playing as Dr. Watson, agencies use the workbook to critically observe Holmes's investigative process. Key scenes from SIXN are selected to help students identify and reflect on the masteries. Key scenes from *Murder at the Margin* are used to decode Professor Spearman's investigative process using SHIM. Finally, individual students, agencies and the class reflect on the introductory performances using SHIM.

The following section describes the enactment of the performance using one scene from SIXN and *Murder at the Margin*.

### *Scene III.II: Performance Enactment*

In the first key scene in SIXN, Inspector Lestrade visits Holmes and Dr. Watson with a puzzling series of events he cannot fully understand (Doyle, 2006, pp. 977–979). He sets out the facts and suggests that they might be best explained by Dr. Watson. Dr. Watson offers a hypothesis which Holmes rejects. This scene is used to illustrate and reflect on how individuals develop hypotheses from what they choose to observe based on their knowledge and the importance of questioning and testing hypotheses.

First, agencies actively read the text and view the scene using the following prompts:

1. What is Watson's hypothesis?
2. What details from Inspector Lestrade's statement do you think Watson is selecting to arrive at his hypothesis?
3. What meaning is Dr. Watson making of these selected observations, and why do you think he makes such meaning?

Agencies discuss how Dr. Watson's hypothesis of an individual suffering from an idée fixe is derived from his selected observations from Lestrade's report and his interpretation of these observations through his medical knowledge. Agencies reconstruct Dr. Watson's abductive reasoning publicly on whiteboards.

Students are then introduced to the masteries encapsulating SHIM using quotes and examples from the Sherlockian canon and then consider Holmes's assessment of Watson's hypothesis using the following questions:

1. What is Holmes's issue with Dr. Watson's hypothesis?
2. What details from Inspector Lestrade's statement do you think Holmes is using to arrive at his critique of Watson's hypothesis?

Through this exercise, students recognize the importance of observation and questioning hypotheses. Holmes observes that Dr. Watson's 'madman' hypothesis cannot account for the apparent use of conscious planning by Lestrade's culprit: ' "That won't do, my dear Watson," said Holmes, shaking his head, "for no amount of idée fixe would enable your interesting monomaniac to find out where these busts were situated" ' (Doyle, 2006, p. 979). Dr. Watson's hypothesis is poor because it is too imaginative, developed without reference to context. It also lacks imagination in that it is 'too "contiguous" to the circumstantial evidence' (Caprettini, 1983, p. 143). Agencies reflect on the importance of being consciously aware of one's problem solving, in particular ensuring that hypotheses account for all known aspects of a phenomenon. Agencies discuss Holmes's refusal to derive a hypothesis for Dr. Watson in the comment, 'I don't attempt to do so' (Caprettini, 1983, p. 143) in terms of his mindfulness of inappropriate leaps of abstraction. Agencies make their reflections public on whiteboards.

The next aspect of the guided performance focuses on transferring SHIM to problem solving with economics. First, agencies decode Professor Spearman's investigative process using a key scene from *Murder at the Margin* wherein Spearman forms a hypothesis that Professor Dyke had murdered Justice Curtis Foote (Jevons, 1993, pp. 179–180). Through this scene, students see how Professor Spearman's selected observations of Professor Dyke's behavior are interpreted through economics' assumption of rationality and the law of demand.

> The curious phenomenon that I observed . . . was this: although Dyke's favorite beverage, planter's punch, was available at zero price, he drank far less of it than at any other time. In short, at a lower price he drank less than at a higher price. . . . I had decided that something had disrupted his normal pattern of life. The only apparent change in his environment was the murder of Curtis Foote. Therefore I concluded he was the most likely candidate to select as the murderer. (Jevons, 1993, p. 179)

Students also witness Spearman's subsequent openness to new evidence falsifying this hypothesis for a simpler explanation:

> On the day of the murder the Times carried an article explaining that the consumption of nutmeg could be poisonous. Now we know that Dyke reads the Times religiously. And we know that nutmeg is a prime ingredient in his favorite drink. A new hypothesis therefore, presented itself. Professor's Dyke's taste for planter's punch could have changed because of the nutmeg scare. That left me with two different hypotheses. . . . When an economist has two hypotheses which can explain the same thing, he is taught to choose the simpler explanation. In this case it is certainly the nutmeg. (Jevons, 1993, p. 180)

Agencies make their reflections public on whiteboards for class discussion.

Next, each student, first in his or her agency and then as a class, uses SHIM to reflect on the introductory performance. These scenes from SIXN and *Murder at the Margin* are used in particular for students to focus on observation using the following prompts:

1. What details of the 'Robin Hood' case do you think your agency observed to arrive at your problem representation (hypothesis) about Robin Hood's problem?

2. What impact on your problem-solving process do you think that your selected observations had on the final solution(s) to Robin Hood's problems?

Agencies make their reflections public on whiteboards for discussion.

Following the guided performance, students' ability to use SHIM in problem-solving performances with economics is assessed in the culminating performance.

## Scene IV: Culminating Performance—From Dr. Watson to Mr. Holmes

Students now role-play as Holmes in his first economics case: The Government's Response to the Housing Crisis (Blackshields, 2008). The structure and style of the problem is similar to the introductory and guided performances. The conceit is that Holmes has been studying introductory economics. It is written for students studying introductory economics. The narrative style and characterization from the Sherlockian canon is maintained to scaffold students' transfer of SHIM to economics problems. Role-playing as Holmes helps to associate the problem solving with economics with SHIM.

### *The Plot*

The detection business is slow. To reduce boredom, Holmes purchases an introductory economics book. The chancellor of the exchequer is sent to Holmes by the prime minister. The housing market is in crisis, and if the problem is not solved, the government might lose the next election. Intrigued, Holmes replies, 'Tell me everything, let no detail escape you, I have been intrigued by the science of economics lately and would very much like to practice my skills. Do go on.'

The case sets out the chancellor's evidence and recommendation. Students develop a 2,000-word memorandum for the chancellor using abductive reasoning and the principles of economics to identify and solve the crisis in the housing market. They do not have to accept either the chancellor's identification of the problem or solutions. As Sherlock Holmes once said, 'the PM may not like my response. I am a scientific man, should my conclusions count against your options, you must accept my counsel.'

Students are advised on structuring memoranda, giving them experience at communicating economics to a noneconomist audience. Students can work individually or in groups of no more than three; facilitating both those who want and do not want peer scaffolding. Students are given specifically designed marking criteria focusing on assessing their problem-solving process in light of SHIM. Students individually develop a reflective journal designed for students to reflect on the level of transformation of their problem-solving processes with economics following participation in EconDec. Students are given 3 weeks to submit their memorandums and reflections for teacher feedback.

## ACT IV: CONCLUDING REMARKS

SHIM evolved in response to Van Sickle's challenge that economics teachers intentionally support the development of students' metacognitive knowledge. Through EconDec, SHIM is used by students to decode the metacognitive qualities of expert problem solving and acquire a metamodel to diagnostically look at their own investigative processes with economics. Students' reflections indicate that EconDec has a positive and, at times, transformative effect on their learning experiences to achieve the understanding goals of EconDec.

The student performance perspective of EconDec is seen as a positive teaching strategy; as one student noted, 'by watching the DVD and filling in the answer book I felt more confident doing [the] assignment.' Students report an increasing awareness and transformation of their own metacognitive knowledge. They report an increasing awareness of the importance of process to effective problem solving—'following from the Sherlock Holmes workshop I have become more aware of the need to set out a clearly defined initial question, followed by comprehensive and intelligent instrumental questions which aim to address the initial question'; observation—'as Sherlock Holmes shows . . . I think that the key to problem-solving is to not let any detail go unnoticed as if you do it could be to your demise' and the need to consciously manage one's cognitive resources—'Those of us studying economics often fall into the trap of seeing every problem as an economic problem as we have been trained to look at things a certain way . . . However, we must always be willing to admit when our range of skills does not meet the requirements of a certain tasks.'

Holmes is seen as a useful metaphor when students are problem-solving: 'every time I now face a problem . . . an image of Sherlock Holmes immediately comes to mind.' However, some students had difficulties transferring SHIM to economics: 'I think I had difficulty in transferring some of the ways that [Holmes] approached a murder case directly over to economics. Though perhaps I was trying to take the idea too literally.' While generally encouraging, supporting students to view learning metacognitive knowledge in a discipline-specific context is a challenge that teachers must be consciously aware of and design strategies to deal with.

SHIM has been used with students taking introductory economics courses. However, with discipline and/or subdiscipline alterations to EconDec's performances, it could be applied as a metamodel in any course within economics or broader business disciplines. Given its focus on abductive reasoning, SHIM could be a vehicle for integrative teaching and learning within and between business disciplines. This is a focus of our own future research on the pedagogical use of SHIM in business education.

Devoting a course unit to the development of students' metacognitive knowledge is a significant use of teacher, student and program resources. However, as 21st-century employability criteria demands that students display what they can do given their education, this investment is appropriate. EconDec's focus on student-centered high challenge and high support builds students' transformative learning capacity. Paraphrasing Kegan (1994), if the goal of business curricula is to support students, then it must enable students to negotiate the complex, interconnected and uncertain curriculum of business life. SHIM, developed through EconDec, enables students to look at their business problem-solving processes, supporting their mental capacity for this curriculum.

**REFERENCES**

Blackshields, D. (2008). The government's response to the housing crisis [class notes]. University College, Cork, Cork, Ireland.

Blackshields, D. (2011). The Sherlock Holmes investigative model (shim) workbook [class notes]. University College, Cork, Cork, Ireland.

Blythe, T. (1998). *The teaching for understanding guide.* San Francisco: Jossey-Bass.

Bonfantini, M. A., & Proni, G. (1983). To guess or not to guess. In U. Eco & T. A. Sebeok (Eds.), *Dupin, Holmes and Peirce: The sign of three* (pp. 119–134). Bloomington: Indiana University Press.

Breit, W., & Elzinga, K. (2002). Economics as detective fiction. *Journal of Economic Education, 33*(4), 367–376.

Brickell, G., Harper, B., & Ferry, B. (2002). *Developing on-line tools to support learners in problem-solving activities.* Proceedings of the International Conference on Computers in Education, Auckland, New Zealand 3–6 December 2002. Auckland, New Zealand. Retrieved from http://www.informatik.uni-trier.de/~ley/db/conf/icce/icce2002-2.html

Caprettini, G. P. (1983). Peirce, Holmes, Popper. In U. Eco & T. A. Sebeok (Eds.), *Dupin, Holmes and Peirce: The sign of three* (pp. 135–153). Bloomington: Indiana University Press.

Davidson, J. E., & Sternberg, R. (1998). Smart problem-solving: How metacognition helps. In D. Hacker, J. Dunlosky, & A. Graesser (Eds.), *Metacognition in educational theory and practice* (pp. 47–68). Mahwah, NJ: Lawrence Erlbaum.

Dew, N. (2007). Abduction: A pre-condition for the intelligent design of strategy. *Journal of Business Strategy, 28*(4), 38–45.

Didierjean, A., & Gobet, F. (2008). Sherlock Holmes—An expert's view of expertise. *British Journal of Psychology, 99,* 109–125.

Doyle, A. C. (2006). *Sherlock Holmes: The complete stories.* London: Wordsworth Editions.

Egan, K. (1995). Narrative and learning: A voyage of implications. In H. McEwan & K. Egan (Eds.), *Narrative in teaching, learning and research* (pp. 116–126). New York: Teachers College Press.

Frank, R. H. (2008). *The economics naturalist.* London: Virgin Books.

Granada TV. (2007). *Sherlock Holmes: The complete Granada television series.* [DVD]. London: MPI Home Entertainment.

Harrowitz, N. (1983). The body of the detective model: Charles S. Peirce and Edgar Allan Poe. In U. Eco & T. A. Sebeok (Eds.), *Dupin, Holmes and Peirce: The sign of three* (pp. 179–197). Bloomington: Indiana University Press.
Hintikka, J., & Hintikka, M. B. (1983). Sherlock Holmes confronts modern logic: Toward a theory of information-seeking through questioning. In U. Eco & T. A. Sebeok (Eds.), *Dupin, Holmes and Peirce: The sign of three* (pp. 154–169). Bloomington: Indiana University Press.
Horsley, L. (2005). *Twentieth-century crime fiction.* Oxford: Oxford University Press.
Jaušovec. N. (1994). Metacognition in creative problem-solving. In M. Runco (Ed.), *Problem finding, problem solving and creativity* (pp. 77–98). Norwood, NJ: Ablex.
Jevons, M. (1986). *The fatal equilibrium.* Princeton, NJ: Princeton University Press.
Jevons, M. (1993). *Murder at the margin.* Princeton, NJ: Princeton University Press.
Jevons, M. (1998). *A deadly indifference.* Princeton, NJ: Princeton University Press.
Johnson-Laird, P. (2008). *How we reason.* Oxford: Oxford University Press.
Jonassen, D. H. (1997). Instructional design models for well-structured and ill-structured problem-solving learning outcomes. *Education, Training and Development, 45*(1), 65–94.
Kegan, R. (1994). *In over our heads: The mental demands of modern life.* Cambridge, MA: Harvard University Press.
Lampel, J. (1991). Robin Hood. Retrieved from http://cac.schulich.yorku.ca/Case%20-%20Robin%20Hood.pdf
McNamara, T. (1994). Knowledge representation. In R. Sternberg (Ed.), *Thinking and problem-solving* (2nd ed., pp. 83–118). San Diego: Academic Press.
Moore, S., O'Neill, G., & Barrett, T. (2008). The journey to high level performance: Using knowledge on the novice-expert trajectory to enhance higher education teaching. In B. Higgs & M. McCarthy (Eds.), *Emerging issues 11* (pp. 51–61). Cork, Ireland: University College Cork, NAIRTL Publications.
Mumford, M. D., Reiter-Palmon, R., & Redmond, M. (1994). Problem construction: Applying problem representations in ill-defined domains. In M. Runco (Ed.), *Problem finding, problem solving and creativity* (pp. 3–39). Norwood, NJ: Ablex.
Myers, D. G. (2004). *Psychology.* New York: Worth.
Oatley, K. (1999). Why fiction may be twice as true as fact: Fiction as cognitive and emotional simulation. *Review of General Psychology, 3*(2), 101–117.
Patokorpi, E. (2007). Logic of Sherlock Holmes in technology enhanced learning. *Educational Technology and Society, 10*(1), 171–185.
Perkins, D. (1998). What is understanding? In M. S. Wiske, (Ed.), *Teaching for understanding: Linking research with practice* (pp. 39–58). San Francisco: Jossey-Bass.
Scaggs, J. (2005). *Crime fiction.* London: Routledge.
Senge, P. M. (1990). *The fifth discipline.* New York: Doubleday.
Sintonen, M. (2004). Reasoning to hypothesis: Where do questions come? *Foundation of Science, 9,* 249–266.
Truzzi. M. (1983). Sherlock Holmes: Applied social psychologist. In U. Eco & T. A. Sebeok (Eds.), *Dupin, Holmes and Peirce: The sign of three* (pp. 81–118). Bloomington: Indiana University Press.
Van Sickle, R. (1992). Learning to reason with economics. *Journal of Economic Education, 23*(1), 56–64.
Witherell, C., Tan Tran, H., & Othus, J. (1995). Narrative landscapes and the moral imagination: Taking the story to heart. In H. McEwan & K. Egan (Eds.), *Narrative in teaching, learning and research* (pp. 39–49). New York: Teachers College Press.

# Appendix
## Scene I from SIXN Text Used in the Guided Performance in EconDec (6.36 to 10.25 in the Granada TV Adaptation of SIXN)

It was no very unusual thing for Mr. Lestrade, of Scotland Yard, to look in upon us of an evening, and his visits were welcome to Sherlock Holmes, for they enabled him to keep in touch with all that was going on at the police headquarters. In return for the news which Lestrade would bring, Holmes was always ready to listen with attention to the details of any case upon which the detective was engaged, and was able occasionally without any active interference, to give some hint or suggestion drawn from his own vast knowledge and experience.

On this particular evening, Lestrade had spoken of the weather and the newspapers. Then he had fallen silent, puffing thoughtfully at his cigar. Holmes looked keenly at him. 'Anything remarkable on hand?' he asked.

'Oh, no, Mr. Holmes—nothing very particular.'

'Then tell me about it.'

Lestrade laughed. 'Well, Mr. Holmes, there is no use denying that there is something on my mind. And yet it is such an absurd business, that I hesitated to bother you about it. On the other hand, although it is trivial, it is undoubtedly queer, and I know that you have a taste for all that is out of the common. But, in my opinion, it comes more in Dr. Watson's line than ours.'

'Disease?' said I.

'Madness, anyhow. And a queer madness, too. You wouldn't think there was anyone living at this time of day who had such a hatred of Napoleon the First that he would break any image of him that he could see.'

Holmes sank back in his chair. 'That's no business of mine,' said he.

'Exactly. That's what I said. But then, when the man commits burglary in order to break images which are not his own, that brings it away from the doctor and on to the policeman.' Holmes sat up again.

'Burglary! This is more interesting. Let me hear the details.' Lestrade took out his official notebook and refreshed his memory from its pages.

'The first case reported was four days ago,' said he. 'It was at the shop of Morse Hudson, who has a place for the sale of pictures and statues in the Kennington Road. The assistant had left the front shop for an instant, when he heard a crash, and hurrying in he found a plaster bust of Napoleon, which stood with several other works of art upon the counter, lying shivered into fragments. He rushed out into the road, but, although several passers-by declared that they had noticed a man run out of the shop, he could neither see anyone nor could he find any means of identifying the rascal. It seemed to be one of those senseless acts of Hooliganism which occur from time to time, and it was reported to the constable on the beat as such. The plaster cast was not worth more than a few shillings, and the whole affair appeared to be too childish for any particular investigation.'

'The second case, however, was more serious, and also more singular. It occurred only last night. In Kennington Road, and within a few hundred yards of Morse Hudson's shop, there lives a well-known medical practitioner, named Dr. Barnicot, who has one of the largest practices upon the south side of the Thames. His residence and principal consulting-room is at Kennington Road, but he has a branch surgery and dispensary at Lower Brixton Road, two miles away. This Dr. Barnicot is an enthusiastic admirer of Napoleon, and his house is full of books, pictures, and relics of the French Emperor. Some little time ago he purchased from Morse Hudson two duplicate plaster casts of the famous head of Napoleon by the French sculptor, Devine. One of these he placed in his hall in the house at Kennington Road, and the other on the mantelpiece of the surgery at Lower Brixton. Well, when Dr. Barnicot came down this morning he was astonished to find that his house had been burgled during the night, but that nothing had been taken save the plaster head from the hall. It had been carried out and had been dashed savagely against the garden wall, under which its splintered fragments were discovered.'

Holmes rubbed his hands. 'This is certainly very novel,' said he.

'I thought it would please you. But I have not got to the end yet. Dr. Barnicot was due at his surgery at twelve o'clock, and you can imagine his amazement when, on arriving there, he found that the window had been opened in the night, and that the broken pieces of his second bust were strewn all over the room. It had been smashed to atoms where it stood. In neither case were there any signs which could give us a clue as to the criminal or lunatic who had done the mischief. Now, Mr. Holmes, you have got the facts.'

'They are singular, not to say grotesque,' said Holmes. 'May I ask whether the two busts smashed in Dr. Barnicot's rooms were the exact duplicates of the one which was destroyed in Morse Hudson's shop?'

'They were taken from the same mould.'

'Such a fact must tell against the theory that the man who breaks them is influenced by any general hatred of Napoleon. Considering how many hundreds of statues of the great Emperor must exist in London, it is too much to suppose such a coincidence as that a promiscuous iconoclast should chance to begin upon three specimens of the same bust.'

'Well, I thought as you do,' said Lestrade. 'On the other hand, this Morse Hudson is the purveyor of busts in that part of London, and these three were the only ones which had been in his shop for years. So, although, as you say, there are many hundreds of statues in London, it is very probable that these three were the only ones in that district. Therefore, a local fanatic would begin with them. What do you think, Dr. Watson?'

'There are no limits to the possibilities of monomania,' I answered. 'There is the condition which the modern French psychologists have called the "idée fixe," which may be trifling in character, and accompanied by complete sanity in every other way. A man who had read deeply about Napoleon, or who had possibly received some hereditary family injury through the great war, might conceivably form such an idée fixe and under its influence be capable of any fantastic outrage.'

'That won't do, my dear Watson,' said Holmes, shaking his head, 'for no amount of idée fixe would enable your interesting monomaniac to find out where these busts were situated.'

Doyle, Arthur Conan. *The Adventure of the Six Napoleons*. Electronic Text Center, University of Virginia Libraryhttp://etext.virginia.edu/etcbin/toccer-new2?id=DoyNapo.sgm&images=images/modeng&data=/texts/english/modeng/parsed&tag=public&part=1&division=div1.

# 13 Action-Based Learning for Millennials
## Using Design Thinking to Improve Entrepreneurship Education

*Blaž Zupan, Anja Svetina Nabergoj[1], Rok Stritar and Mateja Drnovšek*

### INTRODUCTION

This chapter describe an approach to teaching an entrepreneurship course using the design thinking methodology. A connection between some of the key competencies in entrepreneurship and the mind-sets that design thinking develops (Brown, 2008; Fraser, 2007) is made, and we identify several advantages of introducing design thinking in the curriculum.

Entrepreneurship education has long been acknowledged as a key means of making people more entrepreneurial and increasing the supply of practicing entrepreneurs (Drucker, 1999). As a result, a growing body of entrepreneurship research has been devoted to entrepreneurship education (Wiklund, Davidsson, Audretsch, & Karlsson, 2011), where several problems have been identified in the delivery and content of educational programs. To improve the effectiveness of entrepreneurship education, a variety of approaches have been described in the literature, and design thinking has been increasingly recognized as one of the most promising practice-based pedagogies (Neck & Greene, 2011).

The structure of the chapter is as follows. First, both problems and recent developments in entrepreneurship education are discussed. Design thinking as a teaching tool is presented, together with implications for both educators and students. We follow with a practical illustration of a course where design thinking was deployed as a teaching tool and report on the use of the tool and student feedback. Finally, the conclusion outlines the chapter's contribution to the study of using design thinking in entrepreneurship education, the limitations of the study and opportunities for further research.

### RECENT DEVELOPMENTS IN ENTREPRENEURSHIP EDUCATION

Kuratko (2005) states that entrepreneurship 'is about continual innovation and creativity' (p. 591). Entrepreneurial knowledge is highly action based and develops through practice, but only if students are aware of how their experience is connected with entrepreneurial tasks. Since the early 2000s, mainstream entrepreneurship education has received repeated critiques and numerous calls to change its paradigms, values and ways of doing things (Gibb, 2002; Kuratko, 2005), which seldom support what entrepreneurs actually need and do (Collins, Hannon, & Smith, 2004).

There is, however, substantial evidence that new approaches to teaching entrepreneurship are being developed and tested (Heinonen & Poikkijoki, 2006; Pittaway & Cope, 2007). These include virtual courses and e-courses (de Egana & van Dorp, 2011; Turnbull & Eickhoff, 2011), games (James & Olajide, 2011; Neck & Greene, 2011), participatory courses where students interact with entrepreneurs and facilitators (Kickul, Griffiths, & Bacq, 2010), competence-based, tailor-made individual programs (Harkema & Schout, 2008), starting businesses as coursework, simulations (Okudan & Rzasa, 2006; Plumly et al., 2008), design-based thinking and reflective practice (Neck & Greene, 2011).

Most methods are highly personalized, need substantial resources in terms of commitment and time and provide students with valuable firsthand experience. This corresponds with the traits most valued by students in entrepreneurship education: personal qualities of entrepreneurship educators, teaching methodology and delivery, personalized experience and project-based learning (Gatchalian, 2010). As Anderson and Jack (2008, p. 259) note, 'teaching entrepreneurship needs to produce a combination of the creative talents of the artist, the skills and ability of the artisan, yet include the applied knowledge of the technician.' Entrepreneurship pedagogy is increasingly acknowledging the different talents, skills, knowledge and abilities an entrepreneur needs, and in this chapter we describe design thinking as one possible approach to effectively teach those traits.

## DESIGN THINKING AS A TEACHING TOOL

In recent years, design thinking has been receiving increasing attention in both the literature (Brown, 2008; Meinel & Leifer, 2011; Neck & Greene, 2011) and in pedagogy, where some of the most notable examples include the Hasso Plattner Institute of Design at Stanford (Winograd, 2008), the Rotman School of Management in Toronto (Dunne & Martin, 2006) and the Hasso-Plattner-Institut: HPI School of Design Thinking in Potsdam, Germany (Plattner, Meinel, & Weinberg, 2009). Stanford has defined design thinking as 'a catalyst for innovation and bringing new things into the world' (Stanford University, 2007), while Tim Brown defines it as '*a methodology that imbues the full spectrum of innovation activities with a human-centered design ethos*' (Brown, 2008, p. 86). Thus, design thinking has emerged as a promising multidisciplinary approach in teaching and training or, as Rauth, Köppen, Jobst, and Meinel (2010, p. 7) define it: 'a learning model which supports design creativity, utilizing a project and process based learning process by emphasizing creative confidence and competence'.

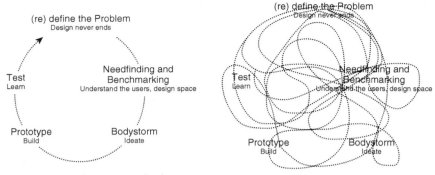

*Figure 13.1* The Design Thinking Process
Source: C. Meinel and L. Leifer, *Design Thinking: Understand—Improve—Apply* (Berlin: Springer Verlag, 2011), 14.

The design thinking methodology is usually represented by five stages of design, which are represented in Figure 13.1 as both a series and a representation of actual cognitive processes. In the beginning, the problem is defined and design thinkers use ethnographical observational methods to understand the user, his or her emotions and motivations and the environment he or she lives in. Information about the user is used in the ideation phase, where design thinkers ideate about solutions by using various idea-generating techniques. Selected solutions are prototyped, first by basic techniques such as sketching and later by actual physical prototypes. Selected prototypes are tested by actual users, and the best solution is eventually implemented. The process at first seems linear; however, as students' progress from phase to phase, the testing phase provides additional insights that may lead to another ideation session, modified prototypes and sometimes even to a redefinition of an actual problem. Sooner or later, due to technical and societal advances, each solution is redesigned to better address user needs. By understanding the phases and acknowledging that the actual cognitive process of design is not linear, students learn valuable skills and develop a mind-set capable of tackling an unpredictable entrepreneurial reality.

The next section presents a case study using design thinking as a teaching tool and describes the techniques used to develop core skills and mindsets.

## DESIGN THINKING CASE STUDY

Since 2006 a novel design thinking–oriented approach to teaching entrepreneurship has been evolving at the Faculty of Economics, University of Ljubljana. Design thinking has been used as a teaching tool in several graduate and undergraduate courses, where students need to develop working prototypes of products, services or businesses. One such course is Entrepreneurial

Opportunity Development, which is taught in the third year of undergraduate studies to a group of about 50 business students by two facilitators: one professor and one teaching assistant. On a weekly basis, the class has two three-hour meetings for six consecutive weeks. Usually the first part of each session is devoted to the presentation of methodology and workshops in various entrepreneurial skills. In the second part, the groups present their weekly progress and work on their problems using the design thinking approach. Students work on two design projects during the twelve sessions. The first project is introductory, where students develop their proficiency in the methodology. The second lasts for about eight weeks and requires students to develop viable solutions to a real-life problem. They go through several iterations of the design thinking process and test the prototypes with real users.

Arguably, the most important tangible outcome of the course is enhancing the set of skills needed in entrepreneurship. As people outside professional design have a natural aptitude for design thinking (Brown, 2008), sometimes all that is necessary is to awaken some understanding of the basic principles of design thinking or the basic skills of a design thinker (Stolterman, 2008), which can be easily applied to the entrepreneurial process. Table 13.1 clearly demonstrates that there are numerous similarities between what entrepreneurs and designers do. Based upon this comparison, one can argue on philosophical grounds that entrepreneurs or entrepreneurship students should not find it difficult to understand design thinking skills and mind-sets.

*Table 13.1* Key Findings of the 2012 Postgraduate Survey

| Designers | Entrepreneurs |
|---|---|
| Primarily deal with what does not yet exist and invent a different future (Liedtka, 2004). | Continually innovate and drive changes in products and services (Kuratko, 2005; Schumpeter, 1934). |
| Listen to, pay attention to, explore, extract, recognize and choose useful information from all potential sources (Stolterman, 2008). | Locate new ideas (Baumol, 1968) and recognize opportunities in the environment (Timmons & Spinelli, 2004). |
| Handle uncertainty and think as part of a team (Dym, Agogino, Ozgur, Frey, & Leifer, 2005; Lojacono & Zaccai, 2004). | Deal with uncertainties associated with new ventures (Vesper, 1990) and are more successful if they act in teams (Macmillan, Zemann, & Subbanarasimha, 1987). |
| Are mindful of the process (Meinel & Leifer, 2011). | Follow the entrepreneurial process and its stages (Bhave, 1994). |

The following sections describe some of the design thinking skills and mind-sets we purposely developed in class but which are relatively infrequently analyzed in entrepreneurship education literature.

## HUMAN-CENTEREDNESS

The importance of empathy in entrepreneurship (Chiles, Tuggle, McMullen, Bierman, & Greening, 2010) and in entrepreneurship education (Hindle, 2002) has already been recognized, especially as part of social entrepreneurship curricula (Smith, Kickul, & Coley, 2010). Similar to entrepreneurs, design thinkers imagine the world from multiple perspectives—those of colleagues, clients and end users (Brown, 2008). Both designers and entrepreneurs have to be able to gather user requirements by observing, listening to and empathizing with the user. During the course, students are taught various observation techniques, ranging from covert methods such as videography to overt methods such as in-depth interviews and researcher participation, which requires them to develop a deep empathy with their target audience. Students use these techniques to understand the users and their needs and later to test prototypes.

## INTEGRATIVE THINKING

Designers rely on analytical processes that not only produce choices but also demonstrate the ability to see all of the relevant aspects of a problem and create novel solutions that dramatically improve on existing alternatives (Brown, 2008). In his book *The Opposable Mind: How Successful Leaders Win Through Integrative Thinking*, Roger Martin (2007) defines integrative thinking as resolving the tension in opposing models by forming entirely new and superior ones. Entrepreneurs do not simply work in one discipline; many of them have significant experience in multiple disciplines. Depending on the problem students are solving, guest speakers in various disciplines from both the academic and business community are invited to work with students and help them develop the knowledge they need to successfully solve the problem.

## EXPERIMENTALISM

Experimentalism and prototyping, an essential part of product development and thus one of the most important steps in commercializing any new product, are repeatedly missing from the literature on the entrepreneurial process (Bygrave & Hofer, 1991). Design thinkers pose questions and explore constraints in creative ways (Brown, 2008), choose from a variety of possible solutions, prototype them, get feedback, revisit the problem and, in the end, similar to entrepreneurs, bring new products and services to the market. Through prototyping students learn that failing early and often in the development process improves the final solution and lowers the risk of market failure. Students are trained in various prototyping techniques such as sketching, mock-ups, three-dimensional modeling and storytelling. The prototyping process is repeated several times, and at each stage students are expected to come up with a more advanced prototype. At each stage, the proposed solution is assessed according to three measures of design: technological feasibility, business viability and human desirability. Students are expected to argue their solution on all three accounts, and feedback is given at each stage on what can be improved. It is not unusual for students to return to brainstorming or even to redefine the actual problem as new insights are acquired about the nature of user needs.

During the final session of the course, students present their market-ready prototypes or solutions to a wide audience consisting of students, professors, facilitators, practitioners, entrepreneurs and other businesspeople. Students are graded on their weekly progress and on the sophistication of their final solution and presentation.

Empathy, experimentalism and integrative thinking, together with optimism and collaboration, are core characteristics of design thinkers (Brown, 2008). Collins et al. (2004) analyzed the literature and found that the skills listed above were practically absent in existing entrepreneurship curricula. Design thinking allows students to develop these skills while enhancing student outcomes in terms of marketable solutions when compared to the more traditional business plan method. Design thinking therefore adds value to entrepreneurship education by increasing the number of skills developed through formal education.

## STUDENT FEEDBACK

At the end of the course, students were asked to complete an anonymous open questionnaire about their work and what lessons they had learned about entrepreneurship and developing marketable solutions. We analyzed the responses and systematically coded the answers to investigate the key learning experiences for students. To increase the validity, the answers were coded by two independent researchers.

Experiencing **group work** was the most common positive learning point emphasized by the students in the course. Most had little experience of participating in interdisciplinary teams or in the demanding task of collaborating prior to the course. The hands-on approach forced the students to actively collaborate from the first session, quickly revealing key challenges that had to be overcome for the group to achieve the required results. The students reported that 'I learned that interdisciplinary teams with students from different faculties bring new knowledge and insights and are more successful,' and 'teams with motivated and knowledgeable members have a much higher chance of success.' The results show that this led to improved **communication skills**, as students reported that 'I learned how to communicate with people with different backgrounds.'

The use of rapid **prototyping** and **learning from their own mistakes** were elements of experimentalism that were often identified as techniques that delivered new knowledge to the participating students. They stated that 'prototyping proved to be a crucial step in communicating our idea with users as well as investors' and 'prototypes really sped up the development of our idea because brains had time to process what eyes saw and hands felt and were not tied in building imaginary images of our product.'

The students also emphasized that the challenges presented by the course would cause them to fail at certain ideas and to be faced with challenges that initially seemed insurmountable. Students trained in an academic environment are rarely used to facing failure and therefore noted **coping with failure** and **creatively adapting** to new markets as important experiences gained during the course. Students came to a conclusion that 'in entrepreneurship there are numerous factors you cannot predict and you need to adapt as you go,' and 'failure often does not mean you have to end the project, you have to learn from your mistakes and go back to the drawing board to see what went wrong and how to improve your prototype.'

Working with customers quickly revealed the importance of **empathy** for understanding the customers' needs and developing a desirable solution. They noted 'we learned how to identify customer needs not only by interviews and questionnaires but, what is often even more relevant, by observing their behavior,' and 'we need to look at things with the eyes of our customers.'

The participants unanimously praised the way the course enabled them to use the theoretical knowledge they acquired through their education in a **practical way**. One student reported that 'even though I have been studying business for almost 5 years because of lack of practical experience I still feel somehow lost when faced with real-life business problems.'

The results from the feedback are well aligned with the goals of the course described above. The course forced students to move from comfortably thinking about how to solve a problem to facing the challenge of actually solving it. This is best shown by these two quotes: 'it does not matter how much time you spend working on a project. At the end only the result counts,' and 'in entrepreneurship there is no fixed salary. You always get paid based on what you deliver.'

## DISCUSSION

While it is still too early to understand all the effects of introducing design thinking into the entrepreneurship curriculum, some conclusions can be drawn from several years of experience, numerous adaptations of the curricula and student feedback. All stakeholders involved were very enthusiastic about the new approach, and students found it to be fun, engaging and motivational. Interestingly, a relatively high number of them became nascent entrepreneurs, planning to develop their own companies based on the opportunities identified and the skills and knowledge acquired during the course.

Scholars who had been working with the traditional business plan method for years found a new enthusiasm and zeal for working with students. Professors working in different faculties joined forces to develop knowledge and solutions that extended beyond the boundaries of a single research field. Companies were actively involved in the process and got the opportunity to generate innovative ideas and even find potential employees.

Our initial observation is that the design thinking approach is an improvement on the business plan method. Students not only think and write about business ideas but actually work on functioning and marketable solutions. However, this new approach also has its limitations and problems. First, the effort of organizing such a class is far greater than the effort put into traditional entrepreneurial education. The number of people involved means that coordination is a serious issue, made more complex by the multidisciplinary character of classes. Second, conflicts within and among groups and negligent students are to be expected and need to be actively managed by educators who have training in conflict management or have a background in psychology. Third, assessing student output is challenging, because there are usually no written exams, or, where exams do exist, they contribute only a small percentage to the final grade. Usually a jury comprised of educators and guests from practice grades the final presentation, which, together with an assessment of effort put into weekly tasks, forms the majority of the final grade. Finally, additional resources are needed to support such classes, because there is a need for lecturers, facilitators, team coaches and suitable classrooms to support action-based collaborative work. Existing classrooms need to be adapted, because as design thinking demands prototyping labs and space where teams can work creatively on their projects. Prototyping equipment is another significant cost, because specialized machines and software are usually quite expensive.

Design thinking has been accepted as an action-based teaching practice in engineering schools. As this case study confirms, it can be successfully applied as a methodology for teaching entrepreneurship. It prepares students to act as real-world entrepreneurs by developing neglected skills and mindsets which, though recognized as important, were not taught or developed by existing entrepreneurship curricula. The methodology itself is flexible enough to be used in courses of any length and at various degrees of proficiency. The level of immersion can be controlled by the educator, who needs to exercise control and guide the students even in apparently unstructured classes. Small groups guided by facilitators with practical entrepreneurial experience and a profound understanding of the design thinking methodology were our preferred mode of delivery. Multidisciplinary classes with students and educators from different faculties should be highly encouraged, and guest speakers should be invited to cover areas where the teaching team lacks knowledge.

Design thinking is slowly finding its way into all facets of education, including entrepreneurship taught at university levels. However, further research is needed to fully understand its role in the classroom environment. Open research questions that are of interest include:

- How can we compare different action-based approaches in entrepreneurship education and measure their effect on the supply of practicing entrepreneurs and their subsequent success?
- What is the most effective way to introduce the design thinking methodology to students?
- To what extent should we complement or substitute existing entrepreneurship curricula with design thinking?
- Can design thinking be successfully applied to other courses throughout the university?

## CONCLUSION

Courses based on design thinking give motivated students a chance to experience entrepreneurship in action and can be considered an upgrade on existing entrepreneurship programs. We do not reject the importance of analytical skills, because we believe that successful entrepreneurs are multidisciplinary individuals, known as T-shaped people, with deep knowledge in specific areas and empathy across disciplines, including analytical knowledge (Kelley & Littman, 2008). Notable differences between business plan and design thinking–based teaching methods support this, as a combination of both gives students the wide set of skills needed to effectively cope with the unpredictable nature of entrepreneurship.

Based on our observations, we can, to a great degree of certainty, assume that design thinking could be a successful way of augmenting existing entrepreneurship curricula. However, it is demanding in terms of resources and can only be applied in small classes. Our experience has shown that design thinking can be incorporated into existing programs to improve students' entrepreneurial skills. Students reported that they learned how to be practicing entrepreneurs instead of only theorizing about possibilities and analyzing the entrepreneurial world without actually living in it. One student concluded, 'until this course I never taught of actually living and not only dreaming my entrepreneurial ideas.'

## NOTE

1. Corresponding author.

# REFERENCES

Anderson, A. R., & Jack, S. L. (2008). Role typologies for enterprising education: The professional artisan? *Journal of Small Business and Enterprise Development*, 15(2), 259–273.
Baumol, W. J. (1968). Entrepreneurship in economic theory. *American Economic Review*, 58(2), 64–71.
Bhave, M. P. (1994). A process model of entrepreneurial venture creation. *Journal of Business Venturing*, 9(3), 223–242.
Brown, T. (2008). Design thinking. *Harvard Business Review*, 86(6), 84.
Bygrave, W. D., & Hofer, C. W. (1991). Theorizing about entrepreneurship. *Entrepreneurship: Theory and Practice*, 16(2), 13–22.
Chiles, T. H., Tuggle, C. S., McMullen, J. S., Bierman, L., & Greening, D. W. (2010). Dynamic creation: Extending the radical Austrian approach to entrepreneurship. *Organization Studies*, 31(1), 7.
Collins, L., Hannon, P. D., & Smith, A. (2004). Enacting entrepreneurial intent: The gaps between student needs and higher education capability. *Education + Training*, 46(8/9), 454–463.
de Egana, A. H., & van Dorp, C. A. (2011). Methodology and evaluation of entrepreneurship courses. *International Journal of Business Research and Management*, 1(3), 132.
Drucker, P. F. (1999). *Innovation and entrepreneurship: Practice and principles* (2nd ed.). Oxford: Butterworth-Heinemann.
Dunne, D., & Martin, R. (2006). Design thinking and how it will change management education: An interview and discussion. *Academy of Management Learning and Education*, 5(4), 512.
Dym, C. L., Agogino, A. M., Ozgur, E., Frey, D. D., & Leifer, L. J. (2005). Engineering design thinking, teaching, and learning. *Journal of Engineering Education*, 94(1), 103–120.
Fraser, H. M. A. (2007). The practice of breakthrough strategies by design. *Journal of Business Strategy*, 28(4), 66–74.
Gatchalian, M. L. B. (2010). An in-depth analysis of the entrepreneurship education in the Philippines: An initiative towards the development of a framework for a professional teaching competency program for entrepreneurship educators. *International Journal of Research and Review*, 5(1), 51–73.
Gibb, A. (2002). In pursuit of a new 'enterprise' and 'entrepreneurship' paradigm for learning: Creative destruction, new values, new ways of doing things and new combinations of knowledge. *International Journal of Management Reviews*, 4(3), 233–269.
Harkema, S. J. M., & Schout, H. (2008). Incorporating student-centred learning in innovation and entrepreneurship education. *European Journal of Education*, 43(4), 513–526.
Heinonen, J., & Poikkijoki, S. A. (2006). An entrepreneurial-directed approach to entrepreneurship education: Mission impossible? *Journal of Management Development*, 25(1), 80–94.
Hindle, K. (2002). A grounded theory for teaching entrepreneurship using simulation games. *Simulation and Gaming*, 33(2), 236.
James, T., & Olajide, J. O. (2011). Developing entrepreneurship teaching approach using 'WORDS and PICTURE' games in integrated science classroom. *European Journal of Scientific Research*, 52(1), 70–74.
Kelley, T., & Littman, J. (2008). *The ten faces of innovation*. London: Profile Books.
Kickul, J., Griffiths, M., & Bacq, S. (2010). The boundary-less classroom: Extending social innovation and impact learning to the field. *Journal of Small Business and Enterprise Development*, 17(4), 652–663.

Kuratko, D. F. (2005). The emergence of entrepreneurship education: Development, trends, and challenges. *Entrepreneurship: Theory and Practice*, 29(5), 577–597.
Liedtka, J. (2004). Design as strategy. *Rotman Management. The Alumni Magazine of the Rotman School of Management*, Winter, 4.
Lojacono, G., & Zaccai, G. (2004). The evolution of the design-inspired enterprise. *MIT Sloan Management Review*, 45(3), 75–79.
Macmillan, I. C., Zemann, L., & Subbanarasimha, P. N. (1987). Criteria distinguishing successful from unsuccessful ventures in the venture screening process. *Journal of Business Venturing*, 2(2), 123–137.
Martin, R. (2007). *The opposable mind*. Boston: Harvard Business School Press.
Meinel, C., & Leifer, L. (2011). *Design thinking: Understand—improve—apply*. Berlin: Springer Verlag.
Neck, H. M., & Greene, P. G. (2011). Entrepreneurship education: Known worlds and new frontiers. *Journal of Small Business Management*, 49(1), 55–70.
Okudan, G. E., & Rzasa, S. E. (2006). A project-based approach to entrepreneurial leadership education. *Technovation*, 26(2), 195–210.
Pittaway, L., & Cope, J. (2007). Entrepreneurship education. *International Small Business Journal*, 25(5), 479–510.
Plattner, H., Meinel, C., & Weinberg, U. (2009). *Design-thinking*. Landsberg: Mi-Fachverlag.
Plumly, L., Jr., Marshall, L., Eastman, J., Iyer, R., Stanley, K., & Boatwright, J. (2008). Developing entrepreneurial competencies: A student business. *Journal of Entrepreneurship Education*, 11, 17.
Rauth, I., Köppen, E., Jobst, B., & Meinel, C. (2010, December). *Design thinking: An educational model towards creative confidence*. Paper presented at the First International Conference on Design Creativity, Kobe, Japan.
Schumpeter, J. A. (1934). *The theory of economic development: An inquiry into profits, capital, credit, interest, and the business cycle*. Piscataway, NJ: Transaction Books.
Smith, B. R., Kickul, J., & Coley, L. (2010). Using simulation to develop empathy and motivate agency: An innovative pedagogical approach for social entrepreneurship education. In Alain Fayolle, (Ed.) *Handbook of research in entrepreneurship education* (pp. 13). [Cheltenham, UK: Edward Elgar].
Stanford University. (2007). Hasso Planter: Institute of Design at Stanford. http://www.stanford.edu/group/dschool/
Stolterman, E. (2008). The nature of design practice and implications for interaction design research. *International Journal of Design*, 2(1), 55–65.
Timmons, J. A., & Spinelli, S. (2004). *New venture creation: Entrepreneurship for the 21st century*. New York: McGraw-Hill/Irwin.
Turnbull, A., & Eickhoff, M. (2011). Business creativity—Innovating European entrepreneurship education. *Journal of Small Business and Entrepreneurship*, 24(1), 139.
Vesper, K. H. (1990). *New venture strategies*. New York: Prentice Hall.
Wiklund, J., Davidsson, P., Audretsch, D. B., & Karlsson, C. (2011). The future of entrepreneurship research. *Entrepreneurship Theory and Practice*, 35(1), 1–9.
Winograd, T. (2008). Design education for business and engineering management students: A new approach. *Interactions*, 15(1), 44–45.

# 14 Enquiry-Based Feedback

*Andy Adcroft*

## INTRODUCTION

The chapter describes, evaluates and advocates an approach to learning and teaching that combines two issues: feedback and enquiry-based learning (EBL). In terms of feedback, the chapter offers an alternative to normal approaches to feedback, which center on individualized comments on a piece of assessed work. There is a broad consensus in both the theory and practice of feedback that, provided feedback is given, received, understood and acted upon, it has a crucial role in the development and enhancement of learning (see, for example, Mutch, 2003; Carless, 2006; Gibbs & Simpson, 2005); as students progress through a program of study, feedback assists them in developing knowledge and skills through the identification of what they did well and badly in each episode of assessment. For feedback to be valuable, it must lead to either a change in learning behavior or the reinforcement of good learning behavior (Adcroft, 2011b). A significant body of literature, however, suggests that feedback often fails to have a positive impact on learning, and this happens for a variety of reasons—usually based on either poor practice such as feedback being too brief, not constructive enough or lacking in specifics (Vardi, 2009) or dissonance in the understanding of feedback between students and academics (Crisp, 2007).

Kahn and O'Rourke (2005) define EBL as a 'broad umbrella term to describe approaches to learning that are driven by a process of enquiry' (p. 1). Within this broad definition, EBL is characterized by partnerships between academics and students whereby academics set tasks and then facilitate the process through which students undertake those tasks. What this usually boils down to is the notion that knowledge and skills are not passed from academic to student but rather developed by the student as he or she engages in intellectual work (Brew, 2003). The main benefit of EBL is that it provides a clear mechanism through which the content and process of study is understood by students (Edelson, Gordin & Pea, 1999). Within the extensive and rich literature on EBL, its characteristics tend to be summarized in terms of engagement with complex problems, the identification of one's own learning needs, the stimulating of curiosity and responsibility for learning falling on students. Thus, EBL develops skills of independent learning, which, among other things, allows students to self-diagnose their own strengths and weaknesses and learn across subject boundaries.

Enquiry-based feedback (EBF) combines these two elements of theory and practice, and the aim is for feedback to have a significant impact on learning through engagement. The approach to EBF in this chapter is built on four assumptions. First, for effective learning to take place, students must view their learning experience as something they actively participate in rather than something they are spectators of. This applies to what happens outside of the classroom and lecture hall as much as what happens inside. In simple terms, students learn best when they work things out for themselves. Second, for feedback to be effective, there is limited value in explaining to students what they may have done well or badly in a piece of work that they will never have to do again. Instead, useful feedback is about providing the necessary resources for students to become more effective independent learners who can self-diagnose their own strengths and weaknesses. Third, good teaching is not necessarily about doing what students want but is rather about doing what is effective in supporting high-quality learning. Student satisfaction and student learning are not always the same thing. Students in higher education should be viewed, and treated, as mature and responsible individuals who want to do challenging work because they want to learn and gain the satisfaction of real achievement. Finally, changing student learning behavior is possible, if difficult, and this can best be done through changing assessment and feedback.

## THE APPROACH

This explanation of EBF will focus on experiences in one module taught in a UK university. The module is a final-year undergraduate module on business strategy, which is a core module across a range of business and management degree programs from generalist programs to more specialist programs such as accounting and finance, retail management and tourism and hospitality programs. The module is also taken by nonmanagement students, typically from engineering and computer science subject areas. In a typical year, the module is taken by between 500 and 600 students. The module runs for 12 weeks, and students have one 2-hour lecture each week and a fortnightly seminar that lasts for 1 hour.

There are two points of assessment in the module: a midterm assignment that focuses on the understanding of theory and an end-of-module exam that focuses on the application of theory. EBF is used in the assignment. The assignment is based on students writing a critical review of an article from the field of strategy which is drawn from the *Harvard Business Review*. In total, eight articles are chosen, and students are randomly allocated one of these articles to review. Allocation is done in the second week of the module, and reviews are submitted in the seventh week. The reviews must cover three equally weighted issues: (1) the position of the article in wider debates in strategy, (2) the theoretical underpinnings of the article and (3) the main strengths and weaknesses of the article. As well as these elements, students are also awarded marks for presentation and style.

The overall aim of EBF is to help students improve their academic performance both in the module itself and in subsequent modules they study as part of their degree program. This aim is met through the development of a number of skills and attributes such as:

- Independent learning, especially self-reflection;
- Critical analysis, especially identifying key issues, synthesis, comparative work and conceptualization;
- Active learning, especially active reading;
- Study management.

To develop these skills and attributes, the approach to EBF views it as a coherent and consistent three-stage process built upon: **preparation** and what happens before the assignment is submitted; the **feedback** itself and how resources are provided to students and **action planning**, which focuses on how students conceptualize their knowledge in preparation for the exam. This process is explained to students in the first lecture of the teaching program and then reinforced and revisited at regular intervals once it is up and running (see Figure 14.1).

## Step 1: Preparation

This phase of EBF is crucial in setting and managing the expectations of students, and those expectations focus on transparency in assessment, students taking responsibility for their own work and active engagement in the learning process. Central to this phase is the marking scheme for the assignment, which is provided in advance to all students. The detailed

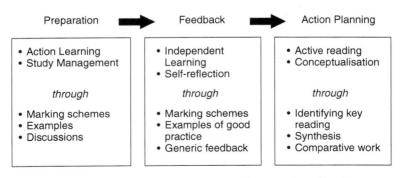

*Figure 14.1* The Three-Step Process of Enquiry-Based Feedback

marking scheme gives a breakdown of marks awarded for each element of the assignment and a description of the characteristics of the work that must be produced to gain different marks. As well as providing transparency to students about how marks will be allocated, the marking scheme also supports the team of academics who assess student work in the module. In a module of this size, there are usually between three and five markers, and having a clear and detailed marking scheme allows for more consistency in marking, which reduces the burden of, for example, second marking and moderation. An example of the marking scheme for the use of theory is given in Figure 14.2.

The second element of preparation support is a discussion in the university's virtual learning environment (VLE), and this element has several important characteristics. First, it is the only forum in which questions will be answered about the assignment. Having a single forum means that all students have access to exactly the same information and thus receive a consistent message about the assignment. Second, the discussion is time limited, thus encouraging students to engage with the assignment at a pace set by the academics. In this element, for example, the first two weeks of the discussion are taken up with questions about the assignment, which tend to focus on either technical issues about word limits, submission dates, formats and so on or on clarifications of the marking scheme. Third, the majority of the discussion is student, not academic, led. Following the initial question-and-answer element of the discussion, a number of examples of good practice from previous years' assignments are given, and students use these as a basis for discussing the substantive content of their

| **Understanding of Theory (30 marks)** | Mark range | Mark |
|---|---|---|
| The underlying theoretical assumptions of the article are identified and discussed. There is clear understanding of how these theoretical foundations influence the conceptual basis of the article. | 30–21 | |
| The underlying theoretical assumptions of the article are identified but the discussion lacks development. Links are drawn between the theoretical underpinnings and concepts. | 20–18 | |
| Attempts are made to identify underlying theoretical assumptions but these are a little cursory and lacking in depth. The link between theory and concept is made but never fully developed and discussed. | 17–15 | |
| There is no real discussion of theory and the review focuses on the conceptual basis of the paper only. Limited understanding of the relationship between theory and concept is shown. | 14–12 | |
| No real understanding of the theoretical assumptions of the article is shown. The work demonstrates no understanding of how theoretical assumptions can underpin strategy concepts. | 11–0 | |

*Figure 14.2* An Example of the Detailed Marking Scheme

own work. In this stage, which lasts for three weeks, academics do not answer questions but simply monitor the discussion and only intervene if it goes significantly off track. Two weeks before the assignment submission date, the discussion is closed for new postings, but its archive is still available for students to access.

## Step 2: Feedback

Once submitted, assignments are marked by members of the teaching team according to the marking scheme, and following this process, grades are made available to students. Students do not receive any individualized comments on their assignment in terms of either annotated comments in the main body of their work or summary comments at the end. The benefit to academics of this approach is that marking takes much less time: typically 550 assignments (of 2,000 words in length) are marked, second marked and returned to students within 10 days. Although students do not necessarily find this a comfortable experience, it is nevertheless a valuable experience because it encourages them toward becoming independent in their learning and helps them develop the key academic skill of self-reflection. The approach to feedback focuses on the provision of a range of feedback resources for students to use as they figure out themselves what they did well and badly, where their strengths and weaknesses are and, most importantly, what they should do next.

The first resource made available to students is a breakdown of marks for their assignment for each element of the marking scheme, which allows students to see where they gained and lost marks. By referring to the marking scheme, students should be able to see what a mark of, for example, 19 out of 30 for the use of theory means. The second feedback resource is generic feedback, which is provided to all students in two forms. First, students receive a statistical breakdown of performance across the whole cohort, which covers information such as mode, mean and median marks; the number of assignments in each classification band; performance comparisons across the different articles reviewed and the marks awarded by each marker (albeit in an anonymous form). This is provided for two reasons. First, a growing volume of literature suggests that students are as interested in their relative performance within a peer group as they are in the marks they achieve themselves (Adcroft, 2009; 2011a) and, second, to ensure as much transparency as possible in the marking process. The other form of generic feedback given to students are comments about what, on the whole, was done well and what was done badly. An example of this feedback is shown in Figure 14.3.

The final element of feedback is a series of examples of excellent practice. For each of the articles reviewed, the best three assignments are posted in the university's VLE for all students to see (after they have been made anonymous and the author's permission given), and a discussion forum is opened

In general terms, where students did not get good marks, it was for the following reasons:
- You did not pay enough attention to the question, or at least all elements of the question. In many cases, students answered one or two parts of the question really well but did not pay enough attention to the other parts-we wanted students to allocate words on the basis of the weighting of each section-one third of the assignment should have been on the position of the article, one third on the theoretical underpinnings and so on. If you used too many words on one section, you had less on other sections and, hence, got lower marks;
- There was limited evidence of wide reading a round the subject matter. In many cases, students only looked at their own article, a couple of other articles from the VLE, the textbook and maybe some lecture notes. As we said, we really wanted you to read as widely as possible;
- Too much time was spent on describing what was said in the article rather than critically engaging with it. For example, there was no real point starting your review with 2 or 3 paragraphs or even a full page saying what the article says. All that is demonstrating is that you have read the article;
- You didn't focus on your article enough in your discussions. For example, some students spent a lot of time explaining the difference between RBV and positioning, or emergent and prescriptive approaches to strategy, but did not spend enough time explaining where your article fitted into that debate, and why you made that judgement;
- Referencing was a big issue, both within the text of the reviews and also in the list at the end. Please note that this is a really important issue in, for example, your final year projects so if you didn't reference well make sure you sort this out for your other modules.

*Figure 14.3* An Example of Generic Feedback

up. The purpose of posting these examples is threefold: First it encourages the whole cohort and acts as a reward for those who have done excellent work; second, it provides a number of different points of comparison for students in assessing their own work and, third, it demonstrates to students that there are no model answers and that there are a number of different routes to achieving good marks.

## Step 3: Action Planning

If the purpose of feedback is to improve performance, then it has to result in a change in learning behavior; doing the same thing over and over again and expecting to get different results is a definition of madness. This final phase of the EBF process focuses on changing learning behavior through students developing action plans and then considering how they conceptualize the knowledge they develop through their reading and research. Changing learning behavior is important as students transition from assignment to exam for the basic reason that the form of assessment is different and hence requires different learning skills. The starting point for this process is that students are given the opportunity to create an action plan that they can then discuss either individually or in a small group with a member of the teaching team in a meeting that usually lasts 20 to 30 minutes. In a typical year, around 20% of students take advantage of this opportunity.

Action plans need to contain two things. First, they must identify what the student sees as his or her own strengths and weaknesses through engagement with all the feedback resources described in Step 2. Second, they must identify what the student plans to do differently in preparation for the exam. The specifics of the action plan are less important than the mind-set that it helps generate; students focus on next steps, change and improvement, and academics must ensure that meetings are positive and forward looking and do not act as an inquest or discussion about the mark awarded for the assignment.

Active reading is a core element of learning behavior that the action planning process aims to foster in students. Active reading, in this context, is defined as reading that has analysis as its fundamental purpose from the start rather than reading simply to acquire information that may be analyzed at some point in the future. For example, a common technique that students use when reading, say, a journal article is to use highlighter pens to identify important points as they read. This is seen as passive reading, and students are encouraged to forego it as a technique for a number of reasons. For example, when using highlighter pens, students will rarely stop or pause to consider whether something is important; instead, text is highlighted in a way and at a speed that rarely slows or interrupts the pace of reading. In most cases, the use of highlighter pens increases as more is read; it is usual to see just a word or sentence highlighted in the first couple of pages, paragraphs highlighted in the middle sections and whole pages highlighted toward the end of a journal article. Indeed, many who use this technique report that, upon completion of reading and highlighting an article, little is remembered of the article, what is highlighted or what is important.

As a counter to this, students are encouraged to read using small pieces of paper or sticky notes to organize their thoughts and ideas. Students are introduced to a simple process that incorporates the following elements:

1. Read the article as normal, but every time they come across something they would highlight they should pause and write it on a note in their own words. If they would have highlighted a sentence, then they should write one or two words; if they would have highlighted a paragraph, then they should distil it into a single bullet point.
2. At the end of reading an article, they will have something like 15 to 20 notes. Any duplicates should be removed and the remainder put in order from most important point to least important point and only the 5 or 6 most important kept. The rest should be discarded.
3. After reading, say, six journal articles, the student will have 6 sets of notes that identify the key points of each article, which should now be reorganized into thematic groups rather than article-based groups. For example, if there are similar notes from three or four articles,

they can be clustered together in a way that allows synthesis to take place. Where notes have very different perspectives on them, they, too, can be clustered together to identify key debates in the literature to facilitate comparing and contrasting. After this reorganization, any residual notes can probably be discarded, (something that is almost impossible to do if the articles are covered with varying degrees of yellow highlighter).
4. Following the identification of key issues in an article, differentiating between important and nonimportant issues and moving from article-based to theme-based knowledge, the final step is to conceptualize that knowledge into a single page through a diagram of some sort. Usually this will take a number of iterations as the student further explores and analyzes issues in a broad area until something like Figure 14.4 is created.

This final step in the EBF process reinforces the elements that preceded it and places a premium on independent learning, critical engagement and performance improvement. Through this process, students no longer act as passive recipients of feedback, where they sit and wait for someone to tell them how well or badly they did and why, but rather have to engage in the process if they wish to gain any benefit from it. The key question, however, is 'does it work?'

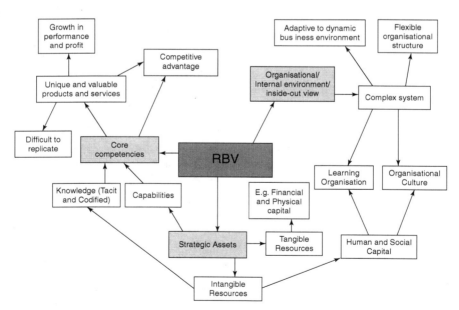

*Figure 14.4* Diagrammatic Conceptualization of a Body of Literature

## IMPACT

Over four years, almost 1,800 students have taken the business strategy module and thus have been exposed to EBF. These students can be split into two groups: action planners and non–action planners. Action planners are those students who have fully engaged with EBF by following the whole process laid out in the previous section, and non–action planners are those students who have only partially engaged with EBF (or who have not engaged with EBF at all). In terms of overall cohort performance, Table 14.1 presents data on how action planners and non–action planners performed in the exam compared to the assignment. Overall, more action planners improved their marks in the exam compared to non–action planners.

Typically, the average assignment mark for action planners is lower than non–action planners, but the average exam mark is higher; action planners start from a lower point than non–action planners but manage to finish at a higher point. Figure 14.5 shows the distribution of the change in marks between assignment and exam for each of the years in which EBF has been used across nine different bands. As is probably to be expected, the largest group of students, for both action planners and non–action planners, is clustered around the central band, which represents a change in mark of between +5 and –5. Well over half of all action planners, for example, appear

*Table 14.1* Percentage of Students Doing Better and Worse in the Exam Compared to the Assignment

|  | Did Better in Exam | Did Worse in Exam | No Change |
|---|---|---|---|
| **All Students** | | | |
| Action Planners | 61.5 | 33.3 | 5.2 |
| Non–Action Planners | 39.5 | 54.0 | 6.5 |
| **Year 1** | | | |
| Action Planners | 67.2 | 27.6 | 5.2 |
| Non–Action Planners | 51.1 | 44.4 | 4.5 |
| **Year 2** | | | |
| Action Planners | 63.3 | 33.9 | 2.8 |
| Non–Action Planners | 33.5 | 59.9 | 6.6 |
| **Year 3** | | | |
| Action Planners | 61.2 | 29.3 | 9.5 |
| Non–Action Planners | 35.4 | 59.1 | 5.5 |
| **Year 4** | | | |
| Action Planners | 57.0 | 40.2 | 2.8 |
| Non–Action Planners | 40.2 | 50.8 | 9.0 |

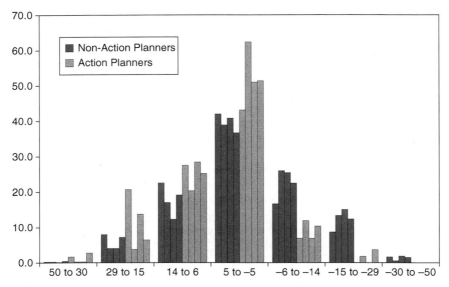

*Figure 14.5* Distribution of Action Planners' and Non–Action Planners' Change in Performance Between the Assignment and Exam Across Nine Bands

in this band. Two other patterns emerge from these figures. First, although a higher proportion of action planners do better in the exam overall, action planners also dominate where improvement is most significant, in the +15 to +29 band and in the +30 to +50 band. Second, fewer action planners appear at the bottom of the scale, where performance has declined most significantly; eight times fewer action planners saw their performance decline by 15 to 29 marks, and no action planners saw their performance decline by more than 30 marks compared to more than 20 non–action planners who had this disastrous level of performance decline.

In a study of the impact of EBF on student performance, Adcroft and Willis (in press) found that this kind of process has a significantly positive impact, particularly for students who do well in assignments and students who do badly in assignments. There is, however, a set of average students in the middle of academic cohorts who seem immune to the effects of feedback whether it is given in the form of EBF or in a more orthodox manner.

## CONCLUSION

Ceteris paribus, students who fully engage with EBF see an improvement in their individual academic performance. Similarly, cohorts of students, again ceteris paribus, who are exposed to EBF will see improvements in overall performance, and more of them will do better in subsequent assessment than will do worse. The problem is that ceteris is very rarely paribus, and this is no more true than in the complicated arena of student learning, which is affected by a range of influences and factors that are student based and environment based, predictable and unpredictable, manageable and unmanageable. While the evidence may be circumstantial (it is, after all, almost impossible to run a controlled scientific experiment in this area without jeopardizing the learning of one group of students), there are still some compelling reasons as to why this has been, and will continue to be in new contexts, a worthwhile experiment in pedagogy.

Notwithstanding the potential boost to performance discussed earlier, for students there are two main benefits to be gained from engaging with EBF. First is the development of skills and abilities of self-reflection, which can have positive outcomes across a whole program of study rather than just in a small component of it. Second is the development of wider skills of independent learning, which are essential to not only higher education but also to what the student does afterward in building a career. The approach described in this chapter requires students to find their own understanding of what they have done well and less well and of their own strengths and weaknesses. Students are, therefore, required to be full and active participants in feedback and not just passive recipients.

For academics, EBF is not a silver bullet that will transform the drudge of marking hundreds of similar assignments into a satisfying and rewarding intellectual experience. It can, though, make the task easier because it requires a reallocation of effort away from marking to providing feedback resources such as detailed marking schemes. It also takes a lot less time to mark because there is no need to comment on each piece of work individually. However, what is saved on marking is used elsewhere in, for example, meeting with individual or groups of students to discuss action plans. This is, though, the main positive for academics: postassessment interactions with students change from often difficult confrontations with surly recipients of marks they don't understand toward positive and constructive dialogue about how someone can do better.

## REFERENCES

Adcroft, A. (2009). The motivations to study of undergraduate students in management: The impact of degree program and level of study. *International Journal of Management Education*, 9(1), 11–20.

Adcroft, A. (2011a). The motivations to study and expectations of studying of undergraduate students in business and management. *Journal of Further and Higher Education*, 35(4), 521–543.

Adcroft, A. (2011b). The mythology of feedback. *Higher Education Research and Development*, 30(4), 405–419.

Adcroft, A., & Willis, R. (in press). Do those who benefit the most need it the least? A four year experiment in enquiry based feedback. *Assessment and Evaluation in Higher Education*.

Brew, A. (2003). Teaching and research: New relationships and their implications for inquiry-based teaching and learning. *Higher Education in Higher Education Research and Development, 22*(1), 3–12.

Carless, D. (2006). Differing perceptions in the feedback process. *Studies in Higher Education, 31*(2), 219–233.

Crisp, B. R. (2007). Is it worth the effort? How feedback influences students' subsequent submission of assessable work in assessment and evaluation. *Higher Education, 32*(5), 571–581.

Edelson, D. C., Gordin, D. N., & Pea, R. D. (1999). Addressing the challenges of inquiry-based learning through technology and curriculum design. *Journal of the Learning Sciences, 8*(3–4), 391–450.

Gibbs, G., & Simpson, C. (2005). Conditions under which assessment supports student learning. *Learning and Teaching in Higher Education, 1*, 3–31.

Kahn, P., & O'Rourke, K. (2005). Understanding enquiry based Learning. In T. Barrett, I. Mac Labhrainn, & H. Fallon (Eds.), *Handbook of enquiry and problem based learning* (pp. 1–12). Galway: CELT.

Mutch, A. (2003). Exploring the practice of feedback to students. *Active Learning in Higher Education, 4*(1), 24–38.

Vardi, I. (2009). The relationship between feedback and change in tertiary student writing in the disciplines. *International Journal of Teaching and Learning in Higher Education, 20*(3), 350–361.

# Part IV
# Ethical Citizenship

# 15 Introduction to Ethical Citizenship

*Elaine Doyle*

In the age of numerous accounting and corporate scandals such as the Enron débâcle and the Parmalat bankruptcy, and in the context of the current global financial crisis, society at large has come to recognize that ethical, sustainable and socially responsible behavior play a critical role in good business practice. Corporate social responsibility (CSR) is now high on the corporate agenda as society demands that companies act more responsibly (Cornelius, Wallace & Tassabehji, 2007, p. 133). In the wake of so many financial and managerial scandals, the role that business schools played, or didn't play, in creating or encouraging unethical behavior has been questioned (Cornelius et al., 2007; Ghoshal, 2005; Pfeffer & Fong, 2004). As Ghoshal suggests, 'business school faculty need to own up to our own role in creating Enrons. It is our theories and ideas that have done so much to strengthen the management practices that we are all so loudly condemning' (2005, p. 75). Cornelius et al. found that, 'by meeting the needs of business, business schools have been less sensitive to, at best, and at worst, more tolerant of the excuses of business' (2007, p. 121). Ghoshal goes as far as to suggest that, 'by propagating ideologically inspired amoral theories, business schools have actually freed their students from any sense of moral responsibility' (2005, p. 76). It is now widely acknowledged that business schools need, as a matter of priority, to address these concerns by making a strong commitment to effectively educate students in the areas of ethics and social responsibility to encourage ethically grounded corporate practice.

Ethics education can be approached in two distinct ways. The first is as a stand-alone, one-semester module, possibly as a compulsory subject within a business program. The second involves integrating the coverage of ethics, corporate social responsibility and sustainability right across the undergraduate and graduate curricula. The latter approach is becoming the norm in many business schools (Nicholson & DeMoss, 2009). Both approaches have elements to recommend them. A dedicated ethics module exposes students to the discipline and introduces ethical frameworks or theories that can serve to guide behavior. Stand-alone modules will be taught by expert faculty members who are typically enthusiastic about the subject matter. However, isolating ethics from other business modules by teaching it as a discrete course may result in separating ethical considerations from real-world business consequences. Furthermore, one module may not afford students adequate time to develop ethical decision-making skills. In a fully integrated model, the student obtains exposure to ethical problems in a contextual manner and experiences the practical application of ethical principles within the domain of the particular business discipline. An added advantage is that ethics, social responsibility and sustainability concepts are communicated and promoted across the breadth of the faculty and are, therefore, not the sole responsibility of one faculty member. It is acknowledged, however, that an integrated approach may necessitate curriculum review, faculty training and ongoing monitoring (see, for example, McDonald, 2005).

In terms of content, ethics education can be reactive (i.e., focused on legal and regulatory requirements) or proactive (i.e., focused on embracing ethically and socially responsible thinking). Cornelius et al. suggest that, 'while much corporate malfeasance would have been avoided by employing and appropriately monitoring "reactive" business ethics practices and procedures, more profound changes to the culture and ethos of organizations are needed to deal with the broader issues of institutional dysfunction due to inadequate social provision or unethical behavior' (2007, p. 118). The authors cite the 2004 Ethics Education Task Force report on ethics education in business schools, which acknowledges that, while reactive ethics education is important, proactive ethics education is crucial in developing flexible ethical management thinking and practice. The task force particularly observes the absence of inputs on 'moral courage' in many business schools' programs and the importance of inputs that heighten moral reasoning, hone ethical decision-making skills and enable the development of ethical leadership (Cornelius et al., 2007).

In a 2006 survey involving 1,600 millennials, Cone Inc. found that 61% feel personally responsible for making a difference in the world, 79% wanted to work for a company that cares about its societal contribution and 69% would refuse to work for a company that is not socially responsible (Cone Inc., 2006). These are encouraging figures that have been supported by subsequent studies. For example, McGlone, Winters and McGlone (2011) found that millennials have internalized the need to make the world a better place and support that attitude by volunteering more. Business schools failing to offer this generation the platform from which they can launch successful business careers while still embracing and enhancing this desire to be socially responsible will be failing this generation and society at large.

It is within this broader context that we showcase how four different business academics are answering the call to integrate proactive ethics into the business school curricula. This section of the book will delineate teaching techniques aiming to enhance students' awareness of the ethical aspects of business decisions and to encourage ethical behavior at both the individual and corporate level. While all of the techniques outlined in this section aim to enhance students' ethical awareness, either in a general sense or in a discipline-specific domain, they are suitable for use in other contexts. All the tools represent examples of active learning, and all involve students working in teams. Positive student feedback on all the teaching innovations showcased in this section is provided by the authors and has been used to improve the teaching and learning techniques as the tools have evolved.

In the first chapter in this section of the book, McCuddy describes how he reverses the traditional student and teacher roles as a means of fostering the moral development of learners. His module is based on the premise that ethics education is about each learner's moral journey in life, and that learners can have a more meaningful moral journey when informed by multiple perspectives that challenge them to grapple with moral issues through active engagement in dialogue with others. Groups of students become 'learning facilitators' for the other students in an ethics in business course. The extensive use of quotes in this chapter allows us to hear students' opinions of the deployed technique.

Evoking the 'learning by doing' methodology, both Moylan and O'Loughlin make use of live cases and projects in teaching ethical citizenship in the context of entrepreneurship and marketing. Moylan's entrepreneurship module involves students not only learning about social entrepreneurship but developing their own social enterprise project, which they must execute during the academic year. The underlying principle of the project is that it is not about making profits but about enhancing and/or adding value to the lives of others. O'Loughlin has designed a marketing module where students are required to apply many of the key concepts covered in the module content to a real social marketing context of importance to student well-being, the campus community and society as a whole. She presents two in-depth cases of student campaigns developed to promote sensible drinking and volunteering to their peers. The aim was to expose students to ethical and moral issues and to foster civic citizenship.

In the final chapter in this section, Killian and Lannon outline the use of the VantagePoint board game as a capstone learning technique in various university CSR courses. They draw on the literature on the use of play in learning which suggests that the use of play will help the class dynamic and students' engagement with both the process and the content of the module as well as ensure that all learning styles are catered for in the classroom. The classes in which the game was used and the way in which it is played as well as practical issues around its implementation are described.

While all the modules described in this section are primarily aimed at enhancing ethical citizenship in students, the development of many other skills was facilitated as a result of the techniques outlined. All the tools involved students working in teams, giving them an opportunity to develop the multitude of skills necessary for successful teamwork. Presentation skills, evidence of creativity and effective engagement with others were also demanded in most of the teaching techniques outlined.

To conclude this short introduction to the ethical citizenship section of this book, we wish to extend a word of caution. While the importance of education in developing ethically sensitive individuals who use principled moral reasoning when facing dilemmas has been widely acknowledged (see, for example, Pascarella & Terenzini, 1991; Rest, Narvaez, Bebeau, & Thoma, 1999), Cornelius et al. (2007) fear that the ethics components of business programs may actually be in decline. They suggest that in an attempt to make business programs more attractive in an extremely competitive market, curricula may be reduced, with ethics being one of the casualties. Business program stakeholders may be indifferent to anything more than a superficial inclusion of ethics and CSR in the curriculum, and the number of qualified faculty to teach the subject is often inadequate (Cornelius et al., 2007). More than a decade ago, Kelly observed that a number of U.S. business schools were reducing or removing ethics education altogether from their curricula (Kelly, 2002). Nicholson and DeMoss (2009) report that there is a trend toward less ethics education overall, while Cornelius at al. (2007) find that most business schools offer only reactive ethics education and caution that, due to the limited availability of qualified faculty members, the nature of ethics education will remain reactive for the foreseeable future (p. 133). Whether these worrying findings are indicative of prevailing business school practice or not, it is critical that this trend does not develop. It is increasingly the case that the most advanced technologies on the planet are designed and developed by corporate entities. The product development decisions taken by pharmaceutical companies will impact upon the health and lives of millions of people. Information technology has allowed business organizations to gather and store vast amounts of data on individuals, redefining centuries-old notions such as privacy. Biotechnology firms are patenting genetic codes and privatizing what would heretofore have always been considered public resources. These are just a few examples of the deeply complex, multifaceted issues raised by the continuous development and deployment of advanced technology by corporate entities. Their resolution is far beyond the scope of this book; however, it is obvious at a cursory glance that the business leaders who are involved in these situations must have the skills required to deal with the ethical issues that they raise. How these issues are addressed will define the shape of the world we live in. Business leaders will be expected to direct companies that will be profitable, abide by the law, behave ethically and give back to the wider community (Carroll, 2000). It is important that we educate the millennial generation in a manner that encourages them to become ethical citizens who not only think critically but also possess a caring attitude and are capable of empathy and commitment.

# REFERENCES

Carroll, A. B. (2000). Ethical Challenges for Business in the New Millennium: Corporate Social Responsibility and Models of Management Morality. *Business Ethics Quarterly*, 10(1), 33–42.

Cone Inc. (2006). *The 2006 Cone Millennial Cause Study*. n.p.: Cone Inc. in Collaboration with AMP Insights.

Cornelius, N., Wallace, J., & Tassabehji, R. (2007). An Analysis of Corporate Social Responsibility, Corporate Identity and Ethics Teaching in Business Schools. *Journal of Business Ethics*, 76(1), 117–135.

Ghoshal, S. (2005). Bad Management Theories Are Destroying Good Management Practices. *Academy of Management Learning and Education*, 4(1), 75–91.

Kelly, M. (2002). It's a Heckuva Time to Be Dropping Business Ethics Courses. *Business Ethics: The Magazine of Corporate Responsibility*, 16(5/6), 17–18.

McDonald, G. M. (2005). A Case Example: Integrating Ethics into the Academic Curriculum. *Journal of Business Ethics*, 54(4), 371–384.

McGlone, T., Winters, J. S., & McGlone, V. (2011) Corporate Social Responsibility and the Millennials. *Journal of Education for Business*, 86(4), 195–200.

Nicholson, C., & DeMoss, M. (2009). Teaching Ethics and Social Responsibility: An Evaluation of Undergraduate Business Education at the Discipline Level. *Journal of Education for Business*, 84(4), 213–218.

Pascarella, E. T., & Terenzini, P. T. (1991). *How College Affects Students*. San Francisco: Jossey-Bass.

Pfeffer, J., & Fong, C. T. (2004). The Business School 'Business': Some Lessons from the US Experience. *Journal of Management Studies*, 41(8), 1501–1520.

Rest, J., Narvaez, D., Bebeau, M., & Thoma, S. (1999). *Postconventional Moral Thinking: A Neo-Kohlbergian Approach*. Mahwah, NJ: Lawrence Erlbaum.

# 16 Actively Engaging Learners in Exploring Business Ethics[1]

*Michael K. McCuddy*

## INTRODUCTION

Moral development 'refers to the growth of moral understanding in individuals. In this respect it concerns a person's progressive ability to understand the difference between right and wrong, to care about the difference between them, and to act on the basis of this understanding' (Parker, 1998, p. 267). Moral development is of particular relevance to the educational application being discussed in this chapter. Specifically, this educational application concerns an Ethics in Business course that focuses on fostering the moral development of learners. The entire course is based upon the premise that ethics education should be about each learner's moral journey in life, and that each learner can have a more meaningful moral journey when it is informed by multiple perspectives that challenge each learner to grapple with moral issues through active engagement in dialogue with others. The focus of this chapter is on actively engaging learners in the exploration of ethical issues in businesses by reversing the traditional roles of teachers and students by having the students become 'learning facilitators' during the second of two phases of the course.

## LEARNING OBJECTIVES IN EXPLORING BUSINESS ETHICS

This approach rests upon a set of learning objectives that is conveyed to the students in the course syllabus. These objectives are:

- To provide each student with an understanding of the fundamental theories and concepts that explain and guide ethical thinking, reasoning, decision making, and actions;
- To expose each student to ethical and moral issues that people encounter in business settings;
- To foster examination of each student's own ethical principles and propensities as they pertain to personal behavior and perspectives regarding the role of business in society;

- To help each student develop an appreciation for the broad-based role that ethics can (*and should*) play in business;
- To help each student understand ethics in a diverse, global context.

## OVERVIEW OF THE BUSINESS ETHICS COURSE

The Ethics in Business course, offered at a private, religiously affiliated university in the United States, is targeted toward third- and fourth-year undergraduate students in a college of business as well as masters-level students in a college of arts and sciences. The course is offered every autumn term, and it meets twice a week for a total of 29 class sessions. Two or three sections of the course are offered each autumn, with each section usually containing 20 to 25 students. Each class session meets for 75 minutes.

The course is divided into two major phases of learning activity. The first phase, consisting of 17 class sessions, focuses on developing students' awareness and knowledge of various ethical concepts and theories and their ability to apply those concepts and theories to a variety of ethical dilemmas. This phase of the course is led and facilitated by the professor, using lectures, discussions, and debates as the primary teaching/learning techniques. The second phase, consisting of 12 sessions, puts students in the role of leading and facilitating class sessions that focus on major ethical issues in contemporary businesses.

## COURSE ACTIVITIES THAT FOSTER INTELLECTUAL ENGAGEMENT WITH BUSINESS ETHICS

In preparation for the second phase of the course, six student groups, with an approximately equal number of members, are formed in each course section. The group formation takes place during the second class session of the first course phase so that the students have ample time to prepare for the facilitation activities that take place during the second phase of the course. Each student group is responsible for facilitating discussion on two contemporary ethical issues in business, selected from a pool of six such ethical issues. Each ethical issue is covered by two groups; thus, two class sessions are devoted to each issue, with one session being facilitated by one student group and the second session being facilitated by a different student group. Consequently, the last six weeks of the course puts student groups in charge of the learning process for themselves and their fellow students, and each group is in charge of two 75-minute class sessions devoted to two different ethical issues.

The ethical issues that are addressed include the following: human resource management, accounting and finance, marketing and advertising, environmental stewardship, technology in the workplace, and moral leadership in business. The student groups are asked to express a first, second, and third preference regarding the ethical issues on which they wish to work. As much as possible, student preferences are honored so long as all six ethical issues are covered twice and each group has two different issues. Determination of which issues a given group works on occurs during the class session when the groups are formed.

The facilitating group is charged with actively engaging other students in learning about business ethics from the perspective of the assigned topic/issue. The facilitating group is expected to challenge the other class members to confront their own ethical ideas and principles and to examine and understand the ethical ideas and principles of other people. The student groups are not restricted in any way, other than reasonable boundaries of social decorum and civility, in how they attempt to engage and challenge the other learners. They are encouraged to use their creative capacity as they seek to engage the other class members in interesting and meaningful dialogue and learning. The two groups assigned to each issue must also coordinate with each other so that both groups do not cover the same territory. Overlap of topical material between the two sessions must be minimized, and preferably be totally eliminated. Each of the six issues-oriented topics is broad enough to accommodate not only two but numerous class sessions with distinctly different content.

What has been described in the preceding paragraph constitutes the entire supervisory direction that is provided to the students for their facilitation projects. They are on their own to research their issues, to plan out content and learning activities for their two sessions, and to execute their sessions. The students know I am available for consultation and help, but that they must take the initiative in seeking such input.

Typically, the student groups will blend a PowerPoint presentation with a variety of other learning activities. The PowerPoint presentations are normally used to convey essential information about the ethical issues. Some of the more innovative learning activities have included adaptations of game shows, simulations, role-playing situations, use of video materials, ethical scenarios and cases, guest appearances by managers, and debates, to name several.

During the student-led facilitation phase of the course, my role as professor—other than providing guidance and input when sought—is twofold. First, I become an active member of the audience—essentially acting as another seminar participant experiencing the learning activities. Second, I take notes on content, facilitation skills, engagement of the other learners, and vibrancy of the discussion in order to provide each student group with feedback that is both evaluative and developmental.

The second professorial role fulfills the assessment function for the student-led facilitation sessions. This assessment utilizes ratings on several standard criteria as well as written comments that are targeted specifically toward the content and process of a given facilitation session. Usually within 24 hours of a group's facilitation session, I send the students feedback via e-mail.

This feedback contains the standard assessment rating, written comments for each individual and for the group as a whole, and, if appropriate, suggestions for improvement.

## STUDENT REACTION TO ACTIVE ENGAGEMENT

At the end of a recent term in which the Ethics in Business course was taught, I invited students to provide 'honest, unvarnished feedback regarding their assessment of and reaction to the student-led facilitation sessions that they experienced during the last six weeks of the semester.' Providing such feedback was entirely voluntary since the request for input was made at the conclusion of the last facilitation session and would require students to provide the feedback during final exam week. Asking for input earlier would not have been appropriate given that students had not had the full experience of the facilitation sessions until the conclusion of the semester.

The students were asked to address three diagnostic questions, providing a one- or two-paragraph response (or longer if the spirit moved them) to each item. The three diagnostic questions were:

- From the perspective of preparing for and facilitating the two class sessions for which your group was responsible, describe how those experiences contributed to your personal learning, growth, and development.
- From the perspective of being an audience member during 10 of the 12 facilitation sessions, describe how those experiences contributed to your personal learning, growth, and development.
- How does your learning, growth, and development under the student-led facilitation session format compare to your learning, growth, and development under other teaching/learning formats (e.g., straight lecture, problem solving, research projects, etc.) that you have experienced during your college career?

## STUDENT FEEDBACK REGARDING QUESTION 1

The first feedback question asked students to describe how their experiences as facilitators of two class sessions contributed to their personal learning, growth, and development. The following quotes provide a reasonable sampling of the student feedback for this question.

- [I]n terms of growth and development, I do think I learned quite a bit. Obviously I learned some about the topics I was presenting on, but since we got to choose our topics, I already did have a good foundation of knowledge about both. One of the other lessons, I suppose, that wasn't quite as obvious, was the idea of teamwork among a class.

- I learned how to better handle working as a team, which is a concept that I was very hesitant [about] in the past. . . . My teammates really made me appreciate others' input, because there were many instances where they made my ideas better.
- Preparing for and facilitating the two class sessions I was involved in was actually beneficial to me. Normally, I loathe group projects. I usually feel like the tasks won't get done or won't be good enough unless I do them. However, the length of the presentations (75 minutes) and the topics to be covered were so enormous and intimidating that it forced me to rely on my group. . . . I learned that it is possible for me to let others do some work, and that the results are usually better than if I were to do it myself.
- Another aspect, in addition to teamwork, that was beneficial to me was the sharing of ideas. It is important to present creativity to one's group, but also to inspire/accept creativity from group members.
- The experience of preparing for the facilitation sessions allowed me to ensure that I was practicing business ethics in the course of creating the presentations. I had to ensure not to plagiarize, had to communicate with my teammates, and had to consider the options available to create a good presentation.
- I learned a lot of time management while preparing the sessions. It was difficult because I did not want to come up short of the time given, yet I did not want to go over. The variable was the audience's participation.
- When the responsibility of teaching other students is required, a larger and more thorough understanding of the topic is also required. As a result, I had to understand both topics that I presented to the class in detail, so that I could share and spread my knowledge with the other students.
- I also learned a lot . . . [about] the material and how to effectively make others understand and retain the material. Making the students actually retain was the most challenging aspect because everyone learns [in] a different way and ethics is something . . . [about which] most people already have a certain idea. . . . It's trying to elaborate [on] and reinforce those ideas that I found challenging but helped me grow as a person and I'm sure will help me in my future years.
- I think that the student facilitation presentations are a wonderful idea and really should be incorporated into every class that we have at this level in our academic careers. For the facilitation sessions that I presented on I probably learned 10 times more than I would have if someone else would have presented the information to me. . . . These facilitation exercises are also great for our own personal growth. . . . I think a great deal of this has been from having to make presentations in classes. This is really getting us ready for some of the stuff that we are going to face in the future. I also felt that I learned more about myself through doing these presentations.

Actively Engaging Learners in Exploring Business Ethics 163

## STUDENT FEEDBACK REGARDING QUESTION 2

The second feedback question asked students to describe how their learning, growth, and development were influenced by their experiences as audience members during those sessions when their facilitation group was not in charge of the class. A representative sampling of students' responses to this question follows:

- We had a class with diverse students from three different countries as well as graduate and undergraduate students, so it was great to hear their differing opinions.
- Being an audience member of the facilitation sessions contributed to my growth by forcing me to interact with the groups and understanding the issues from the perspective of my generation.
- I think it is beneficial to be learning from our peers. . . . [People] always talk about how we are influenced by our peers and maybe this is a form of good peer influence.
- Being an audience member to the rest of the facilitation sessions allowed me to absorb knowledge from the standpoint of a fellow student. . . . I also felt more open when I needed to ask questions or participate in another way.
- I believe the best presentations of all of the sessions were the ones that 'hit nerves' in those in the audience. . . . The more interactive the sessions were, the more everyone learned.
- The variety of subject matter broadened my understanding of how ethics is approached in different arenas. It also made me realize that ethics can vary from profession to profession but at the basis of it all is a somewhat level playing field.
- Many of the topics and issues brought up were controversial and made me think about where I stand and where I would like to stand on these issues.
- There are certain situations where I would think to myself, 'Why should I care?' or 'Why would I want to do that?' After having heard these different topics and participated in different conversations with the facilitators and other members of the audience, I had a change of heart and mind.

## STUDENT FEEDBACK REGARDING QUESTION 3

The third feedback question sought to ascertain how the students' learning, growth, and development under the student-led facilitation sessions compared with their learning, growth, and development under other teaching/learning formats they had experienced. The vast majority of those providing feedback indicated that, in their experiences, the student-led facilitation sessions were preferable to other learning formats. Of course, not everyone responded positively to the student-led facilitation sessions, as is evidenced by two students—one undergraduate and one masters.

A sampling of student feedback of a supportive nature, some of it extraordinarily positive, is contained in the following quotes:

- I would say in 75% of my classes the professor has lectured while the students took notes. I think that this is one of the most ineffective ways of teaching and yet so many professors take this method. . . . I absolutely hate learning like this. I think that it is boring and that I learn very little from it. . . . I am very much the type of person that is hands on and needs to actually do something in order to be able to learn about it. [The] . . . learning methods that we have [used] . . . in this class definitely helped me to learn more and take away more information than I have in previous classes taught lecture style. I also believe that from these facilitation sessions there is some information that I will remember for a long time to come.
- Teaching others is the most effective way I have learned material. While the technique of taking on assignments in groups has always been beneficial to me, I believe teaching the class the material takes the learning process a step further for the presenters.
- Honestly, I felt that doing the two presentations and sitting in the audience for others' sessions was the most beneficial learning format I ever encountered. . . . Most of my classes are straight lecture. These sessions provide so much more. It teaches students how to work in groups, create engaging topics, and submit meaningful comments, among so many other benefits.
- My learning and growth through student-led facilitation (especially when I was the facilitator) was more beneficial . . . because the material presented spoke on my level and in many cases was more interesting than what I have learned in the past. Straight lectures can be somewhat boring and cause my attention to waver, whereas student-led facilitation that includes student participation is more interesting and still maintains an educational purpose. While researching for a class-long presentation I ran across many items that did not even make the presentation but were still interesting.
- When I do the research and work myself, I learn a lot more and feel that I grow more as a person. . . . [F]or me to truly get a good grasp on something, I need to do it myself.
- The uniqueness about leading a session of class is that you get the other perspective of learning. We are able to see what it's like to need to grab the students' attention and participation. It not only encouraged growth among the presenters, it allowed for growth in people in the class as they weren't as hesitant to ask questions.

- I believe these sessions were very beneficial but could only be effective at the upper levels of courses. I do not believe a freshman or sophomore class could handle such sessions as well because they are much more unsure of themselves and are still formulating and defining their thoughts.
- Having lecture after lecture from a professor day in and day out can certainly be boring, but I will recognize the need for it at times. It really depends on the nature of the course. I think it is easy to agree that student-led facilitation sessions for half of a semester would not be a good idea in, say, an accounting class. There, things are much more black and white, and you want an experienced professional to teach you the right way to do things. Since ethics are often more of a gray area. . . , these sessions worked well. Everyone has experiences that can add to the learning of others, so it's good to put those to use. When appropriate, it can really add to the class, and make it better than any one person alone could.
- Thinking about my current classes and the types of teaching/learning formats they used, the student-led facilitation session format is undoubtedly one of the best (and I'm not just saying that, seriously). When this format was first introduced to us, I assumed that it was going to be the same old group project format and results. However, it proved to be much more effective than I had thought. It combined aspects from multiple teaching/learning methods, instead of just focusing on one with no variety. . . . The student-led facilitation sessions forced the class to be involved, and it allowed the students to focus on topics that were important to us. The topics, schedule, and textbook served as a sort of guide to keep us on track, but everything else was left to the students to determine. Since the presentations often relied on heavy audience discussion/involvement, many debatable topics were brought up, often causing me to think further about certain issues once the class was over. If the topics were really good, I often shared them with my family and asked for their thoughts on the topic too.

The two comments that were critical of the student-led facilitation sessions, but not overly critical, were the following:

- On the one hand, I learned a lot about the two topics that my group had covered through the extensive research that was done. For the other five weeks' worth of class, I felt like all I really needed to do was show up.
- I do prefer straight lectures—but the facilitation sessions helped me [to] not be so nervous during presentations. Teamwork is tough, but necessary and a reality in many work and personal life situations. Research projects are always beneficial because one tends to learn something

new. The bottom line for the student-led facilitation session format is it does help you remember better and walk away with new information that will last longer in our brains than [with a] straight lecture format.

With respect to the first comment, students must recognize that they will get more out of the activity when they invest themselves in it, even if they are only audience members. With regard to the second comment, the student acknowledges some useful benefits of the facilitation sessions even though straight lecture by professors is this student's preferred learning method.

## CONCLUDING OBSERVATIONS

Collectively, the students attest to a growing maturity in appreciating, interacting with, and working with others. Other personal development involves rising to the significant challenge posed by the facilitation session expectations and associated work. Still other personal development reflects the students' practice of ethics in the process of creating and executing the facilitation sessions. Other important personal developmental outcomes involve the students recognizing and shouldering personal responsibility for their own learning and recognizing their responsibilities and obligations to others. Students also developed a keen awareness of how the sessions helped to effectively prepare them for their future lives. Finally, the sessions helped students to gain insights into their own personal being.

Active involvement as audience members also contributes to the students' personal development. They come to understand ethical issues from multiple perspectives, and they recognize the potential positive impact of peer influence. They report growing comfort with their involvement with and participation in the process. The students also develop an appreciation for business ethics in different professional arenas. Class members find value in confronting their own ethical values and positions, and they experience meaningful and beneficial changes in their beliefs and attitudes regarding business ethics.

Active involvement through in-depth researching of their assigned ethical issues and being responsible for teaching others about those ethical issues contributed immensely to students' learning. The students recognized the valuable role that teaching others can play in personal learning; this observation is consistent with those of professional educators. For example, Hall (1977/1981, p. 208) asserts that '[m]any people learn better by teaching others, not by listening to professors.' In addition, the student-led facilitations sessions enabled students to connect with the material on their own level.

Many of the concluding observations articulated in the preceding three paragraphs can be applied to many courses beyond business ethics. These insights are relevant to any course where it is appropriate to actively engage students in the creation and delivery of learning experiences where the facilitators and the audience members grapple with important issues and acquire knowledge and perspective through that process.

## NOTE

1. The educational approach discussed in this chapter originally appeared in Steve Halley, Chris Birch, Dirk Tempelaar, Mike McCuddy, Núria Hérnandez Nanclares, Sandra Reeb-Gruber, Wim Gijselaers, Bart Rienties, and Ellen Nelissen (Eds.), *17th EDINEB Conference: Crossing borders in Education and Work-based Learning* (pp. 102–109). Maastricht: The Netherlands: FEBA ERD Press: 2010.

## REFERENCES

Hall, E. T. (1977/1981). *Beyond Culture*. New York: Anchor Books.
Parker, M. (1998). Moral Development. In R. Chadwick (Ed.), *Encyclopedia of Applied Ethics* (Vol. 3, pp. 267–273). San Diego: Academic Press.

# 17 Articulating Competence–Insight in Business Education Through Social Entrepreneurship

*Therese Moylan*

## INTRODUCTION

Traditionally, a significant macro issue for many working in higher education has been the holistic development of the student beyond his or her knowledge domain. This is often articulated in the promotion of active citizenship and the provision of opportunities within the higher education institute (HEI) for civic engagement via the student learning experience. There is an expectation from relevant stakeholders—for example, government, society and the business community—that HEIs consciously engage with this agenda, and the notion of promoting active citizenship in the higher-level educational context has gained increasing traction from both within and external to the sector. This expectation is not new and can be traced back to the educational principles of John Dewey, who posited that education had a role to play in the attainment of social goals (Ostrander, 2004). Those who support the notion of HEIs' civic role argue that universities must be linked to, and rooted in, their communities in order to have relevance.

From an Irish perspective, historically the role of citizenship education has been a feature of the primary and secondary education sectors rather than of the higher education sector (McIlraith, Farrell, Hughes, Lillis, & Lyons, 2007). Recent years have seen a move toward greater engagement from HEIs in the area, particularly in terms of campus community learning outreach activities and more service learning opportunities for students (Ryan & Stritch, 2007). The translation of these aspirations into meaningful outcomes is a challenge facing educators which has been assisted by the introduction of the National Framework of Qualifications in 2004. The associated development of awards standards for specific disciplines has led to a more unambiguous expression of learning outcomes. The most significant impact of the framework has been the shift in emphasis from knowledge-centric learning outcomes to skills and competence-based learning outcomes. In particular, one of the eight dimensions of all national awards in the framework is 'Competence–Insight,' and this dimension offers curriculum designers the opportunity to incorporate and reflect on social and civic engagement at program level.

What does this mean for business education? Arguably, in the context of a deep global recession, business, now more than ever, needs graduates who are critical thinkers to challenge accepted business mores and use their acquired skill set to lead and manage change. Critics draw attention to the limitations of the business curriculum and note its failure to 'expose students sufficiently to the external environment, specifically the social context within which business operates' (Buddensick & Lo Re, 2010). Another critique of many business education programs is that, while they address key functional business issues in depth, they do not integrate across multiple disciplines and tend to devote insufficient attention to the external forces that businesses must engage with (Weber & Englehart, 2011). Some argue for the inclusion of course objectives that deal with civic values and responsibilities and advocate service learning as a means to do this (Steiner & Watson, 2006), and there are those who advocate service learning as a means of 'developing and improving student social awareness and civic engagement' (Berry & Workman, 2007, p. 21).

This chapter presents a case study on how one higher education program has endeavored to embed the business standards around Competence–Insight. In doing so, the lecturing team took the opportunity to develop specific learning outcomes that enable students to engage with the social, ethical and topical issues of the day with a particular reference to social entrepreneurship as a means of achieving and assessing these outcomes.

## CONTEXT

Dun Laoghaire Institute of Art, Design and Technology (IADT) is a college with a particular niche focus, providing specialist programs that equip graduates to work in the arts, cultural, creative and related industries. The School of Business and Humanities runs undergraduate programs with a particular focus on entrepreneurship and enterprise development. IADT has a very active teaching and learning committee, has a strong track record in practice-based and applied teaching methodologies and promotes a proactive sharing of teaching pedagogies across disciplines.

Traditionally the business degrees were based heavily on content. The shift in emphasis from content to program learning outcomes had far-reaching implications and included a much stronger focus on the development of skills and competencies. Particular difficulty arose in working with competence and specifically with Competence–Insight. What are the skills and competencies relevant to the entrepreneur, and what does 'an internalized world view manifesting solidarity with others' mean in the context of an undergraduate program? More importantly, how, as educators, do we explicitly ensure that this occurs, and how do we assess it?

As well as trying to answer these questions, the teaching team was actively engaging with the entrepreneurship education debate. This was driven by a real desire internally to develop a substantial, differentiated and relevant educational program on entrepreneurship. The debate surrounding entrepreneurship education has advanced from the philosophical conundrum of whether or not entrepreneurship can be taught. Current thinking sees a broad remit for entrepreneurship education which enables students to develop appropriate enterprise capacities, and it is suggested that the traditional paradigm of entrepreneurship needs to change in order to facilitate this (Gibb, 2002). Gibb suggests that entrepreneurship existing solely in the dimension of business schools is too narrow and hinders its ability to address major issues in society.

The alternative model of entrepreneurship education, promoted by Gibbs, moves toward a broader societal model, which places emphasis on the values of entrepreneurship and developing entrepreneurial behaviors, attributes and skills encompassing concepts such as emotional intelligence, vision, holistic management and the ability to develop trust-building relationships. This translates into a need to equip individuals with personal entrepreneurial capacities but also the capacity to design organizations of all kinds—public, private and nongovernmental—to support effective entrepreneurial behavior (Gibb, 2007). Therefore, the new challenge for entrepreneurship is that it needs to address a number of personal, organizational and societal capacities. It is worth noting that there is strong alignment of the outcomes identified as important for entrepreneurial graduates with the outcomes associated with civic engagement and active citizenship.

At the heart of a more innovative approach to entrepreneurship education is creating an opportunity for students to feel entrepreneurial, and this requires a teaching methodology that creates opportunities for students to learn by doing. It recognizes that knowledge is not learning until it is in some way internalized either by application or thinking. Very often, this internalizing is achieved by doing. This approach creates very real challenges for higher educational institutes as entrepreneurial learning can be seen as a process of trial and error and incremental improvements, something that can be hard to accommodate within the traditional academic curriculum.

As a result of the simultaneous engagement with the entrepreneurship education debate and the challenges in complying with the National Framework of Qualifications, the program team developed specific entrepreneurial worldview program learning outcomes. In this case the outcome is stated as follows: Appreciate social, community and ethical issues in the entrepreneurial environment. The concept of social entrepreneurship was selected as a means of ensuring the delivery of these outcomes within the context of the discipline being taught.

## PROGRAM DETAILS

The program in question is the bachelor of business in entrepreneurship, which is a three-year undergraduate degree. The typical entrant is 18 or 19 years of age and is embarking on higher-level study for the first time. Surveys conducted with the students on entry to the program indicate that most have aspirations to own and run their own business at some point in the future. A significant number of students come from a family business background. The program also attracts a cohort of direct entry students who transfer into year two or three on successful completion of other higher-level qualifications. The direct entry students often include mature students who have garnered significant work and life experience. The typical class will consist of about 40 students. There is a diverse range of learners in the classroom—within any year there is a significant spread of performance levels, and up to 10% of the group present with some form of learning need.

The program is structured quite simply—six modules are offered in each year over two semesters. There are five main strands introduced in year one, and these are developed incrementally throughout the program—enterprise management, marketing, finance, technology and entrepreneurial competency. Because an entrepreneur must assume simultaneous responsibility for many different functions in the formation and development of a business, the program strives to achieve integration across different subject areas. Central to this is the development of practical projects that are integrated across the modules and are assessed from multiple perspectives by different members of the teaching team. The social entrepreneurship project described next is an example of this program in operation.

## SOCIAL ENTERPRISE PROJECT

The social enterprise project is located in year three in a module currently entitled Advanced Enterprise Management. The module learning outcomes are described below.

On successful completion of this module, the students will be able to:

1. Apply the skills they have acquired in marketing, finance and enterprise to assemble a business plan;
2. Develop and present a funding pitch to relevant stakeholders;
3. Define the concept of social entrepreneurship;
4. Plan and execute a social enterprise project;
5. Work in a team to plan and execute a social enterprise project.

Essentially in this module students learn about social entrepreneurship and develop their own social enterprise project, which they will execute during the academic year. In doing so, they will work in groups to develop a full business plan around their social enterprise project, which moves the idea from a once-off project toward a sustainable social business. The underlying principle in this project is that their idea is not about making profits but about enhancing and/or adding value to the lives of others. In actualizing these objectives, students are drawing on past knowledge and experience from different subject areas and incorporating learning from other modules that they are studying in their third year. The program assessment strategy for the third year is developed by the team, and the social enterprise project is built into the assessment strategy of other modules. This presents opportunities for the teaching team to work collectively on this project.

From a class management perspective, the operation of the module can be broken down into five phases: idea generation, team formation, project development, execution and reflection and evaluation. The first two stages—idea generation and team formation—can typically take 8 weeks, the project development and execution stages last for 14 weeks, and the final phase of reflection and evaluation takes about 4 weeks.

Initially the students spend time considering the concept of social entrepreneurship. This, for many, is the first time that they begin to consider that the entrepreneurial knowledge, skills and competencies that they are developing can be applied in a much broader context. As part of their exploration of the concept, students undertake individual research and produce an academic paper of their findings which is graded individually.

In parallel with their independent research, in-class activities are designed to explore social enterprise ideas that they can realize as a group within a time frame of four or five months. This involves in-class brainstorming, debate and discussion. A wide range of potential ideas emerge at this point. There can be a temptation to short-circuit this process by assigning project briefs prepared in advance to groups. However, experience has shown the team that when students generate and self-select project ideas, the level of motivation and involvement tends to be greater throughout the life of the project. Depending on the scale of the ideas that emerge, students might be engaged in anything from four to seven social enterprise projects during the academic year.

The next step is project selection and team formation. The students vote for the project that they are most interested in, and teams are formed around particular project ideas. The teams are encouraged to develop their own modus operandi and ground rules, which they commit to adhere to for the duration of the project. Roles and responsibilities are assigned to group members. It is a requirement that teams will meet on a regular basis outside of class contact time. The groups are required to develop meeting protocols, set agendas, record attendance, take minutes and develop actions items from these meetings. These are presented at the final stages of the project as part of a portfolio that evidences the work undertaken by the team throughout the life cycle of the project.

To progress, the teams must then develop project plans which are reviewed regularly as the group works through the tasks required for delivering the project. A critical element is the role of the lecturer, which shifts from 'sage on the stage' to 'guide on the side' (King, 1993). The lecturer will typically use one hour in the week as a traditional teaching class, and the remaining time is spent meeting each team individually, reviewing the work done to date and developing and setting goals for the coming week. Where possible, lecturers work together to facilitate and mentor the groups from conception through to execution of the idea. Students are responsible for all aspects of the project. They must raise the funds to execute it, research, develop and market it and take all the risks associated with it.

The assessment of the project is integrated across a number of modules and includes the production of market research reports, project plans, group process logs, a business plan, poster presentations and individual reflective journals. Social enterprise projects that students have successfully implemented include the development of a free sheet magazine that offered financial tips and advice to young people, a recession cookbook geared toward students, a newspaper for the campus and an enterprise trip to Shanghai Expo for graduates and budding student entrepreneurs. They have also identified gaps on campus in terms of business, sport and leisure opportunities and have developed services solutions including soccer tournaments and alumni events. As mentioned, the underlying principle behind each project undertaken is that it must add value and/or enhance the lives of others.

The practical ramifications of running this kind of assessment can be more fully understood by looking at a specific example of a completed project. A recent social entrepreneurship project involved the publication of the first on-campus newspaper, which was distributed free to the student body. An obvious starting point for sourcing ideas is for students to explore their own lived experience and identify gaps in service provision that might in turn lead to potential opportunities. The idea emerged during phase one of the project, when students discussed the perceived shortcomings of student life on the college campus. It quickly became apparent that the sporadic publication of a student magazine was failing to engage the student body, and the class group felt that there was a real opportunity to have a more relevant and more professional news avenue for student issues. There was significant interest in the idea, and a team of six opted to set up and produce the newspaper. The articulated value-added component of the project was to create an open, independent media forum for students to engage with topical issues that impacted on their daily lives. The business model chosen was a not-for-profit free sheet.

For the duration of the assessment, two sets of distinct but related activities took place. The academic requirements of the module demands that students use business planning tools and develop a fully worked-up business plan for the social venture selected. The task for this group was to compile a business plan on the feasibility of publishing a campus newspaper with two or three editions per academic year. Students had to design and conduct primary market research, analyze and interpret the data, develop a marketing and operational strategy, work out realistic finances and put together a comprehensive business plan. They had to draw on their knowledge from earlier academic work to complete this exercise.

In parallel, the students were also creating the first edition of the newspaper, researching news topics, commissioning and soliciting articles, negotiating with printers, sourcing advertisers, looking for sponsorship and ensuring that a newspaper was published. The delivery of both the academic and applied elements of this project was quite complex and depended on good teamwork, division of labor, good interpersonal communication as well as excellent time and project management skills.

The lecturer coordinating the module held one general lecture with the whole class once projects were launched. The objective of this lecture was to ensure that all students were familiar with the standard business planning process. The remaining class time was dedicated to scheduled meetings with each group, where students related progress, discussed problems and set out work to be undertaken for the following week. The lecturer also liaised with colleagues—for example, the research methods lecturer, who was working closely with students on the research dimension, and the finance lecturer, who was ensuring that students had the appropriate financial underpinning and the ability to produce the relevant financial statements.

The outcome for this particular group of students was a well-developed business plan that put forward a solid case for the feasibility of running a student newspaper on campus and the realization of the first edition of a 16-page campus newspaper. As part of the overall assessment, each individual student also produced a personal reflective journal that captured his or her learning throughout the process.

## STUDENT FEEDBACK

An annual review of this module is undertaken via student survey, as is common to all modules taught within the program. Students have responded positively to the experience year after year; however, there is no doubt that differences occur within class groups, and the quality of projects is variable. Interestingly, there can be some resistance to the concept in the early exploratory stages of the project, as heretofore most of the students view business mainly from a for-profit perspective.

Many of the students thrive on the experience of doing, and the less academically oriented learners often excel in this type of learning environment. The production of an individual reflective journal challenges the students to consider how their learning journey to-date has equipped them to deal with the project and also to recognize their own strengths and weakness. From the lecturing perspective, these journals can provide valuable insight into the issues and challenges that have not been raised in the weekly meetings and can contribute to the planning of the module for the following year. A selection of comments extracted from journals and student presentations at the end of the project include:

After this project I have realized that there are many things that I would change about the planning, assigning roles and delegating the workload.

What I have learned is that the academic work is there for a very good reason.

Whereas I used to continuously think about ideas that would make me money, I now find myself thinking about ideas that solve social problems around me.

Year after year, the single biggest issue that emerges from the student feedback concerns the management of group expectations and performance. Real disputes arise, and the individual logs shed light on how students manage or fail to manage these. From an assessment perspective, while there is a reliance on the group working together to achieve both the academic and practical tasks, well over 60% of the module is individually assessed. However, this does not ameliorate the tensions that the experience can create, and in different iterations of this assessment, the lecturing team adapted its approach to managing group projects building on the experience and feedback from year to year.

Another issue that students raise is the marking of the practical component of the project—they wonder whether part of the module grade reflects the quality of website they create or the newspaper they produce and so on. The focus to date has been on the process that students go through to realize the projects, and the grades are assigned to specific staged outputs at particular junctures rather than to the actual realization of the practical project output. The feedback indicates that this has been demotivating for some students.

For some students, their experiences on this module have been very significant. One of the students who participated in the enterprise trip to Shanghai returned with a business idea that he had seen operating in China. He researched and developed the idea as part of his coursework on the degree and subsequently launched the business on graduating from college.

## CONCLUSIONS

Challenges exist in running these types of projects within the traditional academic environment. Setting up group projects of this nature takes time and energy, and problems often occur in managing and marking student group projects. This is dealt with by ensuring that there are significant individual grading components within the overall project, but doing so requires constant monitoring and appropriate training for teaching staff in the management of group assessments. It is also difficult to maintain consistent levels of motivation throughout the life cycle of the project, and this is frustrating for both staff and learners. Timetable constraints and the heavy teaching schedule of individual lecturers make it difficult to organize team teaching when needed. Undoubtedly there is a higher element of risk for all concerned, because there is the potential for exposure to external stakeholders, and on more than one occasion, there has been a very real possibility that the projects undertaken will fail or unravel. However, this experience is surely of critical importance to entrepreneurship students who will engage in evaluating and taking risks to realize their goals in the future.

Other potential developments include the possibility of engaging students with real social enterprises that are rooted in the local community. This has been piloted, with one student involved in developing a business plan for a community sports facility that was successful in terms of the student learning outcomes and the organization involved. However, it requires a considerable amount of time to source relevant projects and to manage the expectations of external stakeholders as to what is feasible within the constraints of student-based projects. The correspondence of the social enterprise's business needs with the academic calendar is also a consideration.

Undoubtedly the time has come to perform a systematic and rigorous evaluation of this project. The annual quality assurance survey is limited and does not yield particularly useful insights. It does not in any way test the impact of the project in either building entrepreneurial capacity or evaluating the effect that the experience has on students' civic engagement. The personal learning logs have been more useful in this respect.

Partly by design and partly by chance, the convergence of the requirement to deliver on the Competence–Insight dimension of the National Framework of Qualifications and the application of the research findings on entrepreneurship education has resulted in the formulation of the social enterprise project described here. It is hoped that the process of engaging with the social entrepreneurship agenda facilitates students in exploring their own worldview and engaging with a wider social application of their business knowledge, skills and competencies.

## REFERENCES

Berry, B., & Workman, L. (2007). Broadening student societal awareness through service learning and civic engagement. *Marketing Education Review*, 17(3), 21–32.

Buddensick, J., & Lo Re, M. (2010). Measuring the effect of service learning on civic awareness. *Review of Business Research*, 10(5), 101–116.

Gibb, A. (2002). In pursuit of a new enterprise and entrepreneurship paradigm for learning: Creative destruction, new values, new ways of doing things and new combinations of knowledge. *International Journal of Management Review*, 4(3), 223–269.

Gibb, A. (2007). Entrepreneurship—Unique solutions for unique environments. Is it possible to achieve this with the existing paradigm? *International Journal of Entrepreneurship Education*, 5(15), 93–142.

King, A. (1993). From sage on the stage to guide on the side. *College Teaching*, 41(1), 33–35.

McIlraith, L., Farrell, A., Hughes, J., Lillis, S., & Lyons, A. (Eds.). (2007). *Mapping civic engagement within higher education in Ireland.* Dublin: Aishe/Campus Engage.

Ostrander, S. (2004). Democracy, civic participation and the university: A comparative study of civic engagement on five campuses. *Non Profit and Voluntary Sector Quarterly, 33*(1), 74–93.

Ryan, C., & Stritch, D. (2007). Active citizenship and higher education. In L. McIlrath, A. Farrell, J. Hughes, S. Lillis, & A. Lyons (Eds.), *Mapping civic engagement within higher education in Ireland* (pp. 30–39). Dublin: Aishe/Campus Engage.

Steiner, S., & Watson, M. (2006). The service learning component in business education: The values linkage void. *Journal of the Academy of Management Learning and Education, 5,* 422–434.

Weber, J., & Englehart, S. (2011). Enhancing business education through integrated curriculum delivery. *Journal of Management Development, 30*(6), 558–568.

# 18 Live Projects—Bringing Learning to Life for Contemporary Marketing Students

*Deirdre O'Loughlin*

## INTRODUCTION

The movement toward more active, experiential learning pedagogies is a phenomenon that has generated interest in recent years (see, for example, Farazmand & Green, 2011). The concept of the 'live case' or 'live project' is becoming recognized in the literature as offering students the ideal opportunity to work on real-life business problems (Thomas & Busby, 2003; Elam & Spotts, 2004). Live cases provide a wide range of learning outcomes and benefits, including teamwork, critical thinking, time management and applied skills (Chase, Oakes & Ramsey, 2007), which are particularly important given the critical role higher education institutions play in preparing graduates for employment. Problem-based or experiential learning (of which live cases is an example) facilitates the effective acquisition of real-life knowledge and skills in addition to helping develop organizational ability, effective planning and strategic thinking, all of which have become increasingly important for the competitive graduate marketplace (Dickenson, 2000). Within the marketing domain in particular, the effectiveness of experiential learning through live cases and projects has been identified as improving marketing pedagogy, providing hands-on experience and fostering a link between theory and practice (Maher & Hughner, 2003). For more detail on the theoretical literature in this area, see the chapter written by Peter Daly earlier in this book.

It is increasingly acknowledged that business schools need to incorporate social, ethical and environmental dimensions into their curricula to enable graduates to adopt a more sustainable approach to business leadership (e.g., Sroufe & Ramos, 2011). Exposure to social and ethical issues through teaching and assessment activities develops a deep internalization of ethical principles and an understanding of societal responsibility in students (Lavine & Roussin, 2012).

Reflecting the mixed success of many social marketing programs (Hastings, 2009), the promotion of responsible drinking attitudes and behaviors by state-funded bodies and alcohol awareness groups are important initiatives that have had varying levels of success in Ireland and elsewhere.

An opportunity was therefore identified to involve students in a live case with the strong societal dimension of promoting responsible drinking directly to their peers. Student volunteering represents another societal practice that offers individual students the opportunity to gain valuable experience and acquire skills while also fostering a sense of community engagement and responsibility (McIlrath & MacLabhrainn, 2007). The live volunteering campaign focused on engaging students in a worthwhile societal issue where civic learning is of value to the individual student, the community and to society as a whole (Wynne, 2011). The next sections of this chapter outline how a live marketing case was integrated into a module undertaken by postgraduate marketing students. One of the student cohorts was required to undertake a social marketing campaign involving responsible drinking, while the second cohort focused on student volunteering. Student feedback on their experience of the live case is outlined, and concluding remarks are provided.

## LIVE CAMPAIGN AIMS AND OBJECTIVES

The decision was made to integrate a live case into a module being taken by graduate students undertaking a master of science in marketing. The relevant module includes a strong societal dimension and engages students in critically reflecting on the role and responsibility of marketing in society and the importance of ethical marketing and consumption issues, corporate social responsibility (CSR) and sustainability. As such, a live case based on a social issue directly relevant to university students was considered an appropriate learning and assessment tool. Both of the cohorts who undertook the live cases described in this chapter were broadly similar, comprising 20 to 25 students from a range of academic backgrounds and disciplines, including marketing, business and nonbusiness graduates, international and mature students. Groups were comprised of between four and six students and included a mix of academic backgrounds, gender, ethnicity, skills and experience to ensure equity across, and diversity within, groups.

The two live cases in question involved responsible drinking and student volunteering and required student groups to develop a live marketing campaign to target and raise awareness among university students using specific themes, concepts, promotional materials and events. In terms of linking the assessment to module learning outcomes, students were required to apply many of the key concepts covered in the module to a real social marketing context of importance to student well-being, the campus community and society as a whole. The idea is that practical marketing experience is gained, and other key transferrable skills, including event and campaign management, are developed, which are of particular importance in an applied discipline such as marketing. The live marketing campaign experience develops genuine engagement among students, particularly of the current generation, who gain direct contextual and applied knowledge, deep learning and understanding and hands-on, relevant experience.

In both cases (responsible drinking and student volunteering), a campaign brief was developed between the module leader and the client, which was a student welfare body in the university. Specific campaign themes were developed and allocated to student teams. A dedicated student welfare officer acted as direct liaison and assumed the critical role of student advisor and mentor throughout the process, ensuring that there was a clear understanding of the brief and receiving regular updates on progress. In regard to both campaigns, the specific aims and objectives are outlined below:

1. Create an innovative and original concept and message around a preset campaign theme and build a marketing campaign upon this creative concept.
2. Demonstrate a clear social marketing strategy involving the budgeting, planning and implementation of the project.
3. Develop and execute a sustainable concept and strategy that could be applied or adapted in future campaigns.
4. Prepare a group report and presentation for a panel of stakeholders, analyzing the key components and outcomes of the chosen campaign and strategy.
5. Showcase the campaign strategy and materials at an exhibition to the university campus community.

Each student group was allocated a specific theme and was charged with developing and running the campaign during a live period of between two and three weeks. Both campaigns are presented in more depth in the following sections, which outline the key processes and outcomes involved.

## CAMPAIGN PROCESS AND OUTCOMES

Each of live cases was seed-funded to a total of €1,000 by the client and an on-campus printing firm, with each student group receiving a total of €150 to fund their campaign. In addition to the student mentoring and support provided by the client, the printing company supplemented printing costs and offered advice to students on the most appropriate printing options for their individual campaign. During the two- to three-week live period, each student team created and ran live, innovative and impactful campaigns using print and electronic media, promotions and events to target and raise awareness of sensible drinking and student volunteering to their peers on campus. In response to student feedback following the responsible drinking project, the live period was reduced from three to two weeks and the credit allocated to the project was increased from 40% to 50% of the module grade in recognition of the time and effort invested by students. Both live campaigns were assessed using a number of criteria, including creativity of concept, appropriateness to target market, effectiveness of strategy in relation to methods and media, effective allocation of budget, quality of campaign materials and events, sustainability, future usability and overall impact. Following the live campaign period, student groups formally presented their campaigns to a panel of experts and exhibited their campaign material on campus, where the winning team was selected and prizes awarded. As a measure of the success of the campaigns, there was promotional coverage in campuswide publications and on radio, local media and (in the case of the responsible drinking campaign) through a national agency for sensible drinking. The next section provides an in-depth outline of specific elements of both marketing campaigns.

## RESPONSIBLE DRINKING CAMPAIGN

The first live marketing campaign focused on engaging student teams to promote sensible drinking through highlighting aspects such as health, identity, sport and anti–drunk driving to students on campus. Student groups were mentored and supported through regular meetings with the client liaison officer and the module leader to develop their creative concept and campaign strategy and identify the most appropriate media and methods to promote their responsible drinking message to the target audience of first-year students on campus. Each of the groups devised a campaign schedule where they used a range of different media (e.g., print, electronic and social media) and methods (e.g., advertising, promotions and events) to promote their message, engage student interest and raise awareness of sensible drinking. For example, the Anti–Drink Driving group developed a dedicated Facebook site to promote its message to its target market. The group created a license plate logo 'Driving Is No Joke' and designed a crashed-car sad clown poster to advertise its drink-free event on campus, a free comedy hour, which was highly effective as a promotional tool and well attended by students. The Facebook page included useful links to official sites such as the Drink Aware site (www.drinkaware.ie), which provides information on responsible drinking and issues health warnings about the dangers of excessive drinking and driving. In a second event, they invited members of the Road Safety Authority and the Irish Police Force to the university campus to display real crashed cars to students. They also highlighted the importance of road safety for anyone walking home at night, particularly after a night of socializing, and provided free high-visibility vests to the hundreds of students who attended the event.

182  Deirdre O'Loughlin

*Figure 18.1*   Alcohol and Identity Poster (Responsible Drinking Campaign)

Figure 18.1 presents a sample poster underlining the link between alcohol and identity, which illustrates how excessive alcohol consumption can adversely affect one's identity and behavior. This group used the occasion of an on-campus Halloween ball to host the event; they invited students in fancy dress to participate in Halloween games while encouraging them to consider the effects of excessive drinking on their identity. They informed participants of the potential risks of binge drinking to their health and reputation among their friends and peers.

Following the live campaign period, student groups collected feedback to ascertain campaign impact and success among their peers and compiled their reports. Each group presented to a panel of experts, including representatives from the Health Services Executive, the Alcohol Working Group and the national agency for responsible drinking, Drink Aware. The overall winning team was selected, and three of the responsible drinking groups were highly commended by the panel for the quality of their campaigns. Each group was invited to present a selection of its campaign materials on the Drink Aware website, aimed at showcasing winning student campaigns to all university students. Furthermore, the Alcohol and Health group produced a highly professional and entertaining video of the effects of alcohol on health and well-being which received over 2,000 hits on YouTube. These examples provide clear evidence of the quality of the students' work and evidence its impact and relevance to the broader student community.

## STUDENT VOLUNTEERING CAMPAIGN

The second live marketing campaign required student groups to promote awareness and take-up of volunteering on campus. This campaign was directed toward generating awareness among all students, regardless of their year of study. It aimed to highlight the personal, community and societal benefits of volunteering at local, regional and national levels. Each project group was assigned a specific volunteering-related issue. They were then tasked with designing a social marketing concept related to this issue and were required to run a relevant live campaign on campus. The four themes developed by students included volunteering in areas of personal interest, volunteering in supportive communities, volunteering and connectedness and volunteering and employability.

Students were invited to use a suite of promotional elements to develop and execute their campaign, including print media such as posters and flyers, electronic media such as e-shots and social media marketing such as Facebook, Twitter and YouTube. They were also encouraged to organize events and activities on campus to build awareness of and interest for volunteering among students. As an example, the Volunteering and Employability group developed the concept of 'putting the V in your CV' (V for volunteering) and held an event involving a musical talent competition based on the X Factor, renaming it the 'V Factor' and connecting it with the universitywide President's Volunteer Award. The V Factor event was very well attended and proved popular among students, whose awareness of the valuable work experience, credit and profile gained through volunteering increased significantly. The group focusing on Volunteering and Connectedness developed the concept of students as ambassadors (see their poster in Figure 18.2) and held an impactful volunteering recruitment road show in various locations around the university campus involving existing student volunteers showcasing their skills and promoting volunteering in order to recruit future volunteers.

The Volunteering in Supportive Communities group used a highly creative and innovative integrated marketing approach that included composing and performing a volunteer rap that exposed the fear and lack of awareness among students of volunteering and how to combat this. The quality of the student volunteering campaigns were highly commended by the panel of judges, which included members from various student bodies in the university, including the Careers Office, the Mature Students Group, UL Clubs and Societies, Student Affairs and the President's Volunteer Award Committee.

184  *Deirdre O'Loughlin*

*Figure 18.2* Connectedness to the Community Poster (Student Volunteering Campaign)

## STUDENT FEEDBACK

To formally capture student feedback on the use of these live projects as assessment and learning tools, a series of in-depth focus group interviews was conducted with each of the nine student groups, comprising five responsible drinking groups and four student volunteering groups. An interview guide was developed, and focus group sessions explored areas such as student expectations and experience of the live project process, the range of knowledge and skills acquired and the ethical and civic responsibility awareness gained by the students through their involvement in these real-life social marketing campaigns. Each focus group was comprised of four to six students, lasted between 45 and 90 minutes and revealed a number of key issues and perspectives that helped the module leader understand how best to manage the process going forward and identified key pedagogical and operational considerations pertinent to the live case as a learning and assessment tool.

## REAL SKILLS, KNOWLEDGE AND EXPERIENCE

Student participants agreed that the live student-run marketing campaigns significantly surpassed more traditional assessment methods in providing real-life marketing knowledge and experience. For some participants, it was the first time they had been required to engage in a practical, live project, and the value of this experience for their CV was highly esteemed. This positive view was further supported by others who compared the live case experience to more traditional approaches, stating 'to actually put something into action like run an event and set up an exhibition stand . . . it's a really good experience' (Anti–Drink Driving Group). Participants also pointed to the personal learning they had acquired regarding themselves and their team members in the context of both transferrable and cognitive skills such as communication, time management, creativity, problem solving, planning and implementation skills as well as a range of marketing, research, public relations and event management skills. One respondent emphasized how he and his teammates had benefited from the process by reporting that 'we all know what our strengths and weaknesses are now . . . it was a good learning experience' (Alcohol and Sport Group). Some students developed specific technical skills and expertise and became, for example, the 'graphic designer in the team' (Volunteering and Employability Group) through mastering software such as Photoshop as a result of working on promotional material. Still others pointed to an overall improvement in their 'organizational, leadership and time management skills' (Volunteering and Connectedness Group).

The live case experience also allowed students to understand firsthand how to cope with and resolve unexpected issues as they arose and engage in brainstorming and problem solving. For example, one participant stated: 'It showed us all the things that could go wrong . . . we had everything planned out as such but there were still glitches . . . it's probably best that you overcome those problems because you are going to be faced with them in the real world' (Volunteering and Personal Interest Group). Students also felt strongly that the overall experience was more realistic because they were treated by the client as marketing professionals who were responsible for producing and delivering high-quality campaigns: 'It was like she had really hired us—it felt like we were doing it in real life and even when it was all over, we were still e-mailing her and writing up our report for her' (Volunteering in Supportive Communities Group). Based on student perspectives, these innovative marketing campaigns developed a range of key transferrable and cognitive skills in students that have both pedagogical and market-related benefits and helped enable students become knowledgeable, confident and capable marketing professionals. Several students stated that they had already presented a portfolio of these live campaign materials at job interviews, which provided the opportunity to outline and sell to prospective employers the key skills and knowledge acquired and the valuable marketing experience gained.

## SOCIETAL RESPONSIBILITY AND ETHICAL AWARENESS

An additional theme emerging from focus group interviews related to the importance of the live case approach in fostering a sense of societal responsibility and in creating a truly rounded graduate. Students on campus were more trusting and accepting of the promotional messages communicated by their peers 'as marketers' than formal university or media communications. Hence, participant students felt a deep sense of both responsibility and personal satisfaction from producing social marketing campaigns that were making a direct difference to their peers' well-being: 'It was great to work on something we all had experience of and try to spread the message of responsible drinking to first years . . . we weren't trying to be preachy and it worked' (Responsible Drinking Group). There was also a strong recognition by participants of the effectiveness and impact of their campaigns: 'I think they really got it—they loved the Halloween theme and they were happy to chat to us about our campaign. They recognized our posters from around campus . . . it was a great feeling to see that they were getting the message' (Alcohol and Identity Group). These views not only illustrate the effectiveness of the campaigns in spreading an important social message regarding responsible drinking to students but also clearly underline the key role played by older students as ambassadors of responsible and ethical behavior and champions of a more balanced approach to drinking for their younger peers. Such live projects help develop a sense of civic duty and responsibility both in the marketers and consumers of these student-run campaigns in addition to creating a culture of community and shared well-being on campus.

Involvement in the campaigns also encouraged students to reflect on themselves as ethical individuals and on their role in society in general as exemplified by the statement: 'you do kind of look at yourself differently . . . being ethical . . . 'cos we can't keep going the way we are . . . you do see the benefits of it for yourself and for everyone else really' (Volunteering in Supportive Communities Group). Similarly, another student stated that she now fully recognized the benefits of volunteering both from a societal and employability perspective and would consider volunteering herself: 'It's not as much hard work as I would have associated with it before I did the project. It is only an hour or two a week and it is not a big deal to get involved in . . . there's so many places you can do it' (Volunteering in Supportive Communities Group). Several students highlighted that, through their involvement in the live project, they were personally more aware of the importance of an ethical mind-set both as a student and as a future marketing professional. Speaking about the importance of student and graduate involvement in civic and ethical activities, one student stated: 'It grows the person in more ways than one 'cos they learn to give their time freely without condition . . . it's not just about the benefit doing your job has for you . . . it kind of gives you a bigger picture . . . the benefit that everybody else will get from you doing your job . . . so even in that sense it's fantastic' (Volunteering and Employability Group). Clearly, engaging students in live projects with a social or ethical dimension integrates a deep understanding and recognition of ethical and societal considerations into student learning and experience and serves to 'broaden their horizon and open their eyes' (Personal Choice Focus Group) to the good that they can do themselves as individuals and the impact they can have on their peers and on society both personally and professionally.

## CONCLUDING REMARKS

Live cases provide an experience that directly enhances a wide range of technical and transferrable skills that are far more significant and valuable than those gained through more traditional assessment formats. Furthermore, live cases that incorporate an ethical or societal dimension, exemplified by the two cases presented, develop a strong sense of civic duty and responsibility in students, not only to acknowledge their own role but in promoting an ethical and societal awareness and orientation among their peers, which is likely to continue throughout their professional lives. The live case model, therefore, used within or beyond the marketing discipline, offers tangible and valuable benefits as a pedagogical tool, leading to deeper learning, enhanced experience, increased employability and, as illustrated in this case, heightened ethical awareness and social responsibility—key graduate attributes for today's millennial generation. Assuming effective project management and student mentoring are provided, it is recommended that appropriate live cases be more extensively adopted in higher education across a wide range of disciplines and levels.

## REFERENCES

Chase, J. D., Oakes, E., & Ramsey, S. (2007). Using live projects without pain: The development of the Small Project Support Centre at Radford University. *Proceedings from the 38th SIGCSE Technical Symposium on Competitive Science Education, 39*(1), 469–473.

Dickenson, M. (2000). Giving undergraduates managerial experience. *Education and Training, 42*(3), 159–170.

Elam, E. L. R., & Spotts, H. (2004). Achieving marketing curriculum integration: A live case study approach. *Journal of Marketing Education, 26*(1), 50–65.

Farazmand, F., & Green, R. (2011). Live-case study learning outcomes: A comparison between students with and without prior internship experience. *Proceedings from Global Conference on Business and Finance, 6*(2), 7–11.

Hastings, G. (2009). Critical social marketing: The role of marketing in a consumer world. In J. French, C. Blair-Stevens, D. McVey, & R. Merritt (Eds.), *Social marketing and public health: Theory and practice.* (pp. 263–279). Oxford: Oxford University Press.

Lavine, M., & Roussin, C. (2012). From idea to action: Promoting responsible management education through a semester-long academic integrity learning project. *Journal of Marketing Education, 36*(3), 428–455.

Maher, J.K., & Hughner, R.S. (2003). Experiential marketing projects: Student perceptions of live cases and simulation methods. *Journal for Advancement of Marketing Education, 7*(Winter), 1–10.

McIlrath, L., & MacLabhrainn, I. (2007). *Higher education and civic engagement: International perspectives.* London: Ashgate.

Sroufe, R., & Ramos, D. (2011). MBA program trends and best practices in teaching sustainability: Live project courses. *Decision Sciences Journal of Innovative Education, 9*(3), 349–369.

Thomas, S., & Busby, S. (2003). Do industry collaborative projects enhance students' learning? *Education and Training, 45*(4), 226–235.

Wynne, R. (2011). The civic learning conundrum. In *Proceedings from NAIRTL National Academy 5th Annual Conference* (pp. 50–51). Cork, Ireland: University College Cork, NAIRTL Publications.

# 19  Making Play Work
## Classroom Use of a Board Game to Teach Corporate Social Responsibility

*Sheila Killian and John Lannon*

### INTRODUCTION

The universal acceptance of the importance of play in early childhood development is demonstrated by its enshrinement as the right in Article 31 of the United Nations Convention on the Rights of the Child (United Nations, 1989). However, the role of play in the lives of adults and the place of play in an otherwise formal teaching environment are less widely understood. This chapter describes the use of a board game to teach corporate social responsibility (CSR) in a university setting. The literature on play and the value of experiential learning for effective learning outcomes are discussed, and the game itself, how it is played and its impact on the class are described. Student feedback is summarized, and the chapter concludes with some suggested refinements and tips for incorporating similar activities into classes.

### DEFINING PLAY

The word *play* is sometimes conflated with *fun*, but, as noted by Vygotsky (1967), it generally involves more than passive pleasure and can even involve displeasure, as when the player loses the game. Krasnor and Pepler (1980) developed a model of four defining characteristics that identify the experience of play. These are

1. an element of make-believe or nonliterality, including role-play and fantasy;
2. a positive effect, or enjoyable experience for the player, particularly as signaled by laughter;
3. intrinsic motivation, meaning that the game is played for its own sake rather than to satisfy external constraints; and
4. flexibility, in the sense that the form and content of the game can be varied, so that the experience of playing it for a second time is not identical to the first.

The significance of these characteristics in defining the experience of play was supported in a wide-ranging empirical study by Smith and Vollstedt (1985). As originally hypothesized by Krasnor and Pepler (1980), no single characteristic is essential; rather, the more of these characteristics that are present, the more likely it is that the activity will be experienced as play. This matters because, as shown in the next section, the experience of play brings specific benefits in a classroom setting.

## WHY USE PLAY IN TEACHING?

A basic reason for incorporating play into the classroom is the fact that it is fun, and therefore engaging. Harris and Daley (2008), studying adult learners in an institutional setting, found that cooperative, educational play had the effect of enriching the learners' engagement with each other, and with materials beyond the immediate classroom. This suggests that, at a minimum, the use of play will help the class dynamic and students' engagement with both process and content. The fact that play is enjoyable will, as noted by Rosato (1995), engender more enthusiasm for the course as a whole.

A second reason is to diversify the teaching and learning techniques in use to ensure that there is something to suit all students in the classroom. Moore and Dettlaff (2005) argue that the use of educational games in the classroom can be useful in a class with diverse learning styles. They contend that many of the more talented students would have their learning needs met best by the competitive and creative aspects of games. They also note that games can afford students opportunities to think critically and strategically in a way that is less straightforward than in traditional written work.

A third reason, depending on the type of play involved, is to develop team skills of leadership, decision making and strategy. When students play games in teams, the natural competition within the class is channeled to increase the students' focus. If, as observed by Magney (1995, p. 3), 'students working in cooperative groups typically achieve higher levels of subject matter learning and more effective communication and other group process skill,' then playing relevant, competitive team games will increase both the students' knowledge of the subject at hand and their group skills.

The importance of teaching CSR in business schools hardly needs restating, particularly as the impact of business on a wide range of stakeholders has come to the fore in the current global downturn (Killian, 2012). In 2008, more than 80% of the world's top 250 companies issued CSR reports, up from 50% a mere three years earlier. As the director of academic programs at Thunderbird School of Management put it in 2012, 'The game has changed—it is essential that all managers consider full stakeholder value over the long-term. Customers seek it, communities in which we operate insist on it, and your clients, business partners and even employees will hold you accountable for making a positive contribution'

(Quacquarelli, 2012). With this in mind, it is relevant that appropriate role-play can be particularly useful in the area of CSR learning. Essentially, it gives students an opportunity to practice dealing with scenarios that might arise in the workplace. Gentile (2010) argues that the skills masters of business administration (MBA) students need in dealing with ethical dilemmas can largely be learned through practice. The idea is that graduates will have to make snap judgments on the job, and they are likely to make better choices if they have practiced similar decisions in a more thoughtful way in class.

## HOW TO USE PLAY IN TEACHING?

In a formal teaching environment, the third defining characteristic of play—intrinsic motivation—will be largely absent. Students play the game in class because this is what has been scheduled for them, not for the game's own sake. This arguably makes it more important that the remaining characteristics are in place: the form of play used should be fun, variable and should involve an element of make-believe or role-play.

To maximize fun, any game can be customized to the level of ability or experience of the students. Beasley (2004) lists some minor modifications that can be made on the spot. These include varying the level of instructor involvement in explaining the rules, providing feedback or arbitrating over disagreements; randomizing events within a game or running the game against the clock for more advanced players; or simplifying the rules for less advanced players.

Very simple games can be used to good effect to teach complex concepts. Lichtenwalter and Baker (2010) used Jenga, a popular game of wooden blocks, as a way to teach structural oppression. Jenga is a straightforward game of skill, strategy and chance, with no intrinsic link to the subject matter of the class. However, the authors focused on the disconnect between the effort of players and their chances of success, and highlighted this to the class as a form of structural oppression imposed by the rules of Jenga itself. By using extensive briefing and debriefing sessions before and after the game to place it in this context, they found that the use of the game increased student engagement and was 'a powerful tool for facilitating students' understanding of the mechanisms underlying structural oppression' (Lichtenwalter & Baker, 2010, p. 311).

A debriefing session during which students reflect on the relevance of the game for their course and the lessons they have learned from playing is critical. Jasinski and Thiagarajan (2000, p. 2) explain: 'People don't always learn from experience. Players can have a great time participating [in a game] but learn nothing. . . . Debriefing provides the opportunity for reflection to take place which hopefully will facilitate the transfer of learning from the game to the work context.'

Games can be used at different stages in a course. A game scheduled toward the beginning of a course can act as an ice-breaker and help in the formation of close student groups. On the other hand, Lichtenwalter and Baker (2010) echo Magney (1990) in observing that a game scheduled toward the end of a course can be very effective as a reinforcing activity for earlier learning. Placed midway in an intensive module, it breaks the pattern of lectures, which can be useful in stimulating the level of engagement with the material.

## BACKGROUND TO THE GAME

The VantagePoint board game was developed by three South African entrepreneurs described as having 'made and lost millions, happily surviving both' (Hove & Agbazue, 2008). It is designed to provide insight into a range of corporate social responsibility and human rights dilemmas encountered in business. The initiative was supported by a Dutch nongovernmental human rights organization called Aim for Human Rights. Collectively the three entrepreneurs had more than 50 years of business experience between them, covering a range of sectors.

It is an interactive and experiential game, played by two to five individuals or teams who, in the course of a game, deal with a series of ethical and everyday business challenges. Players must process sales orders, pay invoices, attract staff, deal with governments, interact with the community and decide how the company will behave toward employees, business partners and banks. Rather like Monopoly, the overall winner is usually the player with the most accumulated money at the end of the game. However, there are also rewards, both direct and indirect, for ethical behavior. For example, ethical behavior may help with winning government contracts, prevent industrial disputes and win community support. The game can also be varied by setting different objectives for winning, such as a high score on the human rights index or accreditation by external standard setters in the areas of health or labor rights.

The game was originally developed for in-company training to emphasize the role of corporations in promoting and securing human rights in a corporate context. It comes packed with a playing board, cards representing sales opportunities, business challenges, and team tokens. Players cast dice and proceed around the perimeter of the board, making business decisions as they go. Each time a player passes a corner square, they can take on a business challenge and make a decision that has both direct (financial) and indirect (reputational) effects that are not always predictable.

The challenges are short, multiple-choice scenarios falling into four categories: employment practices, community impact, supply chain management and overall compliance (see more detail in the appendix to this chapter). They were derived from CSR tools, including the Human Rights

Compliance Assessment, Country Risk Assessment summaries and the CSR Compass (all developed by the Danish Institute for Human Rights), as well as the Universal Declaration of Human Rights, the UN Global Compact, the Organisation for Economic Co-operation and Development Guidelines for Multinational Enterprises and International Labor Organization conventions. Players face the costs and benefits arising from their business decisions and must decide how to make socially and environmentally responsible choices while at the same time making a profit.

In a teaching context, the game is best played with teams rather than individual players. Discussions among players during the game are intended to raise awareness about the risks, challenges and opportunities of human rights issues in the corporate context. These discussions can bring about interesting results as players advise each other, or conversely try to persuade opponents to take poor decisions. Team play also allows a larger group of students to play with relatively few actual games being in progress, making it easier for the instructor to be involved in aiding the discussion.

Each game requires a facilitator who acts as banker, distributor of the cards and reader of the business challenges. The facilitator can take an active part in the game as part of a team or, alternatively, can remain independent and coordinate and recommend actions based on observations, clarify issues of policy, procedure and practice and advise players on likely consequences of their actions.

The game is distributed and supported by VantagePoint (www.vantagepoint.co.za) and is primarily positioned as a business skills development tool for students and entrepreneurs. It has been used in South Africa in retrenchment training and social responsibility initiatives and in entrepreneurship education among war veterans and aspiring cultural entrepreneurs. A number of variants of the original board game are in development. These include a human rights in business game, a customer service game and a soft skills game that focuses on the interrelationships between players to highlight issues around team building, conflict resolution and cultural diversity management.

## USING THE GAME TO TEACH CSR

This section describes two contrasting scenarios in which the game has been used in university business classes to teach CSR.

### The Classes

The game was used in two classes. The first was a small group of executive MBAs who had chosen CSR as a summer school elective at the Kemmy Business School, University of Limerick, Ireland. There were nine students in the CSR module, which ran eight hours a day for four days. They were mostly middle-level managers in multinational companies, taking the MBA program on a part-time basis over two years. The students were aged between thirty and fifty, with extensive business experience. Most of the students were Irish.

The second class was a larger group of undergraduates at Aalto University in Mikkeli, Finland, again, taking CSR as an elective. This course ran each weekday for three weeks with 23 students, all in their early twenties or late teens. They were an exceptionally international group, coming from Finland, France, Japan, Canada, China, Vietnam, Switzerland, the United States and Singapore.

## Preparation

In both cases the game was scheduled toward the end of the module to act as a capstone reinforcing activity for material already covered. The students had already learned about the kinds of international standards on which the ethical dilemmas in the game were based and had engaged in classroom discussions on how to balance the sometimes competing requirements to be socially responsible and profitable. They had undertaken several group activities, and so natural groups had formed within the class with a healthy element of competition between them.

The use of the game was flagged from the beginning. In both cases, the students were very taken by the novelty of playing a board game and looked forward to trying it. The learning objectives of the game were made clear from the beginning of the course, so that it was seen as an integral part of the classroom experience rather than 'time out'.

Because the game is rather complex, some time was spent the day before the game was scheduled on explaining the rules and strategy. The objective of the game—to make as much money as possible—was quickly agreed upon by both the class and the instructor. The students were asked to think about their team as a business, coming up with a company name and a line of business to add realism to the play. Each group or team was asked to choose a captain, and the role of facilitator was explained at that point.

## Playing the Game

Because there were only nine MBA students, they played a single game (one table and board) with three teams of three members. The undergraduates were divided into three games (tables), each with three teams of two or three. Desks and seats were arranged accordingly in the classroom in advance of the students' arrival on the morning of the game.

Once the students arrived and took their places, each table (board) chose a facilitator and a backup facilitator from a different team. The facilitator impacts on the experience of everyone playing the game at their board. It is important to choose a student with good English-language skills, leadership abilities, facilitative skills and enthusiasm. If the class dynamic is healthy and there is a good sense of class identity, the students can choose their own facilitator. This happened in the case of the MBAs. In the case of the undergraduates, the instructor selected the facilitators for each table.

The complexity of the game requires a walk-through of the board initially to ensure that all the players are familiar with the options open to them at each stage. In both classes, the instructor simplified the game somewhat by reducing the number of set-up steps, rationalizing the process of sales orders and pipelines and so on. This simplification process worked well, particularly for the undergraduates, for whom English was not the first language of many.

The MBAs and most undergraduate groups quickly grasped mechanics of the game and began to play competitively. Once they started dealing with the business challenges, discussions became animated and loud, and it was clear that students were very much enjoying the game. The overall structure of the class was kept loose, so students felt free to go and fetch coffee at any time they wanted. The only constraint was that the game would be wrapped up within two and a half hours.

One of the undergraduate tables, however, spent a very long time at the walk-through stage, painstakingly going through every square on the board to determine the options before the game play began properly. The facilitator's rather pedantic style was not compatible with that of several of the players, who were keen to get started and work out the details as they went along. This certainly damaged the experience of playing the game for that group of students, and an earlier intervention by the instructor would have been useful in resolving the conflict and restoring the fun element of the game.

Once the game was on, the students did not tire of playing. While they took short breaks to get coffee, they returned quickly and played enthusiastically for the full timed period. As the allotted time was coming to an end, teams that were losing became reckless, trying to gamble their way back to victory, and winning teams grew cautious in an effort to consolidate their gains. Competition between the teams also grew more intense as time went on, with active efforts made to undermine the leading teams; temporary alliances were made and broken.

Students were given a short window to complete a final round of play, count money, repay loans and work out their final score before ranking the teams. A small prize was awarded for the winning team(s).

After the game was complete, some class time was spent reflecting on the experience of playing the game, discussing how it related to the sorts of dilemmas faced by managers in business, how it related to the theory covered earlier in the module and what lessons could be learned from playing. It was especially useful for students to reflect on their own behavior at different stages in the game and on the impact of groupthink on their individual ethical stances.

## STUDENT FEEDBACK

The reaction from students to the game was very positive, with some suggestions for improvements. They favored teams of three, as they felt this led to the best discussions. From observation, this certainly seemed to be the case. The undergraduates thought that some of the business challenges were a little transparent, making it easy to see which option would result in the best outcome for the game. Interestingly, none of the MBAs, who had far more business experience, felt this. This may be because the undergraduates, having more experience of games than of business, were focusing on the challenges as a game rather than as a business simulation. This difference didn't seem to affect their enjoyment of the activity, however.

Students from both classes felt that the rules were a little too complex. While they appreciated the realism of the game, they spent a long time learning the different squares on the board and working out their own interpretations of the rules.

Perhaps because the content of the game was directly related to the curriculum material, the students were very clear on the usefulness of the game for learning. One of the undergraduate teams observed that the discussions over the board game were more intense than class discussions, perhaps because of the competitive element. This is particularly useful in dealing with affective issues such as ethical dilemmas, because it triggers a high level of engagement by students.

The groups that had chosen their own facilitators were happier and seemed to enjoy the game most. Unsurprisingly, the winners of the game reported the highest level of satisfaction with the activity.

The timing of the game at the end of the course met with general approval, although some better students noted that the game would have been more challenging if played at the beginning, since they would not at that stage have been exposed to any of the material on which the business challenges were based. Some students suggested playing the game both at the beginning and the end. This would, however, use a great deal of classroom time.

## REFINEMENTS AND TIPS

In playing the game in the future, a simplified version of the rules will be prepared to reduce the learning curve associated with the current, rather complex version. The students will be encouraged to choose their own facilitators once the role has been explained to them. The awarding of a prize to the winners, however small, seems to be very important and will be continued. Where class numbers permit, teams of three will be used.

The timing of the game at the end of the course seems to work well, but consideration will be given to using it in the middle of a course as a way of breaking up the pattern of lectures, strengthening groups' formation and making the game itself more challenging.

## CONCLUSION

This particular game was very useful in teaching CSR and could be employed in any university course on the subject. It worked equally well with young, relatively inexperienced undergraduates and business managers in an MBA setting, and with diverse or monocultural classes. Working with teams of three, a class of up to 60 can easily be accommodated with five copies of the game.

Preparation in terms of student expectations, teaching (and simplifying) the rules, classroom layout, and time for reflection afterward are very important in getting the maximum value from a game of this nature. Student engagement was definitely increased as predicted by the literature. The motivation to win gave students who were very quiet in classroom discussions the incentive to debate issues in a smaller group, suggesting that it suited different learning styles, and, in the particular case of CSR/ethics, the opportunity to practice business decisions should help students make better judgments after graduating.

## REFERENCES

Beasley, N. (2004). *A Study of Adult Engagement with Constructivist Computer Games*. Napier University, Edinburgh. http://www.napier.ac.uk/fecci/research students/Documents/exampletransferreprot2.pdf.

Gentile, M. (2010). *Giving Voice to Values: How to Speak Your Mind When You Know What's Right*. New Haven, CT: Yale University Press.

Harris, P., & Daley, J. (2008). Exploring the Contribution of Play to Social Capital in Institutional Adult Learning Settings. *Australian Journal of Adult Learning, 48*(1), 50–70.

Hove, H., & Agbazue, T. (2008). *How Do You Want to Do Business?* Retrieved from http://www.ngopulse.org/article/how-do-you-want-do-business.

Jasinski, M., & Thiagarajan, S.T. (2000, April). *Virtual Games Real Learning: A Seriously Fun Way to Learn Online*. Paper presented at the TCC Online Conferences, University of Hawaii.

Killian, S. (2012). *Corporate Social Responsibility: A Guide with Irish Experiences*. Dublin: Chartered Accountants Ireland Publishing.

Krasnor, L. R., & Pepler, D. J. (1980). The Study of Children's Play: Some Suggested Future Directions. *New Directions for Child and Adolescent Development, 1980*(9), 85–95.

Lichtenwalter, S., & Baker, P. (2010). Teaching Note: Teaching About Oppression Through Jenga: A Game-Based Learning Example for Social Work Educators. *Journal of Social Work Education, 46*(2), 305–313.

Magney, J. (1990). Game-Based Teaching. *Education Digest, 55*(5), 54–57.

Magney, J. (1995, December). *Teamwork and Cooperative Learning in Technical Education*. Paper presented at the American Vocational Association Convention, Denver, CO.

Moore, L., & Dettlaff, A. J. (2005). Using Educational Games as a Form of Teaching in Social Work. *Aretê, 29*(1), 58–63.

Quacquarelli, N. (2012). *QS Global 200 Business Schools Report 2012.* QS Ratings Agency.

Rosato, J. (1995). All I Ever Needed to Know About Teaching Law School I Learned Teaching Kindergarten: Introducing Gaming Techniques into the Law School Classroom. *Journal of Legal Education, 45*(4), 568–581.

Smith, P. K., & Vollstedt, R. (1985). On Defining Play: An Empirical Study of the Relationship Between Play and Various Play Criteria. *Child Development, 56*(4), 1042–1050.

United Nations. (1989). Convention on the Rights of the Child. Retrieved from http://www2.ohchr.org/english/law/crc.htm.

Vygotsky, L. S. (1967). Play and Its Role in the Mental Development of the Child. *Journal of Russian and East European Psychology, 5*(3), 6–18.

# Appendix
Detail on the Game Scenarios

As explained in the chapter, the scenarios used in the board game can be roughly categorized as covering employment practices, community impact, supply chain management and overall compliance with international standards and codes. They are deliberately short, allowing for wide interpretation and discussion among the players. A typical scenario (paraphrased) might be something like this:

> You are a senior executive in a multinational firm, which operates a manufacturing plant in a developing country. You learn that in one of the suppliers to the factory, children as young as 14 are employed on a full-time basis. Your local manager assures you that this is not a problem, as 14 is the minimum working age in that country.
> What action do you take, and why?

In general, the teams will discuss the action to be taken, and the facilitator will allow the discussion to develop on issues of child protection, education, responsibility for the supply chain, and so on. Once the players are converging on a possible solution, the facilitator will present them with three options. In this case, the options might be:

1. Do nothing—no laws have been broken.
2. Switch to a supplier that does not employ children.
3. Work with the supplier to ensure that the children have access to education.

Depending on the choice made, there may be an immediate or deferred financial cost, damage to or enhancement of the company's reputation or other outcomes.

# 20 Conclusion

*Patrick Buckley, Conor Carroll and Elaine Doyle*

This book was conceived, written and edited with the aim of providing educators across the world with a selection of some innovative solutions to the challenges that face business school teaching. In concluding this work, we begin by making the observation that our interaction with academics working at the forefront of contemporary business education has confirmed our suspicion that the challenges we face are common internationally. All our authors struggle with the changing nature of the tertiary education sector. Universities are becoming more market driven. Business schools in particular are exemplars of this trend, as evidenced in Khurana's (2010) sweeping and comprehensive analysis of the history of business school education. State support for higher-level education is diminishing in most jurisdictions, in some cases quite severely. To survive, universities must offer more courses to more students. The advent of funding models that increasingly place the financial burden on students is significantly altering the traditional relationship between academics and courses, students and the institution. Course design has always been a contentious issue for academics seeking to maintain a balance between academic rigor and professional relevance. Competing positions on curriculum design will undoubtedly wax and wane for as long as universities exist, but, at the moment, the changing model of university funding and the necessity of attracting fee-paying students are subtly rebalancing the weighting in favor of professional relevance. Students who pay fees for their education see themselves more as customers and less as students. Institutions are now expecting teaching staff to take on greater administrative loads and drive the development of new courses. All these changes are occurring in an environment that employs, retains and promotes academic staff primarily on the basis of research outputs.

In particular, the emerging prominence of massive open online courses may revolutionize the manner in which higher-level students are taught. Universities, and in particular business schools, need to proactively differentiate the value they add compared with these free and open educational platforms. Educators need to focus on the real value-add of a university-level learning experience. Some educationalists advocate the concept of the 'flipped classroom,' where direct instruction can be undertaken by online videos while problem-based learning and dynamic discussion take place in the classroom. Indeed, the case method may be rejuvenated in the wake of this altered educational landscape, generating participant-centered learning. There is a need for enhanced focus on generating the higher-order learning outcomes of synthesis, analysis and evaluation of academic content. Universities need to play to their strengths, creating dynamic learning environments, developing curricula that reflect the real world and leveraging the digital literacies/competencies of the millennial generation.

In addition to the evolving model of tertiary education, the material in this book validates our experience of the millennial generation as a key challenge facing contemporary educators. Our contributors are united in their conviction that this generation is unlike previous generations. Their modes of information collection, analysis and utilization are significantly different from the generations before. Students are less willing to engage in the sustained periods of reflective learning associated with activities such as reading books. This is often bemoaned as an unwillingness to learn. It is our contention that care must be taken not to rush to such judgments. The millennial generation is the first to be immersed in information technology since birth. Their instinctive dislike of rote learning (the memorization of discrete facts) is not borne of a disdain for knowledge, but rather of an awareness that any factual information they will need is immediately at their fingertips. Indeed, a primary challenge for educators is to equip students with data literacy skills that improve their sense-making capabilities and allow them to synthesize information. As business school teachers, we need to at least explore the possibility that the millennial generation's modes of learning are better adapted to the digital world that they will inhabit than ours are and consider the possibility that we must adapt to them rather than vice versa.

Despite the challenges that business school educators face internationally, what has repeatedly struck us in our interactions with all the collaborators involved in this collection is the energy, innovation and enthusiasm they display in handling the challenges of teaching in the 21st century. The style utilized by the contributors to this book in sharing their teaching techniques and experiences ranges widely—some use a formal, academic style while others adapt a more personal tone. Regardless of the style, however, the contributions provide innovative solutions to practical problems, while also offering beleaguered educators the encouragement that there are techniques that have been developed, tried and tested by fellow business school teachers. It is heartening to observe the enthusiasm with which educators all over the world are dealing with challenges and to see evidence that the academy still has the ability to recruit and retain many of the most competent, energetic and innovative individuals in society as university lecturers.

From the outset, this book was conceived with a specific audience in mind—namely, business educators teaching the millennial generation. A specific focus is necessary, but unavoidably omits many important issues—for example, handling the challenges of back-to-education learners and exploring in depth contexts such as executive education and distance learning. These issues are touched upon in some of the chapters in this book, but a full treatment worthy of these topics is regrettably beyond its scope. We believe that exploring these issues in detail in a similar manner to the approach herein would be a very worthy endeavor.

The specific innovations presented in this book were novel to the editors and were chosen for inclusion in the book for that reason. At a conceptual level however, we wish to conclude this book by examining the trends in tertiary education that emerged from these collective chapters which most surprised or engaged us. Certain themes are common to almost all the contributions. Technology is playing an ever-increasing role in our educational lives—both in teaching and in learning. E-learning is escalating in importance. It is no longer an add-on to courses or a slightly bizarre delivery mechanism practiced by gung-ho proponents who can be safely ignored by the rest of us. Technology has become central to the learning experience, and claiming unfamiliarity with it or suspicion of its techniques is no longer an option for the modern academic. Some references to online teaching and learning resources can be found in the Appendix. Similarly, it is very evident from the chapters within this book that active learning, in its broadest sense, is now the standard we must all seek to achieve for the delivery of all educational programs. The chalk and talk era is over. To use a popular phrase, we are no longer sages on the stage, but guides on the side. Educational offerings are moving away from delivering domain-specific material and instead embracing multidisciplinary approaches. There is an increasing acceptance that we must prepare students for careers rather than jobs, which in turn entails a focus on developing students' transferable skills and metacognitive processes and facilitating them to become lifelong learners.

Another theme that emerged across multiple chapters is the importance of helping students to recognize that they are, first and foremost, members of society. Many fingers have been pointed at business schools for inculcating the philosophies and perspectives that ultimately led to the current financial crisis. While academia is not alone in carrying this burden, there is a certain truth to this, and many chapters in this book explore how we can begin to foster and enhance in our students the ethical and moral sensitivities necessary for the next generation of leaders if the mistakes of the past are to be avoided in the future.

Understanding these emerging themes in business school teaching and learning is important for us as business academics, and we do not seek to diminish their importance. However, two further themes emerged from the chapters contributing to this book which surprised and energized us—we wish to draw particular attention to these in this concluding chapter. The first is the importance of emotion within the teaching and learning context, and the second is the crucial importance of realism in the education environment.

Time and again, our contributors discuss the importance of emotion in various contexts. This mirrors the call by Hawawini (2005), who advocated that business schools need to impart both behavioral and societal skills. Killian and Lannon, for example, discuss how important it is to create 'a positive effect, or enjoyable experience for the [student]'. All our authors discuss to a greater or lesser degree the importance of affect on the learning experience. Teckman highlights the importance of creating educational environments whose raison d'être is creating situations that are emotionally challenging for students. In his chapter on delivering feedback to large groups, Adcroft concludes with the observation that his methods don't necessarily reduce the marking burden on academics, but changes the feedback process from 'difficult confrontations with surly recipients of marks they don't understand toward positive and constructive dialogue about how someone can do better'.

In exploring the issue of emotion in teaching as it emerges within these chapters, we suggest that its impact be considered from three perspectives. First, the best teachers and learning environments move beyond the delivery of skills and knowledge, however technically or conceptually advanced. Excellent teaching involves engaging with students as emotional beings. The contributors to this book are strong advocates of this, and we strongly endorse it. A great learning experience is, to borrow Killian and Lannon's words, 'signaled by laughter'. Indeed, the integration of play into learning can create extremely dynamic learning environments. Play can trigger creativity and productivity, induce fresh perspectives and yield strong social and emotional benefits. The employment of gamification concepts within education potentially yields exciting learning opportunities and may assist in tackling student engagement challenges.

We also suggest that there are two other perspectives on the importance of emotion in teaching that receive less attention. The first is the importance of emotion from the perspective of an educator. We are all professionals, trained both in our subject disciplines and in various teaching approaches and methodologies. However, teaching is a deeply personal activity that cannot be stripped of its emotional component. As educators, we enjoy teaching engaged, motivated classes. At best, the job evolves into something that resembles 'work' much less than a positive learning experience for us as well as for our students. Many of the challenges facing higher-level education, such as larger groups, have had the second-order effect of reducing our emotional connection with our students—creating a disconnect. It is important for educators to appreciate that being innovative does not solely benefit students in terms of a better learning experience. It also makes the job *fun* again, reinvigorating passion and commitment for teaching. What the chapters in this book contain is not just descriptions of better learning outcomes for students but also the voices of educators who enjoy their job more because of the innovations they have deployed. Our authors are excited by their innovations and, as evidenced by their contributions to this book, eager to take time out of busy schedules to share their work with others.

The final perspective on the importance of emotion that emerges from this collection is its importance in students' professional careers. Teckman's chapter is perhaps the clearest exponent of this, but all the chapters reflect on it. The business professionals that our students will become cannot be emotionless automata, the *homo economicus* of Herbert Simon. In their professional careers, our students will face the challenge of managing and regulating their own emotions while also being cognizant and mindful of others and often dealing with emotionally fraught situations. Academic institutions need to embrace the role of developing not only the cognitive skills of students but also their emotional intelligence. Assisting students in the development of these skills will make them happier, more balanced members of society, equipped with the tools they need to successfully operate in the stressful and highly fraught environments that are all too common in the contemporary business workplace. We need to instill perseverance and resilience in our future business leaders. High-level business decision making is very rarely clear-cut and seldom involves a sequential linear process leading to a successful outcome. The real world is messy and fraught with complexity, thus requiring agility and adaptability to situations—Bennis and O'Toole refer to 'the mysteries and ambiguities of today's business practices' (2005). Students need to be assisted in developing empathy for their colleagues and fellow citizens and encouraged to behave morally and ethically.

The chapters in this book emphasize the importance of integrating emotion into the learning environment. Creating emotionally engaging learning experiences for students, managing our own emotions and developing the emotional intelligence of our students are all identified as critical factors in business school teaching and learning. However, failure to embrace the important issue of emotion is just one facet of a larger criticism that universities face. In attempting to create, retain and transmit knowledge in its purest form, universities often stand accused of abstracting problems to such a degree that they lose the power to educate students in any meaningful sense. In this context, we found it fascinating to observe how many of our contributors emphasize the importance of creating realistic educational experiences. McCarthy, for example, discusses the importance of creating authentic assessments. O'Loughlin and Daly outline the meaning of and demonstrate the use of live cases, which differ from the traditional case method in that students solve actual problems suggested by real companies. Zupan and colleagues describe how design thinking is integrated into the curriculum to better mimic the product design processes that occur in the professional arena, while Maiksteniene describes how to position case study work in a manner that allows and encourages students to actively seek information themselves rather than depending on information supplied by the educator.

All these approaches place realism at the core of contemporary business school education. Realistic problems, learning environments and assessment strategies build the crucial bridge that helps students understand how theoretical concepts from academia will be applied in their professional careers. Realism grounds learning, improving student motivation and enthusiasm. It helps students appreciate that the problems they will face in their professional careers will constantly challenge them to learn and develop new skills, thereby emphasizing the importance of lifelong learning. This is consistent with Pfeffer and Fong (2002), who advocate a greater clinical or practice component within the business curriculum. In contrast to more stylized iterations, realistic problems often do not have definitive solutions. The vital skill of learning to choose the 'least bad option' as opposed to 'finding the right solution' is one that is often not developed in the circumscribed problems associated with more traditional educational formats. Furthermore, any form of learning where students work with external stakeholders also enhances the engagement between the university and the wider community.

The importance of emotions and creating realistic learning environments are concerns of all the contributors to this book. They are also tightly interlinked. Only a realistic situation can create an emotional impact, and no situation lacking emotional engagement can be truly considered realistic. As editors, we have chosen to highlight these issues because of their importance to our contributors. We were not unaware of the importance of either issue. However, the weight placed upon them by our contributors emphasized their importance and challenged us to consider how we address these issues in our own teaching. In this way, this book has been a learning experience for us, and our aspiration for this collection is that it facilitates others to enjoy a similar journey.

Teaching is about assisting students to develop the skills and abilities they need to prosper in their future lives and careers. However, and particularly in the case of tertiary education, it is also about developing students as individuals. It is the process whereby students develop critical thinking skills. It is the arena in which knowledge is not just imparted, but where individuals learn how to learn. It is an environment that shapes the moral and ethical qualities of the future leaders of societies. Teaching is a two-way street. When the learning experience is correctly shaped, educators can learn as much as, if not more than, the students—and not simply about the art and craft of teaching. By describing, explaining and exploring the disciplines we teach in the company of students, we arrive at new reflective insights.

There is no doubt that tertiary education in general, and business education in particular, is experiencing dramatic change at the moment. The arrival of the digital natives of the millennial generation poses new challenges that, as educators, we are only beginning to address. This book and our contributors—leading educators from all over the world—attest to these observations. Much more than delineating the challenges we face as educators in the 21st century, this book is a testament to the enthusiasm and innovation with which these challenges are being met. Our final thought is the hope that the reader has found this book as inspiring, challenging and heartening to read as we have found putting it together.

## REFERENCES

Bennis, W., & O'Toole, J. (2005). How Business Schools Lost Their Way. *Harvard Business Review, 83*(5), 96–104.

Hawawini, G. (2005). The Future of Business Schools. *Journal of Management Development, 24*(9), 770–782.

Khurana, R. (2010). *From Higher Aims to Hired Hands: The Social Transformation of American Business Schools and the Unfulfilled Promise of Management as a Profession.* Princeton, NJ: Princeton University Press.

Pfeffer, J., & Fong, C. (2002). The End of Business Schools? Less Success Than Meets the Eye. *Academy of Management Learning & Education, 1*(1), 78–95.

# Appendix
## Online Teaching and Learning Resources for Business Schools

| Website | Description |
| --- | --- |
| Audacity<br>audacity.sourceforge.net | Free open-source software that allows users to record and edit sounds, allowing users to create podcasts. |
| Coursera<br>www.coursera.com | The pioneering massive open online course (MOOC) offering free online classes ranging from gamification to math. These platforms could revolutionize university education, forcing educators to develop new value-add learning experiences within their classrooms. |
| Diigo<br>www.diigo.com | Online information management solution where users can online bookmark, highlight, and annotate. Thus, users can collect an archive online material and access the content remotely. |
| Evernote<br>www.evernote.com | Excellent free online data capture tool, in which content can be stored and accessed online through the cloud. Can store photos, video, notes, sketches and audio. |
| Flickr<br>www.flickr.com | Huge repository of images that can be used in slide shows in accordance with creative commons guidelines/licenses. |
| Gliffy<br>www.gliffy.com | Allows users to create dynamic diagrams, flow charts, organization charts, wireframes and floor plans, among others. |
| Learnist<br>www.learnist.com | A curated website that allows users to provide education content called learning boards, which may be podcasts, blogs, Twitter feeds, slide shows or other online resources. |
| Lore<br>www.lore.com | Formerly called Coursekit. Free online course management site with easy-to-use interface. Features include calendaring, file management, ability to upload lectures, post links and video files, public or private; good discussion time line. |

| Website | Description |
|---|---|
| Merlot<br>business.merlot.org | Digital learning repository where one can access learning materials. Useful resource, but very U.S.-centric. |
| Mindmeister<br>www.mindmeister.com | Useful brainstorming and mind mapping software. Xmind is a similar service. |
| Ning<br>www.ning.com | Empowers users to create their own specialized social network. |
| Participant Centered Learning & Case Method<br>http://hbsp.harvard.edu/multimedia/pcl/pcl_1/start.html | Harvard Business School resource focused on the case method and demonstrating teaching techniques. In the wake of MOOCs, now the case method is of real value-add in the classroom. |
| PBwiki<br>www.pbwiki.com | Can create online workspace for collaborative projects. |
| Pinterest<br>www.pinterest.com | Educators can become online content curators, recommending blogs, books, infographics and articles to their students. |
| Prezi<br>www.prezi.com | A powerful alternative to Microsoft PowerPoint software. Educators can store dynamic presentations in the cloud for free. Excellent animations. |
| Skitch<br>www.skitch.com | Made by Evernote. Allows educators to sketch and overlay images, and extremely useful for editing PowerPoint slide images. |
| Slideshare<br>www.slideshare.com | Large online repository for presentations on diverse topics of interest. Look through what presentations people are marking as favorites to see some excellent ideas and concepts. |
| Top Hat Monocle<br>www.tophatmonocle.com | This company specializes in developing state-of-the-art audience response systems, integrated into mobile devices such as tablets and cell phones. It differs from the traditional clickers in that students buy a license for the software instead of hardware. It allows for real-time interaction opportunities, polling, Q&A and, importantly, text discussion. It is free for academics. |
| TED<br>www.ted.com | Nonprofit organization focused on the central theme of ideas worth spreading. Diverse speakers talk on topics ranging from technology to entertainment and design. |
| Udacity<br>www.udacity.com | Another MOOC provider. Here students can take open and free courses, avail of instructor videos, wikis and online discussion on a variety of material. |

| Website | Description |
| --- | --- |
| Videolectures.net<br>www.videolectures.net | A global catalogue of lectures, tutorials, conference presentations and keynotes from academics and thought leaders. This large video repository has free access. |
| Voicethread<br>www.voicethread.com | This collaboration tool allows users to share images, documents, video and other content while allowing users to add voice or text commentary. |
| Wikispaces<br>www.wikispaces.com | Allows educators to create free dedicated course wikis for their students. Lecturers can post ideas, work, videos or other media in a password-protected site. Administrators can adjust permission settings to allow student access. |
| Wolfram Alpha<br>www.wolframalpha.com | This discovery engine offers fresh insights and comparisons for queries. Very useful for mathematical problems and solutions. |
| Wordle<br>www.wordle.net/create | Creates word clouds, where frequently occurring words gain greater prominence, and then can be copied into a presentation for visual effect. Other word cloud maker equivalent is Tagxedo.com |
| Zoho<br>www.zoho.com | Offers a suite of apps and software, equivalent to the popular Microsoft Office suite. Basic content is free for users, with advanced features being charged a premium. |
| Zotero<br>www.zotero.com | Zotero is a free online bibliography manager, which rivals the likes of Endnote. Online content can be seamlessly organized and collated, capturing all referencing tags and fields. |

# Contributors

**Dr. Andy Adcroft** is the director of academic development in the Faculty of Business, Economics and Law at the University of Surrey, England, where he teaches strategy to undergraduates and research methods postgraduate students and underpinning philosophies of research to doctoral candidates. His research interests are in the relationship between feedback and performance and in how learning experiences are influenced by the motivations and expectations of the learner. Both his teaching and research are built on the view that they are social processes.

**Daniel Blackshields** is a lecturer in economics in University College, Cork (UCC), Ireland. His current research interests are in exploring the teaching of economics, entrepreneurship, cognition and creativity, and economics and the arts. He holds an MBS (business economics) and an MA in teaching and learning in higher education. He is the teaching fellow for Reflective Practice for UCC, and in 2012 he won both the UCC's Presidents Award for Excellence in Teaching and the UCC's President's Award for Research on Innovative Forms of Teaching and Learning.

**Dr. Peter Daly** is professor of business communication and head of the Department of Business Communication and Language Studies at EDHEC Business School, France. Daly gives seminars in business and managerial communication; team building; managerial styles; recruitment and assessment center preparation; and management. He has a BA in languages (French, German, Spanish and English); an MA in applied linguistics, a PGCE in online pedagogy and a PhD in higher education. His research revolves around managerial and learning discourse, future work skills and business apprenticeship.

**Dr. Mateja Drnovšek** is an associate professor of entrepreneurship at the Faculty of Economics, University of Ljubljana. Her research is immersed in cognitive and affective aspects of entrepreneurship and their influence on the formation of entrepreneurial intentions, new venture creation and overall entrepreneurial effectiveness. Her work has been published in journals such as *Academy of Management Review, Baltic Management Journal, Economic and Business Review, Scandinavian Management Journal, Journal of Enterprising Culture, Small Business Economics* and others.

**Dorit Geifman** is a PhD candidate at the Graduate School of Management, University of Haifa, Israel, and is active in the Sagy Center for Internet Research. She holds an MSc degree in computer science a BSc degree with distinction in mathematics and history and philosophy of science. Her research interest lies in the socioeconomic aspects of collective intelligence and crowdsourcing. Geifman's doctoral research deals with the effect of trader's behavior on the performance of prediction markets. As a researcher in the FP7-ICT SocIoS project, she investigates business models for user-generated content in social networks.

**Dr. Sheila Killian** teaches corporate finance and corporate social responsibility at the Kemmy Business School, University of Limerick, Ireland. Her main research areas are corporate social responsibility, critical perspectives on accounting, tax policy and development issues. She has also taught in South Africa and Finland, and her research is published on five continents. She is the author of *Corporate Social Responsibility: A Guide with Irish Experiences* (2012), and she is the founding chair of Soweto Connection.

**Dr. John Lannon** teaches information and knowledge management at the Kemmy Business School at the University of Limerick in Ireland. His research focuses on human rights information management and on assessing human rights impact in a range of policy areas. In 2012 he co-edited *Human Rights and Information Communications Technologies: Trends and Consequences of Use*. He has taught in Asia and Africa and has worked as a consultant with several international human rights and other nongovernmental organizations.

**Dr. Helena Lenihan** is assistant dean, research, and a senior lecturer in economics at the University of Limerick in Ireland. She is an applied economist who researches on public policy issues. More specifically, her research addresses the following interrelated streams: industrial/enterprise development and policy; innovation policy; enterprise and innovation policy evaluation (examining the impact/effectiveness of policy interventions from both ex-ante and ex-post perspectives and a concern with evaluation methods); and the role of enterprise and entrepreneurship/new venture creation in economic development and firm growth. In 2008, Lenihan was a visiting fellow at the Centre for Business Research at Judge Business School, University of Cambridge, UK. She spent June 2008 as a visiting academic at the Centre for Small and Medium Sized Enterprises, University of Warwick, UK. In

2009, Lenihan received a National Excellence in Teaching Award from the National Academy for the Integration of Research and Teaching and Learning. She is also twice winner of the University of Limerick's Excellence in Teaching Award.

**Kristina Maiksteniene** is senior lecturer and head of marketing strategy and management programs at ISM University of Management and Economics in Vilnius, Lithuania. Maiksteniene holds an MBA degree from Kellogg School of Management (Northwestern University, USA), an MA degree in dconomics from Central European University (Czech Republic), an MSc degree in applied mathematics from Kaunas University of Technology (Lithuania), and is currently working toward her PhD degree. Her previous experience includes brand management at Procter & Gamble Baltics, Poland and Belarus, as well as years of extensive business consulting to domestic and international corporations. For 12 years, Maiksteniene has been a keen advocate and implementer of case pedagogy at ISM, has coauthored one of the first books on case methodology in the Baltics (*Stories Told in the Classroom: How to Write and Teach Case Method*, 2010) and serves on the editorial advisory board of *Baltic Journal of Management*. Maiksteniene has been developing her professional and pedagogical competencies at leading business schools (including Harvard Business School, the Wharton School, Copenhagen Business School, Fudan University, BI Norwegian Business School) and last year became an alumnus of ITP—a faculty development program organized by the International Schools of Business Management.

**Dr. Grace McCarthy** is a senior lecturer and teaching and learning coordinator at Sydney Business School, University of Wollongong, Australia. Following many years in industry, McCarthy completed her PhD in leadership and now specializes in leadership and coaching. Her combination of academic expertise and real-world experience is valued by her students. McCarthy sees authentic assessment and reflection as important ways for students to make their own connections between theory and practice. She is a University of Wollongong accredited peer reviewer of teaching and is particularly interested in challenging interactive sessions, learning from and with her students.

**Dr. Marian McCarthy** is co-director of Ionad Bairre, The Teaching and Learning Centre in University College, Cork, Ireland. Her research interests are in teaching and learning in higher education, specifically Teaching for Understanding; the scholarship of teaching and learning and the dramatic and the visual arts in educational contexts. She has won the UCC's President's Award for Teaching Excellence, the President's Award for Research on Innovative Forms of Teaching and Learning and a National Award for Teaching Excellence (Special Commendation, team award). In 2011, she received her PhD (UCC) for research entitled *Teaching for Understanding at University College Cork: Advancing the Scholarship of Teaching and Learning*.

**Professor Michael K. McCuddy** is the Louis S. and Mary L. Morgal Chair of Christian Business Ethics and Professor of Management at Valparaiso University in Indiana, USA. His teaching interests focus primarily on business ethics and secondarily on high performance aspects of organizational behavior. He has published extensively on the science and art of teaching, drawing on experiences with a variety of innovative educational approaches. He also pursues a variety of research interests in business ethics. His current work focuses on four primary areas: relationships between freedom and corruption in a global context, the fundamental moral nature of human beings and its relationship to stewardship, the roles that stewardship and financial acumen play in the success of large corporations and methods for educating people regarding the ethics of emerging technologies. He has coauthored award-winning papers in two of these four areas of research interest.

**Professor Sarah Moore** is the associate vice president academic at the University of Limerick in Ireland. Her research interests include learning orientations and environments in work and education, gender in education, cognitive style, student retention in third-level environments, professional development in academia, teaching innovation and diversity awareness and management. She is responsible for the continued development of teaching and learning strategies at the University of Limerick, and is Strand leader of the Shannon consortium's teaching and learning strategy. She regularly publishes books and journal articles in the areas of academic practice, student development and learning dynamics. She has recently joined the UK's SEDA papers committee, serves as external advisor to the teaching grants committee at University College Dublin, is a member of the Irish Institute of Training and Development and is an appointed member of the Higher Education Authority.

**Therese Moylan** is head of the Department of Business and Enterprise at Dun Loaghaire Institute of Art, Design and Technology, Dublin, Ireland, where she has responsibility for a suite of undergraduate programs. Moylan is a board member of INTRE (Irish Network of Teachers and Researchers in Entrepreneurship) and a member of the expert group that developed the HETAC Guidelines on Enterprise and Entrepreneurship Education. Her work history includes higher education management and teaching experience in the areas of entrepreneurship, marketing and business planning. She has also worked in senior management in retail and publishing. Her research is in the area of entrepreneurship education and female entrepreneurship.

**Fran Myers** has been with the Open University Business School (OUBS) in the UK since 2002, where she has held a variety of posts, including tutor and regional manager for OUBS and as assistant director for Aimhigher. Prior to joining the OU, Myers started out in retail, undertaking a variety of management and project management roles before transferring to the communications industry in the late 1990s. Myers has her first degree in history from the University of Birmingham and her MBA from the OU. Her current research interests include business as an agent of social and political change, student retention and digital pedagogy.

**Dr. Anja Svetina Nabergoj** is an assistant professor at the Faculty of Economics, University of Ljubljana, where she teaches design thinking and entrepreneurship courses. Recently her research is focusing on the impact of integrating design thinking into the entrepreneurship curriculum. She has been visiting at Hasso Plattner Institute of Design at Stanford since 2010, coaching for various courses and teaching executive education programs. She is also a founding member of the Research as Design group at Stanford University, which focuses on teaching design thinking to the scientific research community and conducts research on the role of creativity in scientific research.

**Dr. Deirdre O'Loughlin** is a senior lecturer in marketing in the Kemmy Business School, University of Limerick, Ireland. Her research interests include branding and relationship marketing, consumer behavior, social policy and ethics, marketing pedagogy and teaching quality. Deirdre has published in a broad range of international peer-reviewed journals and has presented at many international conferences. She has secured a number of grants to fund research into consumption and teaching quality studies. She is a recipient of the University of Limerick Teaching Excellence award and has been nominated twice for the Shannon Consortium Regional Teaching Excellence award in Ireland.

**Mike Phillips** has been a tutor with Open University Business School, UK, since 2000, supporting students through the certificate in management and work-based learning modules. He became a regional manager with OUBS in 2008, and subsequently took on line management responsibilities with the undergraduate program regional teaching and learning team. He has extensive experience in marketing, finance and operations management roles in commercial organizations—with twenty years in the retail motor industry—as well as senior roles with a sector skills council and a training provider. His research interests include student retention, work-based learning and the retail sector.

**Dr. Daphne R. Raban** is a senior lecturer at the Graduate School of Management, University of Haifa, Israel, and head of the Department for

Information and Knowledge Management. She is active in the Sagy Center for Internet Research. Her broad area of research interest is the value of information, including topics such as information markets, economics of information goods, information/knowledge sharing, the interplay between social and economic incentives and games and simulations. In collaboration with IBM HRL, she conducts social computing research and she is also a partner of the FP7-ICT SocIos project.

**Paul Raby** joined the Open University Business School in the UK in 2009, after having worked for thirty years in banking and finance. He has worked closely with the Institute of Financial Services as a tutor and examiner on its distance learning courses. Raby is also a tutor with the OU for its business studies degree and with Manchester Metropolitan on its finance and law modules. Raby's first degree was in financial services, acquired by distance learning while in full-time employment. He is also a Fellow of the Institute of Bankers and a Fellow of the Higher Education Academy. Raby's research interests are in bank regulation and the use of digital technology in the delivery of professional and higher education courses.

**Carey Stephens** joined the Open University Business School in the UK in 2002 after leaving Manchester Metropolitan University and is a regional manager for the business undergraduate orogram. Stephens line-manages the business degree tutors in the North West and Yorkshire and is also a tutor and co-chair. A believer in lifelong learning, Stephens achieved an OU MBA in 2003 and a BSC (Hons) in criminology and psychology in 2010.

**Rok Stritar** is a teaching and research assistant at the Faculty of Economics, University of Ljubljana. He is involved with most undergraduate entrepreneurship courses in the faculty. In addition to studying and teaching entrepreneurship, he is also an active entrepreneur. He was part of the team that introduced the design thinking teaching approach for entrepreneurship at the faculty.

**Jon Teckman** is an associate faculty member of Ashridge Business School in the UK. He is also the chief executive of the Phoenix Education Trust, treasurer of the British Board of Film Classification and director of Fletcher Teckman Consulting Ltd. He was previously chief executive of the British Film Institute, where he had overall responsibility for the leadership and development of more than 500 staff. Before that he was a civil servant, where he learned at firsthand how not to manage people. His leadership hero is Ernest Shackleton, and his favorite film is *It's a Wonderful Life*.

**Blaž Zupan** is a teaching and research assistant and a PHD candidate at the department of entrepreneurship, Faculty of Economics, University of Ljubljana. His research interests include family business, entrepreneurship education and the impact of integrating design thinking into entrepreneurship curriculum. In addition to teaching entrepreneurship to numerous classes at various faculties and to diverse closed groups, he is an active entrepreneur having worked in both his family business and his own ventures.

# Index

Page numbers in *italics* indicate figures or tables.

Aalto University *see* VantagePoint board game
abductive reasoning 110–11, *111*
academics *see* instructors
action plans 83, 144–6, *146*
active learning 20–1, 202
active reading 145–6, *146*
adaptation, creative 134
Adcroft, A. 94
adult learning theories 82
agility 39
alcohol campaign 178–9, 181–3, *182*, 185, 186
andragogy, as term 57
Arts Council of England 97, 98
Ashridge Business School *see* The Leadership Experience
assessment, authentic *see* authentic assessment
assignments, authentic 83–4
Association of American Colleges and Universities 70
Association to Advance Collegiate Schools of Business 90
authentic assessment: about 57, 81; action plan with SMART goals 83; adult learning theories 82; applicability 89–90; assessment design 82–3; assignments, authentic 83–4; assignments, linked 85–7; class profile 82; coaching assignments 83, 85–6; codes of conduct assignment 84, 87; feedback, generally 85–8; grading guidelines/rubrics 87–8; learning, student facilitation of 84; listening skills 83; research project 86–7; sales presentation assignment 83; self-assessment and reflection 84–5; student feedback on course *88*, 88–9; timing of feedback 87
authentic assignments 83–4
Awak'iT 75–7; *see also* live case study

Baker, P. 191, 192
Bean, J.C. 106, 107
board game *see* VantagePoint board game
Burglar Problem 44–5, *45*, 48–9
business coaching program *see* authentic assessment
business education challenges/trends 1–8; about 1–2; financial models, changing 3–4; globalization of education 5–6; massification of education 4–5; millennial generation 2–3; pedagogical challenges 7–8, *8*
business ethics course *see* "learning facilitators," students as
business strategy module *see* enquiry-based feedback
buzz-group exercises 23–4

cafés, student 33
calling, warm 23
Carr, M. 94–5, 99
cascading effect 48–9
case study, traditional 59, 61–2, 71; *see also* live case study
challenges: business education 1–8; higher education 200–1; large group teaching 14–15

## Index

chapter headlines, in ten-sentence cases 65
chronological events, in ten-sentence cases 64
civic role of higher education 168–9
clients, in live case study 73–4, 74–5, 76, 78
coaching program *see* authentic assessment
codes of conduct assignment 84, 87
communication skills 134
conceptualization of body of literature 146, *146*
confidentiality, client 74, 78
Cornelius, N. 153, 154, 156
corporate social responsibility (CSR) 153, 190–1; *see also* VantagePoint board game
critical incidents 94–5
critical thinking: about 105–8; components 105; definition, lack of universal 105; importance of 105–6, 108; interaction and 19–20; millennial generation 35, 36; pedagogical challenges 7–8, *8*; pedagogical design and 106; *see also* design thinking; enquiry-based feedback; Sherlock Holmes Investigative Model
CSR *see* corporate social responsibility
culminating performance ("From Dr. Watson to Mr. Holmes") 115, 121–2

debriefing: games in teaching 191; live case study 77; Sherlock Holmes Investigative Model 117; ten-sentence cases 66
design thinking 128–36; about 107; benefits 134–5; case study 130–3, *131*; defined 129; design, stages of 130, *130*; designers and entrepreneurs, compared *131*, 131–3; entrepreneurship education developments 128–9; limitations and problems 135; research questions, open 136; skills and mind-sets 132–3; student feedback on 133–4; as teaching tool 129–30, *130*; uses 135–6
detectives, economists as 110, 118, 120–1
Dettlaff, A. J. 190
Dhaliwal, S. 94

digital native generation *see* millennial generation
discussion round, in ten-sentence cases 66
diversity, student 14–15
drinking responsibly campaign 178–9, 181–3, *182, 185, 186*
Dun Loaghaire Institute of Art, Design and Technology *see* social entrepreneurship
DVDs 26
dynamic learning environments 7, *8*, 55–8; *see also* authentic assessment; enquiry-based feedback; The Leadership Experience; live case study

EBF *see* enquiry-based feedback
economic turmoil 106
economists as detectives 110, 118, 120–1
EDHEC Business School 75–7; *see also* live case study
education *see* business education challenges/trends; higher education; *specific topics*
educators *see* instructors
e-learning 25
elevator speech 65
Ellet, W. 61
emotion, importance of 94, 100, 203–4, 205
empathy 132, 134
enquiry-based feedback (EBF) 139–49; about 107–8; action planning 144–6, *146*; aim 141; assessment 140–1, *147*, 147–8; assignment, midterm 140–1, *147*, 147–8, *148*; assumptions underlying 140; benefits 148–9; components 139–40; exam 140, *147*, 147–8, *148*; excellent practice examples 143–4; feedback 143–4, *144*; generic feedback 143, *144*; impact *147*, 147–8, *148*; marking scheme 141–2, *142*; marks, breakdown of 143; preparation *141*, 141–3, *142*; skills and attributes 141; virtual learning environment 142–3
enquiry-based learning 139–40
entrepreneurship education 128–9, 169–70; *see also* design thinking; social entrepreneurship
Equis 90

ethical citizenship: about 153–6; curricula cautions 156; ethics education approaches 153–4; globalization of education and 6; importance of 153, 156; millennials 154; pedagogical challenges 8, 8; technology, issues raised by 156; trends in higher education 202; *see also* "learning facilitators," students as; live marketing campaigns; social entrepreneurship; VantagePoint board game
excellent practice examples 143–4
exercises, buzz-group 23–4
experiential learning 70, 72–3
experimentalism 132–3

facilitators, learning *see* "learning facilitators," students as
facts, key, in ten-sentence cases 64
failure, coping with 134
feedback: about 139; generic 143, *144*; good practice in 87; millennial generation's desire for 81; timing of 87; *see also* enquiry-based feedback; *specific teaching methods*
fees, course 4
financial models for business education 3–4, 13
flexibility 39, 78, 185
flipped classroom concept 55, 200–1
forums: online 25–6, 142–3; tutor group 32–3, 37–8
"From Dr. Watson to Mr. Holmes" (culminating performance) 115, 121–2
funding for business education 3–4, 13
Future Leaders' Experience *see* The Leadership Experience

games: customizing 191; as interactive technique 26; in MBA program 45–6; ten-sentence cases, improving 68; *see also* VantagePoint board game
generation Y *see* millennial generation
generic feedback 143, *144*
Gentry, J.W. 72–3
Gerber, L.E. 81
Ghoshal, S. 153
Gibb, A. 170
Glaser, E.M. 105
globalization of education 5–6

goals, SMART 83
grading guidelines 87–8
guided performance ("Watching the Detective") 115, 118–21, 125–7

Hidden Profile Task 43, *44*, 48–9
higher education: civic role of 168–9; massification of 4–5, 13; trends 202–5

incentives 48
incidents, critical 94–5
independent study 15
inference development, mastery of 112–13
information technology revolution 106
instructors: availability before and after class 21; classroom activities, explaining rationale of 21; emotion, importance of 203–4; greeting students outside of class 22; live case study 73, 74; role 160–1, 172–3, 174, 175–6; students, connection with 21–2; traditional case study 61; walking around during class 22
integrative thinking 132
interaction: about 22–3; buzz-group exercises 23–4; critical thinking and 19–20; effectiveness of 27; e-learning 25; encouraging 22–7; games 26; online forums 25–6; problem solving, large group 26–7; students' notes 24–5; videos/DVDs 26; voting 25; warm calling 23
international students 5, 6
introductory performance ("Our First Case: Solving the Problems of Robin Hood"): about 114; debriefing performances 117; deliberation 117; performance design 115; performance enactment 117–18; plot 115; presentations 117; reflections 117–18
ISM University of Management and Economics 63, 67–8; *see also* ten-sentence cases

Jenga (game) 191
Jevons, M. 110

Kemmy Business School, University of Limerick *see* live marketing

campaigns; VantagePoint board game
Knapsack Problem 44–5, *45*, 48–9
Knight, S. 35
knowledge: mastery of 112; metacognitive 109
Krasnor, L.R. 189, 190

large group problem solving 26–7
large group teaching: about 13–16; business education challenges/trends and 7, *8*, 13–14; challenges 14–15; connection between teacher and students 21–2; criticism of 18; funding models and 13; interaction, encouraging 22–7; massification of higher education and 13; numerical definition of 20; *see also* Open University Business School; prediction markets
LCS *see* live case study
The Leadership Experience (TLE) 93–101; about 56–7; aims and objectives 94–5; Arts Council of England feedback 97, *98*; critical incidents 94–5; described 95; development of 94–5; emotional impact 94, 100; feedback to students during 96; impact and long-term results 97–100; realistic nature of 95–6; student feedback on 93, 97–9
learning: active 20–1, 202; adult 82; e-learning 25; enquiry-based 139–40; experiential 70, 72–3; from mistakes 134; personalized 38–9; *see also* dynamic learning environments; "learning facilitators," students as
learning environment, virtual 142–3
"learning facilitators," students as 158–67; about 155; authentic assessment 84; course activities 159–61; course overview 159; ethical issues 159–60; groups, student 159–60; instructor, role of 160–1; learning objectives 158–9; personal developmental outcomes 166; responsibilities 160; student feedback on 161–6
lecturers *see* instructors
Lichtenwalter, S. 191, 192
listening skills 83

literature, conceptualization of 146, *146*
live case study (LCS): about 56; advantages 73–4; advice for using 77–8; business education, use in 72; client presentation to students 76; confidentiality 74, 78; debriefing, plenary 77; defined 71–2; disadvantages 74–5; EDHEC Business School approach 75–7; experiential learning potential of 72–3; features, distinguishing 71; material development 76; preplanning 75–6, 77; stakeholders 72; student teamwork and presentation 77; traditional case study compared to 71; types 72; *see also* social entrepreneurship
live marketing campaigns 178–87; about 155, 178–9; aims and objectives 179–80; process and outcomes 180–1; responsible drinking campaign 178–9, 181–3, *182*, 185, 186; student feedback on 184–7; student volunteering campaign 179, 183, *184*, 185, 186–7

management courses, prediction markets in *see* prediction markets
marketing campaigns, live *see* live marketing campaigns
markets outcome 48–9
massification of higher education 4–5, 13
metacognitive knowledge 109
millennial generation: about 34–5; business education challenges/trends and 2–3; critical thinking skills 35, 36; curriculum design implications 35–6; educational needs 60–1, 61–2, 200; ethical citizenship 154; feedback, desire for 81; Open University Business School case study 36–8; traditional teaching methods, disenchantment with 35–6; traits 2–3, 34–6
mistakes, learning from 134
Moore, L. 190
moral development, defined 158; *see also* ethical citizenship

*Murder at the Margin* (Jevons) 110, 118, 120–1
Mystery Puzzle 47

National Framework of Qualifications (Ireland) *see* social entrepreneurship
negativity bias 49
newspapers, on-campus 173–4
notes, students' 24–5

observation, mastery of 112
online courses, open 200; *see also* Open University Business School
online forums 25–6, 142–3
online spaces, personal 33–4
Open University Business School (OUBS) 30–9; about 15–16, 30, 31–2; agility and flexibility, need for 39; entry criteria for students, lack of 31; millennial generation case study 36–8; millennial generation traits 34–6; online curriculum, evolution of 32; online spaces, personal 33–4; pedagogical model and research context 31–2; personalized learning, demand for 38–9; student cafés 33; student retention 31–2; tutor group forums 32–3, 37–8; undergraduate student cohort 36
opinion potpourri 64–5
OUBS *see* Open University Business School
"Our First Case" *see* introductory performance ("Our First Case: Solving the Problems of Robin Hood")

passive reading 145
pedagogical challenges 7–8, *8*, 13–14
pedagogy, as term 57
Pepler, D. J. 189, 190
performances, in Sherlock Holmes Investigative Model: culminating 115, 121–2; guided 115, 118–21, 125–7; introductory 114, 115, 117–18; sequencing of 114–15, *116*
personalized learning 38–9
personal online spaces 33–4
plans, action 83, 144–6, *146*
play, defining 189–90; *see also* VantagePoint board game

Poole, E. 94–5, 99
Powdthavee, N. 100
prediction markets 41–50; about 16, 41–2; Burglar Problem 44–5, *45*, 48–9; business game in MBA program 45–6; considerations and lessons learned 46–9; feedback from students 49, *49*; Hidden Profile Task 43, *44*, 48–9; incentives 48; instructional approaches 42–3; Knapsack Problem 44–5, *45*, 48–9; markets outcome 48–9; Mystery Puzzle 47; trading topics 47; training 47–8; uses 41–2
Prensky, M. 61–2
preplanning of live case 75–6, 77
Prisoners' Dilemma game 26
proactive ethics education 154
problem solving 26–7, 109; *see also* Sherlock Holmes Investigative Model
professors *see* instructors
progress, gauging 14
prototyping 132–3, 134
purpose, clarity of 14

questioning round, in ten-sentence cases 66
questions, asking right 113

reactive ethics education 154
reading: active 145–6, *146*; passive 145
realism, importance of 95–6, 185, 204–5
reasoning, abductive 110–11, *111*
Reitz, M. 99–100
responsibility, societal 186
responsible drinking campaign 178–9, 181–3, *182*, 185, 186
revenue streams 4
rubrics 87–8

sales presentation assignment 83
Sherlock Holmes Investigative Model (SHIM) 109–27; about 107, 110–13, *111*; culminating performance 115, 121–2; in economics education 113–22, *114, 116*; economist as detective 110, 118, 120–1; guided performance 115, 118–21, 125–7; introductory performance 114, 115, 117–18; problem solving, nature of 109;

student reflections 122; uses, other academic 122–3
Simkins, B. J. 72
simulation *see* The Leadership Experience
*Six Napoleons, The* (Doyle) 118, 119–20, 125–7
skills: communication 134; listening 83; team 190
SMART goals 83
social entrepreneurship 168–76; about 155, 168–9; assessment of project 173, 174, 175; benefits 176; challenges 175–6; as concept 172; context 169–70; instructor, role of 172–3, 174, 175–6; learning outcomes 171; newspaper, on-campus 173–4; operation of module 172–3; program details 170–1; project plan development 172–3; project selection and team formation 172; social enterprise ideas, exploring 172; social enterprise project 171–4; student feedback on 174–5; student profile 170–1
Social Learn (personal online space) 33, 34
societal responsibility 186
solution rounds, in ten-sentence cases 66
Spearman mysteries (Jevons) 110, 118, 120–1
story time line 64
student authored case method 72; *see also* live case study
student cafés 33
students: as case informants 68; diversity of 14–15; emotion, importance of 204; instructors, connection with 21–2; international 5, 6; notes of 24–5; purpose, clarity of 14; teachers greeting outside of class 22; voting 25; *see also* "learning facilitators," students as
student volunteering campaign 179, 183, *184,* 185, 186–7
summary, strategic, in ten-sentence cases 64
Sydney Business School *see* authentic assessment

Tassabehji, R. 153, 154, 156
TCS (traditional case study) 59, 61–2, 71
teachers *see* instructors
teaching: classroom activities, explaining rationale of 21; emotion, importance of 203; philosophy of 19–20, 205; traditional methods 35–6; *see also specific teaching methods*
teaching for understanding (TfU) framework 113–15, *114, 116*
team skills 190
technology 106, 156, 202
ten-sentence cases: about 57–8, 60; acquainting students with 65; business issues, prioritizing 63–4; clarifying questions, prioritization of 65–6; constructing 64–5; debriefing 66; development of 60; groups, assigning students to 65; improving 68; objectives 62; questioning round 66; selecting source case for analysis 63; solution and discussion rounds 66; student feedback on 67, 67–8; teaching technique, described 63–6
tertiary education *see* higher education
TfU (teaching for understanding) framework 113–15, *114, 116*
thinking, integrative 132; *see also* critical thinking; design thinking
throughlines 114, *116*
time line, story 64
TLE *see* The Leadership Experience
trading topics 47
traditional case study (TCS) 59, 61–2, 71
trends: business education 1–8; higher education 202–5
tutor group forums 32–3, 37–8

University College, Cork *see* Sherlock Holmes Investigative Model
University of Haifa School of Management *see* prediction markets
University of Limerick *see* live marketing campaigns; VantagePoint board game

University of Ljubljana *see* design thinking
University of Surrey *see* enquiry-based feedback
University of Wollongong *see* authentic assessment

Valparaiso University *see* "learning facilitators," students as
value, adding 55–6, 200–1
Van Sickle, R. 109
VantagePoint board game 189–99; about 155, 189; background to 192–3; classes 193–4; debriefing session 191; facilitators 193; games, customizing 191; game scenarios 192–3, 199; play, defining 189–90; play, process for using in teaching 191–2; play, reasons for using in teaching 190–1; playing 194–5; preparation 194; refinements and tips 196–7; student feedback on 196; teams as players 193; timing 192
videos 26
virtual learning environment 142–3
volunteering campaign 179, 183, *184*, 185, 186–7
voting, student 25

walking around during class 22
Wallace, J. 153, 154, 156
warm calling 23
"Watching the Detective" (guided performance) 115, 118–21, 125–7
Wilson, M. 81